ASKING PROPERLY

THE ART OF CREATIVE FUNDRAISING

ASKING PROPERLY

THE ART OF CREATIVE FUNDRAISING

GEORGE SMITH

THE WHITE LION PRESS LIMITED

LONDON

Published by
The White Lion Press Limited
White Lion Court
7 Garrett Street
London EC1Y 0TY.

First published in 1996.

© George Smith/The White Lion Press Limited.

British Library Cataloguing in Publication Data
A CIP catalogue record for this book can be obtained
from the British Library.

ISBN 0 9518971 1 X

Designed by Bradbury and Williams
Designer: Jessica Caws

Printed and bound in the United Kingdom
by the Lavenham Press, Lavenham, Suffolk, CO10 9RN.

CONTENTS

Foreword   7
Acknowledgements   8
Introduction   10

PART 1
THE PROCESS OF ASKING
  1. By Charing Cross station I sat down and gave…   12
  2. What does the donor want?   36
  3. But what does the donor get?   47

PART 2
FUNDRAISING CREATIVITY
  4. What really matters creatively   64
  5. Writing fundraising copy   82
  6. Thinking visually in fundraising   96
  7. Meanwhile back at the offer…   119
  8. A postscript on fundraising direct mail   139
  9. Who needs envelopes?   148
 10. I just called to say I love you   166
 11. What price TV and radio?   172
 12. Working with suppliers   179

PART 3
WHERE DO WE GO FROM HERE?
 13. The two great priorities   186
 14. Fundraising in a changing world   211
Bibliography   217
Index   218

FOREWORD

When asked to write this foreword I thought it only polite to read *Asking Properly* thoroughly. But politeness didn't come into it. This is good stuff.

George Smith is not at all keen on being labelled a guru, but in the field of fundraising he is widely acknowledged as one, whether he likes it or not. Throughout this book George challenges our thinking, liberally illustrating his arguments with current examples of fundraising from Britain, Europe and America. With great humour he lambasts his way through much that we hold dear as accepted fundraising practice. On one or two occasions I allowed myself a smug smile as I read. All too often though my smile was one of rueful recognition, as yet another fundraising truism was held up for scrutiny — and found wanting. But this is not a book that knocks you down, far from it. *Asking Properly* is full of ideas and suggestions that help all of us think about how we can be better fundraisers.

Most of us wish that we could find the time to take a step back from the day-to-day workload to look anew at what we are doing. *Asking Properly* enables us to do just that, because it leads us on a broad-ranging review of fundraising that is never dull, frequently funny and always perceptive and informative. Whether you have been in fundraising for 20 minutes or 20 years, you are sure to find this an enjoyable and thought-provoking book.

Susan Wilkinson
Fundraising Director
The National Trust

ACKNOWLEDGEMENTS

No one writes a book like this without an enormous amount of help from other people. I certainly didn't.

The list that follows is a reflection of that help. All these people gave me their opinions, their experience and, in many cases, their response figures. This sort of co-operation is all too rare and I must thank everyone for it, for in some cases they could have been understandably wary of being so very helpful to a competitor. To all these people I offer a potential apology as well as thanks — I may occasionally have misheard or misinterpreted what they told me. If that is the case, the fault is mine.

My apologies, too, to the many people I cannot directly credit. They are clients and ex-clients, colleagues and ex-colleagues, hundreds of fundraisers with whom I have been privileged to work all over the world. They may be anonymous but they have all helped me write this book. I should express particular gratitude to my former colleagues in the International Fund Raising Group and, of course, to Harold Sumption, without whom none of our books could ever have been written.

Let me record the support of Ken Burnett in commissioning the book. That support cannot have been easy at a time when he was completing his own successor to *Relationship Fundraising*, but he has said wise and supportive things at regular intervals. Marie Burnett had the lousy job of checking my grammar, my punctuation and my notoriously eccentric vocabulary. If coherence has emerged, it is as much her achievement as mine. Marc Nohr at Burnett Associates had the first draft thrust at him and told to give a younger person's reaction, a challenge to which he rose with characteristic flair and helpfulness, also managing to supply superb case histories from his international collection of fundraising mailings. Simon Pell at Pell & Bales was good enough to vet the telephone chapter for me and David Ford at Smee & Ford updated all my legacy statistics as well as giving me valuable advice on the subject area.

In the United States, I must thank Charles Orasin from the Defenders of Wildlife, Hal Malchow from Malchow, Adams and Hussey, Jonathan Abbott from PBS and Judith Nichols. And I must particularly thank Rich and Aine Fox in Washington who so kindly gave me their spare room during a crazy blizzard-swept week, which fractured Rich's careful and invaluable schedule for my fact-finding mission there.

Steve Thomas of Stephen Thomas and Associates in Toronto proved a stalwart supplier of information on everything Canadian.

The list of British contributors is inevitably long. But compatriots who gave me their time include Jackie Fowler at Burnett Associates, Stephen Pidgeon and Pauline Lockier at

Target Direct, David Strickland-Eales at Chapter One, Alison Jelfs at Sheard Thomson Harris, Maria Phillips at WWAV Rapp Collins, Jeremy Shaw and Sylvia Benaim at Smith Bundy, Marc Gilden at Occam Direct Marketing and Joe Saxton, late of Brann. Roger Millington was, as ever, an invaluable source.

David Brann at the Royal National Lifeboat Institution, Mavis Rennie at CARE UK, Karl Holweger at the Royal National Institute for Deaf People, Jane Rose at the National Society for the Prevention of Cruelty to Children, Sue Wilkinson at the National Trust, Karen Sherlock at Amnesty International, Lindsay Cooke at Charter 88, Margaret Bennett and Tracy Horner at WWF UK and Daryl Upsall at Greenpeace International in Amsterdam all played a part in this book, either by supplying information direct, or by agreeing to its use when supplied by their agencies. Roy Williams produced the original design and Jessica Caws laid out each and every one of the text pages. Celia Cole supervised the printing. Barry Cole read the proofs. My gratitude to all of them. And to the many other people who probably qualify for such gratitude – my apologies for having to curb the length of the list.

Asking Properly was written between February and May 1996. I mention this not as a record of writing machismo but to make the point that whatever I have said is firmly rooted in the time in which I said it. I will probably have different experiences and different attitudes in a year's time. I do not subscribe to the 'tablets of stone' theory of fundraising, so *Asking Properly* is merely how I felt about things in those months.

Lastly, and at the risk of turning this into an Oscar-winning speech, I really must thank my wife, Stella, and my youngest daughter, Jenny. They were wise enough to tiptoe around me, close doors on me, turn down radios and generally avoid my temperamental excesses during the process of creation. Such understanding on their part was crucial.

George Smith

INTRODUCTION

The world of fundraising, like any other contemporary tribe, is subject to verbal ugliness. And that happy and functional three letter verb 'Ask' became a noun about five years ago. It had probably existed as such in America for decades previously but it took a presentation by Bernard Ross called 'Making the Ask' at the International Fundraising Workshop in Holland to inform me of the transformation. Soon and inevitably, the new noun became modish. 'What's the ask?' queried the writer in search of a brief. 'Here's the ask' said the agency-wallah making the presentation. 'I think we should vary the ask' said everyone.

I am inevitably a curmudgeon when it comes to language but I know when to give in, when to start spraying new words about if it helps the cats get fed. So, the really snappy title for this book was going to be *The Creative Ask* on the basis that it sounded right for the management booklist. But the curmudgeon took over again, aware that *The Creative Ask* is just too near parody for personal comfort. Welcome to the comfortable substitute: *Asking Properly*.

My mother always told me to 'ask properly' for things. I got told off if I was impolite or over-aggressive. I was reprimanded for asking in sloppy language or incomplete sentences. I was scorned for asking for the impossible. I was honoured when, on occasion, I did manage to ask properly.

The reward in those days must have been a bag of sweets or fourpence for a bus fare. But it does seem to me that charities are beginning to commit the same sins as that snot-nosed child. This book is dedicated to the difference.

I have had to range wider than the narrow and traditional agenda of apparent creativity for it seems to me that the issues of fundraising creativity are not just to do with technical processes; they are to do with the whole ethos of fundraising – why we do what we do as much as how we do it. To that extent, this book inevitably becomes a treatise on fundraising generally.

One last thing. It is inevitably a British book, written by an Englishman and with a heavy emphasis on the home market. It would be silly to apologise for this, if only because British fundraising has developed so much in the last decade. It has learned a great deal from the United States, reworked many American practices and, in some cases, enhanced them. In any case, we live in a global village now where there are valuable lessons to be learned from everywhere – Singapore turns out to know a lot about payroll giving and South Africa produces some of the most cost-effective direct mail in the world. But I may have become a little parochial on occasion and I do ask the reader's indulgence if that is the case. I still think that the point of view expressed in *Asking Properly* is of universal application.

THE
PROCESS OF
ASKING

'Ask, and it shall be given you;
seek and ye shall find;
knock and it shall be opened unto you'
The Gospel according to St Matthew 7:7

CHAPTER ONE

BY CHARING CROSS STATION I SAT DOWN AND GAVE...

Charing Cross is one of London's great commuter railway stations. I use it when I travel to and from my Kentish home. It is a busy place, used by tens of thousands of harassed travellers every day. Most of them are in frenzied transit to or from work. Others arrive bemused, laden with cases and peering at the train information. And some people are downright lost, looking for friends, staring at maps and sometimes finding that they have simply come to the wrong station. It is my regular, somewhat patrician, habit to ogle this throng over a double espresso at the excellent Costa Café.

For this is a fundraising arena. Just about every night, someone is asking these hordes of careworn people for money. There are panhandlers looking for a cigarette or the price of a cup of tea. There are people selling the *Big Issue,* London's excellent magazine whose revenues go to help the homeless and the street-dwellers. And there are charity collections galore. One of the characteristic sounds of Charing Cross is that of rattling collection tins. And a lot of money changes hands. There are a lot of fundraising lessons to be learned in the nightly ritual of watching it all.

Some of the lessons are obvious. The panhandlers would profit by looking a little less terrifying, staying off the booze and working on a new presentation. Indeed, the practice of outright, shameless begging already offers some usable tuition about asking people for money. The guy who shimmies up to you, scarred from last night's brawl and reeling with canned lager is only ever going to get the occasional coin and you are only going to bestow the coin to get the beast off your back. But the beggar with a story – that's already a difference! I have been daft enough in recent months to have given £5 to a young man who spun me some story about a dying relative, a stolen car, a bank that didn't open till morning and a hopeless quest to get to the deathbed that night. Bear in mind that I am a grizzled old sceptic and you will see the power of the narrative in fundraising.

But the biggest lesson is to do with noise, literal or metaphorical. There are collectors who have so obviously been pressed into service. They look self-conscious and their muteness underlines the perception. They rattle the cans with diffidence, they press themselves against the wall and they hope that they might never ever meet anyone they know in such a shaming situation (listen to their collecting tins – the slight jangling of coins tells its own sad story). And there are *Big Issue* sellers who give off the same diffidence, the same weariness and ennui.

Contrast them with their more confident colleagues. All they usually do is say things – banal, repetitive, loud things, 'Buy *Big Issue* now and help the homeless'; 'Support Cancer Relief'; 'Every penny helps'. And the can-rattling is insistent, a drumbeat to action. The verbal barrage is actually illegal but it works.

And they are not physically reticent, these collectors. They dart about, thrust the cans under your nose. If they are really sporty, they dress up – as doctors for a hospital appeal if they want to stay in logical mode, but as animals, monsters, cartoon characters, or footballers if they just want to make a splash. They eyeball you individually, making the collection a difficult-to-resist, direct, personal responsibility.

And they tend to say thank you. Indeed, they usually make a meal of it. Not just 'Thank you', but 'Thank you very much indeed…you're very generous…have a good journey now.' 'Take care'.

No, I don't like them much either, these brash egotists, these unavoidable irritants who part you from your coinage. But they are raising a multiple of the sums earned by their more diffident colleagues. It is a primitive illustration of two important, indeed imperative, fundraising mottoes.

The first says that if you're going to do something, do it wholeheartedly. Diffidence in fundraising only makes you unhappy, the shrinking violet of a collector pressed against the station wall. The noisy guys aren't just making all the money. They are actually having all the fun.

And the second is maybe the only fundraising motto worth commemorating. Tap it out in 72 point on your word processor, print it out and stick it above your desk. Or sew it on a sampler, frame it and put it above the bed. But, always remember it. It is simple, obvious, logical, banal and profoundly ordinary. And it says this.

You don't get what you don't ask for.

And I am bound to repeat the thought and, quite probably the exact words, in the pages that follow. It is the difference between the successful and the unsuccessful collectors on Charing Cross station. It is the difference between successful and unsuccessful fundraisers everywhere.

And, also at Charing Cross station, I stood up and blubbed a little...

I offer you one other little *aperçu* from Charing Cross. For the whole of the month of December, fundraising there goes all seasonal. Every night a children's choir sings carols to raise money for a whole sequence of good causes – it almost doesn't matter which. For the choirs are neither senior nor musically very adept; these are groups of primary schoolkids, wrapped up in their winter coats, brought in from their schools by their teachers to sing in public. Collectors, probably parents, walk around the crowd that inevitably gathers, with seriously jangling tins.

And they don't have to dress up to do it. Or to eyeball you, or engage in hearty verbiage. They can just collect quietly in the knowledge that the kids have created the atmosphere in which you want to give.

It's not a religious atmosphere that they create. It's just an aura of decency and hope and moist-eyed emotion. You're watching an eight-year-old tot not quite making the descant in 'Away in a Manger', you're watching the kids who are so tired that they've stopped pretending to sing, you're watching the teachers trying to keep them in line.

Look around the crowd and you can see that everyone is *beaming*. The old-fashioned word for this is goodwill and the new-fangled term is probably the feel-good factor. All I know is that I have wandered over from the Costa Café to beam. And that, when the teacher comes round with the tin, I give a pound. And that, on occasion, I blub inwardly at the sheer niceness of it all. You should know that I am more Scrooge than Bob Cratchit when it comes to Christmas.

So, never let anyone tell you that fundraising is finally anything but an emotional business. It always was. It always will be.

Who gives, how and why

British charities live in a very well-ordered world, at least statistically. The Charities Aid Foundation produces an invaluable volume of data every year that analyses the sector in pitiless detail. I know of no other 'business' that can define itself with quite this degree of numerical accuracy.

But a certain kind of corporate pomp always comes with macro-statistics and it sometimes does with charities in the UK. Significantly, the later editions of the CAF report are called *Dimensions of the Voluntary Sector* and it is the work of professors, research fellows, statisticians and analysts from a whole swathe of seats of learning. This is inevitable and proper, but the sight of a cold collation of enormous statistics sometimes makes you purblind. I know of several charities who study these league tables every year and chart their organisational priorities accordingly. I have one director's report right here on my desk that bewails the fact that his charity has 'slipped out of the top 20' in an effort to goad his staff into superior fundraising mode. This is as daft as it is vulgar. Charities are not pop albums and their current performance is usually the dividend of their recent history and a whole sequence of social accidents as much as the practice of their incumbent fundraisers.

But, if you allow for the frigidity of the charts, the academic bent of the narrative and the growing air of self-importance (the annual survey used to be called plain *Charity Trends*), then *Dimensions of the Voluntary Sector* is one hell of a fact file. All of the statistics I shall use, and some that I shall question, are taken from the 1995 and 1996 editions.

I KNOW OF SEVERAL CHARITIES WHO STUDY THESE LEAGUE TABLES EVERY YEAR AND CHART THEIR ORGANISATIONAL PRIORITIES ACCORDINGLY.

There were 178,609 charities in the Charity Commission register in 1994. The total income of registered charities in 1991 was £9,100 million. Their total expenditure during that year was about 93 per cent of that income – £8,500 million. This is as it should be – charities are clearly not salting away their reserves.

It's when you get into the subsidiary tables that you begin to identify some usable truths. Over 178,000 charities sounds a massive number and in fact it's something like one for every 33 people in the country. But 27,000 of these charities are subsidiaries of other charities. And the vast majority of all charities are small. Indeed the average charity turns out to have around the same income as a village shop.

A full 88.8 per cent of all UK charities had a 1991 income of less than £100,000. Nine per cent had an income of between £100,000 and £1 million. Which means that only 2.2 per cent had an annual income of more than £1 million. The 'giants' with more than £10 million in annual income are just 0.2 per cent of the total. Having said that, the £1 million-plus charities account for 73 per cent of the total charity income 'cake'. There can be few other kinds of 'business' or 'sectors' that are so sprawling numerically but where 'brand share' is so skewed to the few major players. On the narrower definition of the voluntary sector offered in the 1996 edition – one that excludes educational establishments and housing associations – the skewing is even more apparent: 91 per cent of such charities have an income of less than £100,000 and the major players with more than £10 million become just 0.1 per cent of the total – 86 out of 97,748.

I call them major players but no one should assume that all are household names. In terms of 1994 voluntary income the Lawn Tennis Association Trust is at number 47, ahead of Shelter and UNICEF. And you don't see too many appeals from the Civil Service Benevolent Fund at number 60 or the Redwings Horse Sanctuary at number 80. It is a fascinating list with all the silly excitement of the pop charts. Sceptical foreigners will enjoy the fact that the Donkey Sanctuary enjoyed a slightly greater voluntary income than the Prince's Trust. The rest of us can welcome the stratospheric climb of Feed the Children in the 1995 edition, climbing a full 128 places and straight in to the top 50 at number 37.

There is a temptation to see all this charity income being engendered by what we call fundraising. Nothing could be further from the truth. Voluntary income of all charities as a proportion of total income was no more than 51 per cent in 1991. And no more than 18 per cent of the income of registered charities came from individuals – and that includes all legacy income! Even a charity like Oxfam, which one presumes to be more or less totally dependent on the direct financial contributions of its supporters, received nearly £25 million (over 28% of total income) from either British Government or European Community sources in 1993/94. Very many top-line British charities are more dependent on statutory income than they are on voluntary income. This is entirely as it should be for those organisations whose work – child care, medical research, social welfare, etc – comes close to governmental responsibility, and I only use these statistics to chasten the fundraiser into a degree of humility. For the voluntary organisations with whom we work, we are neither architects nor even engineers. We are toolmakers – an honourable trade but a subsidiary one.

But who does give?

My biggest quarrel with the CAF statistics is in the area of individual giving. Much of the statistical tracking in *Dimensions of the Voluntary Sector* has to be done on a sample basis – how else can you measure corporate giving for example? And what matters about the *Individual Giving and Volunteering Surveys* is less the size of the sample – 1,005 is quite respectable statistically – but the great dumb question that's asked. For the infinitely repeated index of how generous the British are is based on asking whether the respondent has given to charity in the last month.

Well, did you? What's giving anyway? Does it include the 10 pence exchanged for a lapel badge in the High Street last Saturday? Does it include the recently renewed subscription to the National Trust, or the book of raffle tickets bought from the local school, or the half-forgotten direct debit mandate to WWF? It takes a peculiarly organised person to be able to answer the question with any degree of integrity. And why bother with integrity when the question is so morally loaded? It takes a peculiarly malevolent person to say no. All in all, ask silly questions and you get silly answers.

Which is what I fear CAF publish. Apparently in 1994 only 19 per cent of us failed to give to charity in the last month (any month, remember) and a thumping 81 per cent of us managed to spread a little philanthropic cheer. The fiction increases with the claimed amount for giving. The average (mean) amount given per month by a woman was £14.08 and by a man was £11.39. There are regional variations on this theme of generosity with which I won't bother you. But I did like the answer to one ancillary question: three-quarters of respondents agreed that charities' postal appeals were a waste of time. Agreed? What sort of question was that?

I sneer too easily. The *Individual Giving and Volunteering Survey* is a brave attempt to do the impossible – measure people's charitable giving. Extrapolate the figures and you have data suggesting that the British adult population gave between £4,300 and £6,300 million to voluntary organisations in 1993. Sadly, we have already looked at macro-statistics that confirm that they did no such thing. People are getting into the habit of telling pollsters whatever they think they want to hear. When the subject is so morally charged as giving to charity, they obviously tell whoppers. And I fear that the volunteering side of the survey is equally flawed – apparently 21 per cent of respondents volunteered for something in the last month!

Statistics like this are harmless until they are repeated and repeated beyond their natural environment, their individual components sheered from context. Thus, the annual journalistic story built on these very findings, 'Why Britain is less charitable'; 'Stormclouds gather for charities'; or alternatively, 'Charity giving rises as recession fades'. You will hear politicians and charity heads and sociologists solemnly debating such ersatz topics. The next time you do, know that the whole debate is mounted on really silly foundations. A thousand people have been asked whether they gave to charity in the last month. Many of them won't have remembered, some of them won't have understood the question and most of them will have fabricated the answer. The 'great issues of our time' turn out so often to be self-fulfilling mendacities.

There are useful asides, though, from the *Individual Giving and Volunteering Survey* – the clear imbalance between male and female giving, the superior giving performance of the 25 to 34 age group, the bigger donations made (or at least claimed) by the 35 to 44 age group. These things check out with one's common sense observation. More clinically, they will check out with what you see on your donor files.

Moral: don't quite believe every statistic quoted at you. Never let anyone guide a fundraising programme with overdue deference to league tables, pie charts or comparative data. This is an inspirational business that needs analysis to check the power of the inspiration, *c'est tout!* It really doesn't matter that Save the Children plunged from number one to number four between 1992 and 1993. It matters much more that they raised nearly £54 million in voluntary income in that second year. And what really matters is they helped hundreds of thousands of children and families. I asked the Princess Royal about this and she agreed.

The charitable instinct

The fundraiser is nervous of the word 'philanthropy'. It smacks of the sententious and the preening. Only in the USA would a fundraising journal dream of calling itself the *Chronicle of Philanthropy*.

In fact, the word is an innocuous one. The Shorter Oxford Dictionary offers 'love towards mankind; practical benevolence towards men in general; the disposition to promote the well-being of one's fellow-men'. Which is all a bit masculine, of course – political correctness will doubtless add in the other half of the human race at some stage.

And every culture, every religion and every human society built so far has managed to find its own mode of philanthropy. The Romans gave alms and in Middle English the word 'dole', which has come to mean so many other things since, was used to describe a charitable gift. 'Charity' itself is a key word in all Christian teaching and philanthropy is a key component of Islam – the Koran ordains *Zakat* for all Muslims owning property or earning income, a full 2.5 per cent of income, which must be distributed to the poor and which should be supplemented by *Sadaka,* the spontaneous giving of charity. The Jewish Torah offers similar instruction, using practically the same word though it demands a higher moral tariff of 10 per cent.

PHILANTHROPY IS A KEY COMPONENT OF ISLAM – THE KORAN ORDAINS ZAKAT FOR ALL MUSLIMS OWNING PROPERTY AND SADAKA, THE SPONTANEOUS GIVING OF CHARITY.

Christianity is not so directive but it has harboured the philanthropic tradition to this day. Many of us were educated in schools and colleges that were created by Christian philanthropists from previous centuries. Similarly with hospitals, libraries and other institutions of social care – they were paid for and founded by acts of Christian charity. We often forget that we only just easing into the second century where the State is seen to have a role in social welfare. The religions – Judaism, Hinduism, Buddhism, Quakerism included – continue to exert a major influence on how people give money to charity.

But the link between charity and religion has sometimes carried a price in terms of social perception. The words 'do gooder' have been used for at least 150 years to describe a certain sort of interfering, know-all, sanctimonious type. The novels of Dickens are studded with such characters and Trollope's Warden Harding lives in an almshouse where he is subject to the hypocrisy and chicanery of archbishops and crusading journalists alike (someone ought to update *The Warden* by the way – you could set it in a contemporary women's refuge and the story would still work).

So, philanthropy is not always celebrated and charity is often resented. Today's social worker is still bearing the brunt of this historic suspicion of the art of altruism. It is all very unfair but the fundraiser needs to remember that he or she is not automatically 'a good thing'.

It's time to look at the reasons why people give. Ask them directly and you will get a range of woozy answers. Being good is a difficult thing to report with accuracy; it brings out both the braggart and the blushing violet in us. Especially the British who often combine conceit and reticence in about equal parts.

But it seems to me that there are five primary reasons for giving to charity. Each of them has subclauses and most human giving probably stems from a combination of several of them. But these instincts would seem to be universal and perennial.

Religious or political conviction

I've touched on this on previous pages. Charity effectively started with organised religion and religion effectively infuses acts of giving in any part of the world. Many of our leading charities have formal Christian roots. The Salvation Army is a top 10 charity in Britain and just about everywhere else. Christian Aid raised over £22 million in voluntary income in 1993/4 and CAFOD, its Catholic equivalent, a further £15 million. Our new Asian communities are building temples and social centres as part of a religious imperative. The Jewish community in Britain embraces just about 200,000 adherents yet two of the top 40 British charities are wholly Jewish. Oxfam, Help the Aged and ActionAid were effectively all initiatives by members of the Society of Friends – and there are no more than 20,000 practising Quakers.

Look across the Atlantic and you see an even greater demonstration of the power of religion in charity. A large number of the major US charities are denominational in origin and structure. And the new wave of born-again Christianity has fundraising as a very visible subtext – watch any one of the three Christian TV stations that are usually available to any cable subscriber there and you will hear a fundraising appeal within 10 minutes.

Whatever the nature of your God, it is clear that philanthropy is part of your adherence to the faith. It can take the form of a contribution at the place of worship, it can take the form of a covenant to the church or its wider works, it can take the form of a donation to a faith-related charity. But the instinct is finally a religious one. And it is one that clearly persuades people to make choices between organisations. Why else should CAFOD exist as an organisation other than to offer a conduit for Catholics?

There is an irony here in terms of current fundraising practice. To an extraordinary extent, British charities of denominational origin seem to feel uncomfortable with their respective religions. The Church of England Children's Society dropped its denominational prefix upwards of 10 years ago and became the Children's Society. NCH Action for Children has been through a number of name changes but none of them has celebrated the Methodist roots of the organisation. They have acknowledged, of course, that they exist in a basically heathen country and look after families and children of all religions and none. But does this make the faith that created the mission a cause for effective apology? I would personally urge every religious-based charity to 'come out' and say religious things. I speak as a complete agnostic. But I am still prepared to admire someone else's religion in terms of what it persuades them to achieve. The Salvation Army is a superb example of a charity whose reputation for good works transcends any inhibitions we may have about its evangelism. The fact that they wear odd uniforms and bash tambourines may be quaint, their hymns may be less than profound musically but oh, that gusto, that clear-eyed sense of mission, that no-nonsense worldliness! These are the people I trust to run soup kitchens and administer hostels for the homeless. If it's the love of Christ that motivates this zeal, then I am willing to be impressed. Can you imagine the Salvation Army without the upfront Christianity?

But, for many people, politics has replaced religion – offering a set of ethics that is at best dedicated to produce a better world. I say 'at best' deliberately, for it is difficult to look around the world of politics these days and spot an ethic.

At this point I'd better declare an interest. I was an active member of the British Labour Party for over 20 years. Indeed I represented it for seven of those years on Lambeth Borough Council, a remarkable political finishing school that also managed to produce Ken Livingstone, Tony Banks and a chap with glasses called John Major all within a short space of time. Since then, the faith has wavered. I can only regard New Labour as merely the latest incarnation of the ruling class on the make. So, think of me as a curmudgeonly old leftie and weigh my remarks accordingly. End of apologia *pro vita sua*.

But political conviction has always carried fundraising baggage with it. The analogy with religion is almost complete. You fund your political party as much as you fund your church or place of worship. Your social life is likely to revolve around dutiful fixed fundraising points – the dinner and dance, the jumble sale, the raffle, the targeted drive to mend the church roof, or finance the next election campaign. You are a believer, sacred or

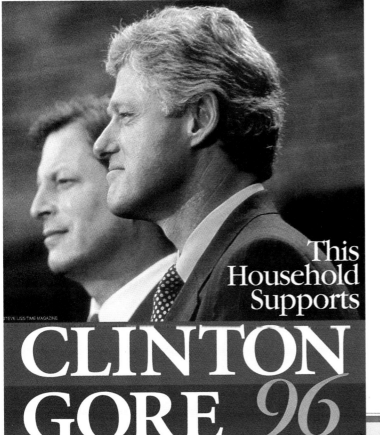

This Household Supports

CLINTON GORE 96

BILL CLINTON AND AL GORE, JR.

hereby recognize

Michael F. Ruane

as a member of the National Steering Committee
of the Clinton/Gore '96 campaign.

President of the United States   Vice President of the United States

CLINTON ★ GORE 96

secular. It's no coincidence that a political party is fond of referring to itself as a 'broad church'.

But those parties are not the only receptacle for the donations of the politically committed. There are myriads of special interest groups that stem from the political agenda and true believers, whether of left or right persuasion, will pursue their politics into the support of these groups. In fact, the obvious examples are mostly from the political left – human rights organisations or small organisations dedicated to constitutional reform, gender-specific issues or progressive

Direct mail fundraising is now a component of political campaigning throughout the democratic world.

overseas development policies. The right is probably more covert but it still spawns think tanks and pressure groups of its own and they all raise funds.

In fact fundraising has become a major feature of the political scene throughout the democratic world. In late 1995 the Democratic National Committee in the States mailed 30 million addresses on behalf of President Clinton's re-election campaign. Even as I write, otherwise sensible American citizens are paying thousands of dollars apiece to share a lunch-table with Clinton, Gore, or Dole. The British Labour Party is now exerting all the lessons of off-the-page advertising and direct mail to recruit members and raise funds. The telephone is now a regular medium for political fundraisers throughout Europe as well as in the USA. Major donor programmes continue in the under-reported uplands of the party hierarchies.

People will continue to give because of their politics, just as people will continue to give because of their religion. And the continued growth of single subject organisations and pressure groups merely amplifies the variety of the political ask. In the States you can choose between the National Rifle Association or the Anti-Handgun Control League, both of them ruthlessly professional fundraisers. There are, and there will continue to be, plenty of political or neo-political products on the fundraising market.

Giving as a thank-offering

We are all guilty of something. Mostly we are guilty of leading easeful lives, eating good food, living in comfortable homes and raising children who are bright, clear-eyed and altogether privileged. And we are guilty of enjoying good health.

Guilt is one heck of a fundraising stimulus. Indeed, it is a rare piece of fundraising that does not evoke the reaction, however subliminally. It all goes back to ancient times when Greeks and Romans would make an offering to the gods – essentially a thank you gift for not getting leprosy, or for surviving the Goths, or whatever. Then you offered a libation to Zeus, or maybe sacrificed a pig. Now, you give to Oxfam or Shelter. It is no mere cynicism to suggest that the instinct is the same.

THEN YOU OFFERED A LIBATION TO ZEUS, OR MAYBE SACRIFICED A PIG. NOW, YOU GIVE TO OXFAM OR SHELTER.

But guilt is a difficult thing to trap. It is a private thing. Only the most melodramatic or deranged donor is going to stand up before you and say, 'I'm guilty – take my money'. Whatever dark thoughts lurk in our psyche, few of us actually admit rational guilt for the terrible things that happen to other people. I do *not* accept that my comfortable house causes homelessness. I do *not* accept that the food on my table is reprehensible because there's another famine in Africa. I do *not* accept that my children are well educated because other children are on drugs.

But I *am* besotted by a sense of privilege. And when I give to charity it is often a thank-offering that I am making. The reflex donation to the depiction of need is admission, if not of guilt, then of gratitude that you and yours do not share that need.

I see no harm in fundraisers pressing this available lever, this suggestion that your very comfort gives you a greater responsibility to help.

But, stress the privilege and not the guilt. An AIDS charity can secure my support by making the point that the disease will have affected people I have known (which, tragically, it has), and by inferring that I, as an intelligent but unharmed observer, should do something to help. But they lose me totally if they begin to imply that AIDS is somehow my fault or the fault of people like me. And I only use this lurid example because I once received a telemarketing call that suggested just that. I was not proud of my verbal reaction that night.

Guilt is a slender string, to be brushed gently and never twanged. I once wrote a really plonky line at the end of an Oxfam ad. It said, 'Give thanks for your own family's well-being with a gift to Oxfam.' It lasted for years, that line. It was gentle, modestly provocative and, in fact, downright banal. It would sit ill with contemporary expression of the same idea. But I still think it's why lots of people give to charity.

Social pressure and convention

The role of fashion in charity giving is much under-reported. Indeed, it seems tasteless to mention it, let alone dwell on it. But it exists and any attempt to categorise donor motivation without mentioning the role of social fashion and cultural mores would be just slightly meretricious.

Social and media pressure dominate our lives to an extent that we rarely admit. Women, thinking women at least, scorn those newspaper fashion pages replete with barmy new outfits and styles. They titter over the designer price tags and wonder out loud who this side of the Princess of Wales ever buys the stuff. And next year, when the styles have turned up in the High Street, they tend to spend long Saturdays searching for the said stuff. It was ever thus.

Men do likewise, maybe in different fields of human performance. How else do you explain the respective social cachets of various fizzy beers? Or that shirts are now worn outside trousers? If you want a demonstration of peer pressure in our society, think baseball caps. Where did they come from? And who said you have to wear them back to front? It is all very mysterious.

Don't think that causes and charities are immune to these pressures. Fashion still applies and is applied by forces over which we have very little control as fundraisers.

Oxfam was the fashion charity of the early sixties in Britain, replaced by Shelter in the latter part of that decade. The environmental organisations all peaked in the late eighties. The AIDS constituency assembled itself at the same time.

A lot of this is caused by the media power of individual personalities. Shelter's rise was the work of one charismatic figure, Des Wilson. The rise of the environmental lobby was accelerated by the likes of Jonathan Porritt and David Bellamy, media-friendly types who put a credible human face to the anxieties about global warming and the hole in the ozone layer. The prominence of AIDS organisations has been fuelled by show business personalities ranging from Elizabeth Taylor to Elton John.

And it is probably true that one unlikely pop singer, Bob Geldof, single-handedly reactivated the British conscience when he launched the extraordinary BandAid and LiveAid phenomena in the mid-eighties as a reaction to the current famine in Ethiopia.

Then, you have that more traditional area of cause promotion – royal or aristocratic patronage. I forget how many charities have how many royals on their letterheads, but it would take a rare, snivelling republican to pretend that it is not important in fundraising. I speak as a snivelling republican but I'm not that rare.

The horrid fact is that the Princess of Wales, diligently deployed a couple of times a year, should add hundreds of thousands of pounds to your annual income. She is a superstar and likely to remain so, a fact which makes her resignation from dozens of worthy causes a considerable blow to many of them.

Other royals will achieve less or will achieve more in different ways (no one should demean the contribution made by the Princess Royal to the Save the Children Fund over the last decade). But such patrons will always make some of your supporters happy and somehow, mystically indeed, persuade them to give.

It is all very odd. But maybe it isn't. For social pressure applies at much lower reaches of the fundraising scale. My wife is annually terrorised into running a stall at the village horticultural society's annual fair. My daughter seeks my sponsorship for her participation in a walk for school funds. The good Doctor Wood collects for a dozen charities a year by knocking on a dozen doors down this country lane. If I refused him ever, if I denied my daughter, if the wife let the horticultural society down, then social obloquy would crowd in from all sides. Multiply these homely anecdotes by a factor of several and you have an explanation of how about £50 disappears from the household budget each and every year. Never under-estimate the role of social pressure and convention in fundraising.

It is reflex giving, obviously. It is affirmation of one's social role, little more. It breeds neither affection for, nor knowledge of, the recipient cause. Those classy young men and women dancing away at a Mayfair ball will have little idea whose charity will benefit. The businessmen who form a line to shake the royal hand will often be equally ignorant.

But, let's not be reverse snobbish about it. The donor who phones in a massive donation to a broadcast telethon is playing the same game – the reward is having your name read out by Terry Wogan. And I have to confess that I can't remember the charity to whom I last gave through the powerful agency of my neighbour, Doctor Wood.

All we can acknowledge is that social pressure, social convention, fashion and personalities all play a part in successful fundraising. We seem to need the self-esteem that comes with these things.

Social responsibility

Giving as an act of social responsibility is an ancient tradition, now being hastily reassembled in the last decade of the century.

Think of all those schools and universities endowed in the Middle Ages and later. As I have recorded, the instinct was probably a Christian one. But the rationale was usually a worldly one. To educate the sons of gentlefolk, to train the young of the ruling classes in the ways of administration and diplomacy, to bring learning to the bourgeoisie in dame schools and grammar schools and, later, to assist the lower classes with 'mechanical institutes' and the like. All these initiatives were the result of private benefaction, pure altruism by rich people who could see a social need and were willing to pay for a solution. Indeed, the tradition goes back even further – the wretched Crusades were essentially paid for by stay-at-home gentry willing to subscribe to the fight against the Saracens. Barmy though it looks 900 years later, this was a prime social responsibility of the day.

THERE WAS AN INCREASING BELIEF THAT THE ILLS OF SOCIETY SHOULD BE CURED BY SOCIETY AT LARGE, THROUGH THE AGENCY OF THE WELFARE STATE.

For about 150 years between the 1840s and the 1980s, this ancient tradition was disturbed – though never quite dislodged – by the new role of the State in Western democracies. For, while private philanthropy still flourished, there was an increasing belief that the ills of society should be cured by society at large, through the agency of the Welfare State. Bad health, lack of education, unemployment, poor housing, poverty generally – all these things and many more crept on to the public agenda and became a public responsibility to be discharged through State spending of tax revenues.

Because most of us will have grown up in that world of assumed State responsibility for social intervention, it is difficult to acknowledge that it appears to have been an interruption of a historical process and not the culmination of it. For it begins to look like it was transient.

Dickens reported regularly on poverty and suffering.

Even in Dickens' day, it would have been inconceivable that hospitals and schools could have been paid for and administered by the State. He may have railed against the workhouse and the awful schools to which his young heroes and heroines are subjected, but there is barely a hint that government should intervene. And, while he writes so tellingly of poverty and suffering in Victorian England, he would have regarded the idea that the State should pay someone for being unemployed or poor as merely a new kind of social irresponsibility, doubtless to be satirised in turn. Characteristically, nearly all Dickens' happy endings are caused by the intervention of private philanthropists. It is the Cheeryble brothers who sort out Nicholas Nickleby's problems and Mr Brownlow who rescues Oliver Twist from his particular cycle of deprivation. Even the escaped convict, Abel Magwitch, turns out to be Pip's benefactor in *Great Expectations*. If Dickens had lived in our times he would have been a rather amusing Thatcherite.

The foundations of the German Welfare State were actually being laid – by Bismarck of all people – within years of Dickens' death. Other Welfare States, including the British and the Australian, emerged in the early years of the twentieth century and only the USA, of the major democracies, stayed relatively immune from the process, giving itself some of the tools of social intervention but never quite convincing itself that the State had total responsibility for its citizens.

The decay in that belief is now visible throughout the world. The retreat of the State is now the prevailing political credo in countries as far removed as New Zealand and Russia, Sri Lanka and Sweden. Even a hardened old statist like myself has to admit that the experiment (which is what it now looks like) is finished. You do not have to accept the shibboleths of the New Right to reach this conclusion; you just have to acknowledge that most of us are exercising our democratic rights in favour of not paying more tax. The dream is over.

But three, perhaps four, generations will have lived through the experiment, a time when the prevailing ethic was a collective one, decades when the idea of social responsibility was widely held, years when we accepted, however generally, the need to help others. My own three children, none of them particularly political, still subscribe to that belief, despite having been reared through the time when the belief was in decay. The State structures that we built around this collective altruism may be tumbling, but the belief lingers. It is as if Christianity were to survive the collapse of the established church. Which it almost certainly will.

This very recent traumatisation of society has left many people anxious, dismayed even. For we now know much more about need. Television tells us about it every night, whether it be a natural disaster in a far-flung part of the world, conflict and atrocity as near as Northern Ireland, famine and grinding poverty in countries we have only recently heard about. The average television documentary is now about need, about cash-strapped hospitals, about unemployed youngsters, about disadvantaged minorities. Walk the streets of London, Amsterdam, San Francisco, or Paris and you stumble through the visual evidence of need – the homeless, the alcoholics, the mentally ill and the junkies. The media and the evidence of our own eyes combine to rub our faces in this constant depiction of need. No generation in history has ever been less immune from the constant depiction of how much help the human race should have.

And not just the human race either. For new anxieties, again amplified daily by the media, have now forced themselves on our consciousness. The environmental movement is less than 40 years old. It has succeeded in telling us how much harm we have done to our planetary home. Schoolchildren can now talk knowingly about carbon dioxide emissions, endangered species and the greenhouse effect – all of them concepts totally unknown to at least their grandparents. More issues, more anxieties, more need...

So, we have a Western world more acquainted with need than ever before. We have a Western world whose governments are annually dispensing with the responsibility for meeting need. It is simply logical that we have a Western world where increasing numbers of people will seek to meet need in other ways. In other words, by using the voluntary sector. And by giving money – and time – to charity. This will probably prove to be the 'age of giving as social responsibility'.

I don't propose to get overwrought about this thesis. At worst it contains a sentimental subtext that has the guilty middle classes rushing about giving away their tax gains to the voluntary sector. It will not be as simple as this. But we should allow of that analogy I offered earlier – that the collective altruism that forged and maintained the Welfare State will survive its demise, that the religion will live longer than its established church. Hard-headed Tory voters in the UK are strangely robust in their defence of the National Health Service, even if they are by now investing in private health insurance. We still want 'good' to be done, even if organised, State-provided good is falling off the agenda.

Indeed, we will use voluntary organisations as political substitutes. If political parties cannot be seen to do the right thing, we shall vest such demands elsewhere. Greenpeace is a classic case of a political substitute, a brave and radical cause group that gives its supporters the same feeling of campaigning zeal that political parties used to offer. Famously, it had more supporters than the British Labour Party for most of the last decade. And, if you total the number of supporters of all the British environmental organisations you reach a figure that is a multiple of all the supporters of political parties. It is no coincidence.

But you can look further afield and see the growth of giving as social responsibility. The foothills of the fundraising business in the UK offer wholly new patterns of giving with schools and hospitals beginning to build fundraising support groups on the American model. Donors may resent this new demand to make a personal donation for school books or ambulances, but all the signs suggest that they are responding to the demand.

Look too at the continuing growth of those charities working in the development field. When I first worked on Oxfam in the sixties you still had to argue the case for supporting what were then described as 'under-developed' countries. Britain was then more insular, giving our research groups attitudes that said, 'They wanted their independence – let them get on with it'; or 'Charity begins at home'.

You rarely hear these crudities any more. The responsibility for rich countries to help poor countries now seems to be implicit in our national mind-set, as does the desire to be kinder to the environment, to grieve about political prisoners overseas, to acknowledge sexism and racism, to care about battered children, to worry about whales. Maybe we just know more about these ills. But we still have to be fascinated by the extent to which millions of ordinary people are moved by them and respond to them. We are, after all, supposed to live in a more selfish society, one where sturdy independence has replaced collective responsibility. If that were true, then Oxfam and ActionAid should have contracted and Greenpeace and Amnesty should have dwindled to the margins of the fundraising process. The reverse has been true, despite (or perhaps because of) the shift of our societies rightwards.

Giving as social responsibility can be argued to be a reflex movement against that rightward shift. The waters of the Welfare State may have retreated but the very ebbing seems to have exposed reefs of goodwill, altruism and decency. This is why I remain optimistic about the immediate future of fundraising throughout the world. There is no evidence that people are becoming nastier.

Pity and emotion

The first of these words is deeply unfashionable, the second admitted by fundraisers only under pressure. The great debate about how far the emotionalisation of need demeans those in need is never-ending and has fuelled more meetings and working parties than the average donor might think possible.

It is a proper debate. The constant depiction of malnourished, fly-blown children and skeletal parents in Africa must build a picture of a hapless and forever dependent society. The portrayal of disablement, mental or physical, can easily relegate the people concerned to the status of simple suffering objects, devoid of feelings. We do well to mark these excesses that do indeed demean the people we are trying to help.

Yet pity and emotion remain the mainsprings that underpin support of just about every charity. Pity, after all, is no more than 'a feeling of tenderness aroused by the misfortune or suffering of another, and prompting a desire for its relief'. Odd then that fundraisers have expunged the word from their vocabulary. And, while fundraisers try and keep the emotional impulse at arm's length, it is about as successful a posture as pretending that sex has nothing to do with lust. For once, I will be other than equivocal – *fundraising will not work without an emotional component.*

By which I do not mean that all fundraising needs to jerk tears. There are of course a number of human emotions other than pity. There is anger for one – the environmental organisations thrive on it. There is pride – Oxbridge colleges were founded on it. There is love – another highly charged word strangely absent from fundraising communication.

But of all these emotions, pity – however carefully aroused and however subliminally supplied – remains the key word, even though it dare not apparently speak its name. Too many fundraisers rue this known truth. At which point they elevate political correctness above one of the highest of human qualities.

We beguile ourselves sometimes with the belief that the educated donor has finally arrived. This is a creature who gives to Oxfam because he/she appreciates the role of development in the South, who gives to WWF because he/she knows all about biological diversity, who gives to a cancer charity because he/she reads *New Scientist*.

He/she may exist. Indeed he/she may represent five per cent of donors. But there is no evidence whatsoever that we have increased the proportion of these knowledgeable and erudite people. At the risk of being totally overbearing (a daily occurrence, my colleagues would say) I would suggest that most people give to Oxfam because they want hungry people fed, that they give to WWF because they want tigers saved and that they give to ICRF because they know a cancer sufferer. These are awkward truths for charities who have tried for decades to present a more rounded picture of their mission, who have indeed wasted money in pursuing the laudable object of explaining themselves more accurately. It is genuinely sad that most people do not want to listen.

Pity and emotion will always override the content of the charity's message.

A children's charity can properly campaign against the minutiae of new family legislation. It can report in utter detail the professionalism of its social work. It can publicise its latest research into child abuse. But what moves the donor to action? It will rarely be the research statistics, agreement with the charity's position on new law, or admiration for social workers. It will be that same old image of an abandoned, frightened, or love-starved child.

Similarly with development charities. For all the campaigns about trade imbalances and debt charges and for all the project reports demonstrating the efficacy of long-term development work, the depiction of need in the public mind remains the obstinate one of hungry people, of women walking eight miles for water, of refugees and famine camps.

Even Greenpeace, whose fundraising has so often eschewed the emotional in favour of the cerebral or, at least, the mischievously provocative, is stuck with a couple of images from its past. One shows the seal cubs being clubbed on the Canadian snows; the other, regularly repeated, shows the bloody carcass of the whale being hauled up the slipway of the whaling ship, its body pierced with harpoons. Neither image is a reflection of Greenpeace's current priorities. But both refuse to vanish from the public memory.

The public see what they want to see, hear what they want to hear. We are privileged in fundraising to have provided utterly memorable images of need. We cannot idly complain when they refuse to vanish and be replaced by the newer images that we know to be more accurate. For they still work in evoking response.

I can recall two vivid memories from my own subconscious. One is of the dying Rock Hudson, sunken-cheeked, frail and thin as he faced that last press conference and told the world that the rumours could be confirmed and that he did in fact have AIDS. The sight of his face and body allied with the implicit admission of his sexuality (then, as now, a brave thing for a Hollywood actor) jolted me into sympathy for that cause for the first time. And in the age of black-and-white television I once watched an anti-smoking message by a big-name American TV personality who was dying of lung cancer and who did indeed die months later. Here was a dying man, visibly so, telling us to give up smoking because it was going to kill him. Images like these have untold power – they echo down the years.

I suspect that someone, somewhere, would find these images less than satisfactory – why should you need dying personalities to proclaim a social truth? But I suspect that millions of people like me promoted that known social truth into the front of our heads as a result. And why was that? Was it the half-known statistics of AIDS or smoking-related diseases that really made you think? Perhaps they helped clinch the argument. But what really got to you was the sight of one man dying. And your reaction was the deeply personal one of compassion. I'll say the word again: pity.

WHAT REALLY GOT TO YOU WAS THE SIGHT OF ONE MAN DYING. AND YOUR REACTION WAS THE DEEPLY PERSONAL ONE OF COMPASSION.

I suspect we cannot win this fight against our own, most memorable images. In the early sixties we ran ad after ad for Oxfam that featured starving children. Round about the middle of that decade we came under proper attack from inside the organisation – we were simplifying the issues, we were indeed demeaning the people we were trying to help. So we changed dramatically, showing positive images wherever possible and never featuring a starving child unless a current crisis such as Biafra made it a fair depiction of a particular situation. I don't think I've seen an Oxfam ad since that used the starving child.

But as recently as two years ago I was still being interviewed by journalists and academics who wanted my views on the 'starving child' issue. When I pointed out to them that the issue had been resolved nearly 25 years previously and that the ads from development agencies had never stooped to such crudity since, they expressed suspicion and annoyance. And when I challenged them to find such ads, they could only point at the latest offering from ActionAid, a child-sponsorship agency that will always – perfectly logically – feature children from Africa and Asia in its recruitment material. 'But this child is not starving', I said, 'she looks healthy. In fact she's smiling.' 'Ah', said the interviewer, 'but people *think* she's starving.'

I rest my case.

So, why do people give? I said right at the start of this section that the impulse to give was usually a complex one, probably involving at least one of my five major motivations and maybe combining aspects of all of them. Indeed, they may well sometimes be sequential. Donors may be motivated at first by a basic religious belief. They may well be further motivated, through greater understanding of the issues, to a sense of overt social responsibility. And they may well be mobilised to more regular participation or activity through social pressure. But at the heart of even such a logical linear development such as this (which will be close to the heart of some of our more cerebral fundraisers), there still lurk those old-fashioned words like 'love' and 'pity' and 'compassion'.

I make no apology for constantly repeating the words. Or for restating the one big lesson of the last 35 years – that fundraising is to do with arousing emotions. There is absolutely no sign that this will ever change.

But *what* do people give?

I want to try and widen our view about the nature of giving to charity. Quite deliberately I quoted earlier the mischievous statistic that we fundraisers are responsible for not much more than half of charities' total income (there is a case for saying that the fraction is actually much less). I do this to cut us down to proper size. And indeed to take the argument a little further.

For we make our own mythology and we are happy for the mythology to be repeated and amplified in the media and in all our many conferences, magazines and seminars. The mythology says that mass marketing has changed fundraising, that the old, quiet charitable tradition has been replaced by a new vulgar hucksterism, that donors are being battered into action by a barrage of new-found, hard-sell techniques that reduce the charity gift to the level of a soap-powder purchase. Thus, the use of press advertising, direct mail, telemarketing, research, TV commercials, radio commercials, on-pack offers, trading catalogues and the like. Fundraisers are seen to be screaming all the time. The public are quailing before all this, offering up the occasional donation to try and still the din.

The facts are a little less exciting. True, charities are spending more than ever before on marketing and communication and they have certainly emerged as very considerable players in the fast-growing field of direct mail. But nothing is new. Both press advertising and direct mail were being used by Dr Barnardo's Homes in the first decade of the twentieth century. The classified columns of *The Times,* which comprised its front page until the 1970s, were replete with charity appeals. Oxfam put its supporters on a database as long ago as 1965. Only telemarketing is a truly recent development, imported from the States with much suspicion and considerable success. And there would have been radio and TV appeals long ago had not the then idiotic broadcasting laws precluded them.

The picture of a society dumbstruck by aggressive fundraising is a total myth. Over 32 per cent of the total voluntary income of the top 500 charities in 1993/94 came in

One of over 5,000 charity shops in the UK.

through the quietest and most private of routes – bequests from the recently departed. And legacies still provide over 70 per cent of the income of some senior charities. This dependence on the bequests of a very small proportion of the population (only one in eight of people who make wills leaves money to charity) barely suggests a gung-ho business that is extracting large amounts of money from its captive public at regular intervals. The public is far from captive.

The grisly truth is that people probably give more time than money to charities. The CAF finding (1995 edition) that 21 per cent of respondents to their *Individual Giving Survey* had volunteered in the previous month may be a mite overwrought, but it points us in the right direction when we try to analyse the nature of charity support. 'I am a charity helper', or 'I do work for charities' are common phrases; they rarely refer to a financial contribution.

There are now well over 5,000 charity shops in the United Kingdom – Oxfam alone has 842, Imperial Cancer Research Fund 470. Multiply those numbers by the volunteer teams who woman them – a very slight joke but it is always women, isn't it? Add in the stalwarts who serve on committees – a charity such as Cancer Relief Macmillan Fund has over 700 such committees; make a further addition of the house-to-house collectors, the flag-day tin-rattlers, the sponsored walkers and the great network of friends and colleagues that get whipped into a major fundraising event (again to quote Cancer Relief Macmillan Fund – it calculates that its Great Coffee Morning involves 600,000 people) and you begin to count in millions. And remember, this is just volunteers in fundraising mode – charities like The Red Cross, or even environmental organisations like Friends of the Earth and Greenpeace make plentiful use of volunteers in the discharge of their basic operational mission.

So, we can begin to make a quiet case that charities actually have more volunteers than they have donors – this is certainly the case with some of the organisations I have mentioned in the previous paragraph. So much for the mass-marketing revolution that has bludgeoned the population into submission-by-donation. As so often in Britain, things are seen to go on much as they have always gone on.

SO MUCH FOR THE MASS-MARKETING REVOLUTION THAT HAS BLUDGEONED THE POPULATION INTO SUBMISSION-BY-DONATION.

But does voluntarism preclude donation? Conventional wisdom says yes. Indeed, *Dimensions of the Voluntary Sector* in 1995 offers a substantive statement from an anonymous piece of research, 'People tend to either volunteer, or to give money – seldom both. Charities' attempts to stimulate both together are likely to be counter-productive.' It is a verdict that would be endorsed by most charities with whom I have worked – volunteers are simply too precious to be subjected to fundraising. They are giving their all and their all should be respected.

There is absolutely no point at sneering at this piety. Like all sweeping generalisations it contains a smidgeon of truth. There are doubtless old ladies helping in shops, swinging an annual collecting device, or pushing envelopes through their neighbours' letter-boxes who are truly doing all they can and who would be offended into inaction by being asked for money. But I still must see this ring-fencing of volunteers as a self-fulfilling prophesy – they don't give money because they are not asked for money. Or at least because they are not asked properly.

For once I must assume that famous hard-boiled marketing hat. There are probably five million people in this country doing voluntary work for charities. They are, by definition, among the most socially aware, altruistic and altogether dedicated and decent people we have. They are also likely to have more money than most – even apparently indigent old ladies. Put with true marketing crudity, they are the key targets for successful fundraising.

So, why presume forever that they are immune from a fundraising request? For the presumption is an arrogant and finally patronising one. It says that Mrs Jones is good only for humdrum duties around the shop, or making the numbers up at a bridge evening. I sometimes think that Mrs Jones might just enjoy a larger role in the pursuit of her philanthropy. We shall never know until we ask her.

In the last year I have recommended to two large British charities that they target the first stage of a badly needed legacy drive at their thousands of committee members. The first charity has found every reason not to do it, the second will likely argue this simple idea into total inaction. The reasons are identical — fear of upsetting people, important people. It is a deeply conservative posture that does no credit to organisations who badly need every pound they can raise. For it celebrates the *status quo* more than the opportunity, the organisational structure more than the fundraising potential of that structure. I actually find it positively irresponsible.

Not that it matters what I think. What matters is that they have probably sacrificed millions of pounds of potential legacy income through a strange social conservatism.

Nothing works until you make it work. I speak with all the moral authority of the man who told Rich Fox that telephone fundraising would never work here. We were far too conservative, I said.

WHAT DOES
THE DONOR WANT?

Accept the five main donor motivations in the last section and you begin to see what the donor wants to achieve with a donation. Isn't it odd that fundraisers spend so little time in discerning these needs and practically none in meeting them?

To talk of a 'rewards structure' in fundraising is somehow vulgar. But no marketer of a commercial product or brand would spend millions of pounds on communicating that product or brand without due care to what the consumer thinks he or she is acquiring with its purchase. Eat Shredded Wheat and you achieve health. Drink Gold Blend coffee and you are somehow sexier. Buy Windows 95 and you stay ahead of your competitors. These are the apparent rewards of purchase.

In fundraising, the only reward we seem to acknowledge is a warm, human glow. Give to us, we say, and somehow – mystically almost – you will feel better.

This will not do. We need to define the warm, human glow with greater precision. Such an exercise does not make us sinister, hidden persuaders. It makes us more responsible human beings. For is there anything more presumptuous than the automatic, unthinking acceptance of thousands of millions of pounds of other people's dosh?

Again, mix and match these five donor demands. Or add to them, for no list can be truly comprehensive. But they seem to me to capture the unspoken, but deeply felt, desires of the vast majority of donors.

1. Assuage my guilt!

As I have indicated previously, guilt is a difficult quality to trap. But there can be no doubt that it is the subtext of many acts of philanthropy. The donor is comfortable, healthy, well fed; the donor's children are getting an education, spending untold amounts of money on clothes, food, leisure and their own entertainment. No man or woman is an island and it would take an unusually insensitive version of either to preside over such privilege without the occasional pang of concern for others who do not.

But the process of guilt arousal is intuitive and subliminal. A headline that said, 'Feel guilty that you pay £70 for your kids' trainers while Romanian orphans are chained to their beds' would not work. And it would not deserve to.

2. I want to achieve something!

W.H. Auden called the 1930s the 'age of anxiety'. Heaven knows what he'd have called the 1990s!

For the spirit of this age is total personal insecurity. No one now has a job for life. One in three marriages ends in divorce. Sportsmen, authors, film directors and pop groups are accorded the status of genius in one year and reviled as mediocre has-beens the next. Even business leaders now seem to be seasonal – masters of the universe in spring, outmanoeuvred dinosaurs come autumn.

So how on earth can you acquire any sense of personal achievement? In days gone by, it came with a career of modest upward mobility, the raising of a stable family, the buying of a house, the acquisition of a car that would last a decade or more. And it came with a society where more people actually *made* things – retired people are able to tell you that they worked on a particular aircraft, or helped build a particular kind of furniture – few of us can define ourselves in relation to such practical achievements.

But a donation to charity can help infuse this spiritual vacuum with a true sense of well-being and self-esteem, however marginal. It is at least something that you can do to demonstrate your human worth, or even the point of your very existence. We all want to achieve something even if the achievement is private and utterly personal.

In *The Raising of Money* by James Gregory Lord, he quotes George G. Kirstein (no, I've never heard him either). 'Apart from the ballot box, philanthropy presents the one opportunity the individual has to express his *(sic)* meaningful choice over the direction in which our society will progress.'

Some charities have it easier than others. A child-sponsorship charity like ActionAid or World Vision can point to the individual sponsored child and tell the donor that he or she is achieving the education, the training, the communal skills that will give that child a better future. A university can tell a businessman that his endowment is buying a new science block. Most charities lack this clear-cut relationship between the donation and the achievement.

But they should not dismiss the power of the idea, even when it must be expressed metaphorically rather than literally. It is always worth writing down the headline, 'This could not have happened without you' in a donor communication and listing the practical results of donor generosity. It may have to be a generalised summary, but ordinary donors will find their own personal place in it.

All of us want to achieve something. Charities can always offer a distinctive answer to that need. How strange that they rarely seek to impart it.

3. I want to belong!

The human race remains deeply tribal – we need the sense of belonging, of fraternity or sorority that confers a sense of pride, of solidarity, of common purpose. A lonely hearts ad in *Time Out* a few years back started 'Woman, 30s, Amnesty, Literature...'

In previous centuries it was the Church that met this need to belong with all its sub-tribal passions. More recently, political movements and parties offered the same degree of social involvement, the same ability to wear your tribal mark with pride – as recently as the early 1950s, the British Labour Party had a membership approaching a million and the French Communist Party could count its card-carrying membership in the millions as late as the Pompidou presidency.

In Europe at least, the Churches have dramatically waning memberships (although the Christian revival in the United States has reversed this trend there). And political parties are numerical shadows of their previous selves – the British Labour Party is currently preening itself after years of aggressive recruitment at having achieved a membership not much more than a third of the figure 40 years ago.

We need to look outside these traditional areas of bonding to see the continued power of the need to belong. Football clubs still offer an answer – the traditional support on the terraces has now been amplified by club-specific chants and songs, by individual, supporter-produced magazines and newsletters, which report on results, developments, club gossip and club jokes. (These 'fanzines', as they are called, are quite often brilliantly written and produced, yet they seem to have passed the analysts of popular culture by. They are a far better expression of working-class culture than all those doomy left-wing plays that Arnold Wesker thought we should watch.) Football fans now no longer confine their support of a particular club to match days. They call up dedicated telephone hot-lines to get the latest news. They wear the club shirts on the streets. They buy club videos.

And look at pop music. I have often rued on public platforms the growing tribalisation of the music that has marked all our lives. In the sixties, I say – rising to my theme like a

Colonel Blimp bewailing the calumnies of the young – we used to have universal pop music. Everyone could enjoy everything without fear of tribal damnation. Gad, even your parents could admit to liking the Beatles – and the rest of us could swing entirely subjectively from the Stones to Motown, from Pink Floyd to Dionne Warwick.

Not now. You are no longer a pop music fan. You are into hip hop, heavy metal, club, indie, reggae, soul, rap, or techno, while we old fogies are left with something called easy listening. This is yet another display of social tribalism, a sad one because – like football club affiliation – it soon descends into stupid combativeness. But it does underline the continued need of people to belong and the power of communications that feeds the need. Why else does my daughter receive postcards from Oasis, telling her of their upcoming tour dates? This is the tribe that has secured her current affiliation.

In charities, as so often, the 'belonging' message is a subtext. A formal membership, or at least a formal mass membership is usually out of the question – who needs supporters who put down awkward resolutions at annual general meetings? But the instinct is still there. It is almost always profitable to surround a high donor appeal with the imagery of the 'club' – that special feeling of being on the inside of things, of being close to the organisation, of belonging better and more visibly.

There is a danger of banality in such literal responses to the need to belong. But fundraisers badly need to be more imaginative and full blooded about meeting the need, of giving donors a sense of being 'on the team', as the Americans would say. Few of us want to be alone in our enthusiasms. We enthuse the more by knowing that the enthusiasms are shared with thousands of others.

Some of the humblest and most traditional forms of fundraising acknowledge this. Why else do we sport stickers and little badges when we have put a coin in a tin? Why do millions of us walk round wearing poppies in early November? Why do young people carry on wearing their AIDS ribbons months after World AIDS Day? To be sure, there is an element of posturing in this – I wear a poppy so I am a deeply caring person, I acknowledge my debt to war veterans. But so what? We should not resent the display if we can secure the commitment.

Belonging is increasingly important to people and charities could offer the best kind of belonging. If we turned round many of our staple means of communication and saw them in this mode, we might be very surprised at their new efficacy.

Take the telephone. It now has an honourable place in the process of 'upgrading' donors and a less-honourable place in recruiting them. But CARE UK had a very bright idea in 1995. It put a recorded message on a dedicated telephone line, a message that had one of its field workers from Africa reporting on the week's work there. And donors were invited to call to check out the latest developments on the project. Being diligent, CARE tested the idea as back-up to a routine house mailing. A free 0839 number was even tested against a regular 0171 number. This simple low cost idea increased response by up to 60 per cent on a mailing that yielded an average donation of better than £20. And responses to the 0171 cell were higher than those to the 0839 cell.

Just a gimmick? I don't think so. It genuinely offered an imaginative means of belonging better.

4. I want to stop something, start something, eradicate something!

Well, don't you?

I guess you'd like to abolish hunger, secure harmony in the former Yugoslavia, find a cure for multiple sclerosis, plug the holes in the ozone layer, sustain growing numbers of pandas, release political prisoners and ensure that old people didn't die of hypothermia. You'd be a louse if you didn't.

Every charity appeal offers intimations of these universal human ambitions. But, in that drive to political verbal correctness, the rhetoric, the excitement of wanting to change the world tends to become increasingly lost. The language has become prolix and proper, the thrill goes missing. You are being sold a set of technical programmes, but you really want that sense that they add up to a historic achievement, one to which you can attach your name. And the two things are not mutually exclusive. It is perfectly possible to report with diligence while still retaining the sense of colossal achievement.

Just add sentences like these to the prose.

'God knows when we'll find a cure – or even the beginnings of a cure – for this terrible disease. But we intend to find it. Continue to help us and we'll find it quicker.'

Or, 'People like yourself helped us feed 200,000 refugees in Rwanda. That is why I ask you to help us deal with this new challenge in Burundi.'

Or, 'We cannot win this battle overnight. But it is possible that we can remove the threat of CFCs during your lifetime – if you continue to support our campaign.'

Each of these simple pieces of rhetoric elevates the appeal just slightly. It gives the donor what the donor wants to have – the belief that the world may be a little better, or at least more promising, as a result of that donation.

Not that donors are daft. They know that a donation to Greenpeace will not seal the holes in the ozone layer. They know that a donation to WWF will be unlikely to save a single rhinoceros. They know that a donation to the Motor Neurone Disease Association

THIS is an open letter to all my friends in Great Britain:

The first non-racial democratic elections ever known in South Africa – on 27th April 1994 – could at last bring the peace and freedom for which so many South Africans earnestly pray.

Much ground has already been gained. But we still have an urgent problem. We do not have enough money to fight this election. **Yet it is absolutely vital to convince people that the peaceful and democratic road is the only viable route for our country.**

Our present position on the Transitional Executive Council is no guarantee of achieving democracy. We must have a decisive electoral majority to ensure our reconstruction policies are carried out.

'Votes for Freedom' is our campaign to raise one million pounds from within the United Kingdom to help us win this critical election. I am asking you, right now, to support the campaign. We need your support today.

Apartheid and its resultant violence has blighted South African lives for the last thirty years. The movement I have the honour to lead, the African National Congress, represents all sections of South African society and has spoken out against repression for over 80 years.

Who will win?

I know that we have justice on our side. I believe our years of struggle and sacrifice have earned us the right to lead South Africa into a future free from every vestige of apartheid.

But the National Party, and its allies on the right, are strong. They are a minority but they have access to enormous wealth – and they are past masters of media manipulation. They have hired Sir Tim Bell, architect of Mrs. Thatcher's most formidable electoral triumphs, as an adviser.

I am asking our friends in Great Britain – and I hope that means you – to come forward now. We have to know how much help we can rely on.

Freedom is the greatest gift.

If you really want democracy for South Africa – and many have suffered and died for that dream – then do not be lulled into a false sense of security. The result of this election is by no means a foregone conclusion.

We of the ANC are the natural guarantors of democracy in South Africa – whereas the National Party's history makes its continuation in power a threat to any democratic future.

We have earned the respect and a place in the hearts of most South African people – we are a non-racial alliance of men and women representing all classes in South Africa.

But this overwhelming support must be translated into an overwhelming number of votes. Most of our supporters have never had the opportunity to take part in any kind of election before – let alone a secret ballot, with all the complexities involved.

After years of brutal repression freedom is within sight.

Participation in conventional political activity has been denied our supporters ever since whites only rule was imposed 83 years ago. Yet these disadvantaged voters must now learn, instantly, a whole new language – the grammar and syntax of democracy.

There is so much to do. We must ensure that people from remote country areas can get to the polls. And when voting takes place, we must ensure the rules that apply to voting slips are fully understood: every accidentally spoiled ballot paper would be a vote lost for freedom.

Let us not forget, either, the ability of our opponents to play a very dirty political game. For the experts in dirty tricks to rob us of our achievement now, would be the last and dirtiest trick of all!

Why we need the support of people in Britain.

Somehow we must match the vast resources of our opponents. That is why I am asking for your help. We need you to tell us we can count on you. Fill in the coupon opposite and you will help us achieve our goal.

Votes ☒ for FREEDOM

PHOTO: IDAF

Can we count on you?

Achieving that goal – the political liberation of every adult human being in South Africa – will require skills which under-privileged people have been denied the freedom to develop. Our election workers must learn to organise, to manage, to communicate and administer. And all at short notice.

Consider the scale of the problem. This is the minimum we need to do:

● Train 210,000 volunteers to help newly enfranchised people understand their right to vote
● Set up 94 properly equipped regional offices: canvassers and party workers need proper resources
● Teach 140 trainers and organisers to direct the efforts of ANC volunteers more efficiently
● Set up a proper communications network: the 'phones and faxes that party workers in Britain would take for granted
● Invest in detailed constituency research so we can relate our policies to the issues which directly concern each locality
● Buy bicycles and motorbikes so our representatives can travel unrestricted around South Africa

The cost of all this will be many millions. We are not asking our British friends to carry all, or even most, of this great burden. But I hope that those who have provided such encouragement

Will young South Africans grow up in a free, non-racial democracy? Your help will decide.

through the long years of our struggle will be able to help us to raise our target of £1 million within the United Kingdom.

When you make your contribution it will be put to good use straight away. There is a crying and immediate need for sufficient funds so that we can mount our election campaign in South Africa effectively. We have a great objective before us, and I hope your hearts will be generous.

This is history. It's happening now, and you can be part of it.

As soon as we have your address 'Votes for Freedom' will be able to keep you in touch with news from South Africa. It will be real news, about real people, and sent to you with all possible speed.

The South Africa that I want to see cannot become reality unless we can turn the overwhelming support for democracy amongst all South Africans into an overwhelming majority of votes.

The under-privileged majority in South Africa still need to be convinced of the importance of each individual vote. We have to make it clear to everyone that for a democratic future they must exercise this hard-won right. Many are still nervous, and understandably fear retaliation by the old regime.

They need reassurance and for that we need your help. We need to know we can count on you now. Please give us your support today.

[signature] Nelson Mandela

We have set ourselves the target of raising one million pounds within the UK to fight the South African election. We need to know <u>now</u>, how much of your help we can rely on. We are asking friends of democracy in Britain to:

1 Make a donation to '<u>Votes for Freedom</u>' now by returning this form.

2 We will then keep you informed about our election campaign in South Africa.

An extraordinary fundraising story: £1 million was raised for a political party on the other side of the world.

SEPTEMBER 1996

OCTOBER 1996

NOVEMBER 1996

FEBRUARY 1997

MARCH 1997

APRIL 1997

MAY 1997

YOUR GUESS IS AS GOOD AS OURS

BUT, WHATEVER THE DATE OF THAT GENERAL ELECTION IT'S NOW JUST WEEKS AWAY!

Dear Supporter,

This could be our last appeal for financial help before the next General Election.

I mean it. We may not have the time and we may not have the money to ask a certainly have a mound of other things to do. When you are running a small c organisation like Charter 88 and doing it on a knife-edge budget, then you can promise that this is the last time you'll be asking for money (it would be irres But I am willing to make you, the individual supporter, your own version of th

If you can give to this one appeal, then I promise that you will not be ask financial support between now and the calling of a General Election.

I take my life in my hands when I say that and I ignore the advice of some of when I do so. For the wretched fact of fund-raising is that the bulk of the mon in from a small minority of totally dedicated supporters. This letter, for instance twenty odd thousand of Charter 88 supporters who have given us money in th than a third of the total number if signatories. And a third of you are already g make your financial commitment by standing order - in doing so, you have pr Charter 88 in business these last few years.

So, in making a promise not to ask again, I may be denying us future income It is only the utter urgency of our situation that has me doing such a thing. I j that I have got the equation right.

Mobilising a pressure group: Charter 88 supporters are regularly treated to rhetoric and regularly respond to it.

it's NOW?¹²³

HAVE YOU EVER BEEN INVITED TO A REVOLUTION?

or NEVER

will not secure a cure to that terrifying disease. But they want to buy the dream – and fundraisers should not sneer at this dream, this deeply rooted human instinct that the whole world could somehow change for the better if decent people did decent things. There is no soppier pop song than John Lennon's 'Imagine', but its wide-eyed lyrics are still capable of moving rational people to tears – and I include myself in their number.

Never convince yourself that donors are immune from the dream of doing amazing things, of eradicating this evil or ending that atrocity, of starting something quite remarkable in history. Nothing else can explain the astonishing success of the campaign that WWAV Rapp Collins ran for the African National Congress in the 18 months before South Africa's first democratic election. The campaign was mounted in Britain, for a political party in a faraway country. Yet it recruited 24,000 supporters from scratch and raised more than £1 million.

I have been writing for Charter 88 for the last six years. It is that most apparently boring of causes a constitutional pressure group whose 60,000 supporters comprise academics, political activists, lawyers and a host of ordinary people who want a new, written constitution for the United Kingdom. If ever there was a bunch of people who should be immune from rhetoric, wary of excitement and suspicious of vulgar rallying calls, it is surely this band of sophisticates. But the appeal they received in January 1996 had the banner headline 'When's the last time you were invited to a revolution?' And the letter embroidered the revolutionary theme.

> *We have been expressing ourselves with proper and diligent politeness. It's time we began to shout. So that the message, our message, is sure to be heard. Let me restate that message. It says that we are fed up to the back teeth with our current political system, with its arrogant political masters, its culture of secrecy, its lack of individual participation, its sleaze and its corruption, its cynicism, its uselessness. Britain can do better than this. And the people of Britain must demand that things change – quickly, radically and profoundly. So, yes, you are invited to a revolution in the making...*

Phwoooer! It matters less that you can probably hear the tub-thumping of Lambeth Borough Council in there somewhere. What matters a lot is that supporters were roused by a rousing message.

People want to change the world. Don't deny them the privilege. We all want to buy a dream and it is not just cynicism that should make the fundraiser articulate the dream and constantly offer it. For it was the dream that started our charities in the first place. Who are we to betray the dream with the language of bureaucracy rather than that of mission?

5. I want to be *seen* to be good!

For the religious, it might be a place in Heaven. For the rest of us it might be a badge, a certificate, an invitation, a State decoration even.

But the fundraiser is well advised to acknowledge the donor's need, not just for reward but for perceived reward. It is not everyone's need — any list of major benefactors will always include a good smattering of Anons and many good people would run a mile if threatened with any public celebration of their generosity.

But that still leaves a lot of equally good people who will not demur from such commemoration. In some cases, the commemoration is literal. I think of the book in the reception area of WWF UK that lists all its legators and which is constantly updated. I think of those annual reports that find room to list all major donors. I think of Wolfson College, Oxford and the Midland Bank season at the Birmingham Royal Ballet — for what is sponsorship other than the most commercial variant on the theme of wanting to be seen to be good?

Few of us are so self-effacing that we can sneer at this need. My own study is bedecked with business certificates, awards and ceremonial photographs of me in the company of my peers. And how many people throw away their school examination certificates?

My local butcher in Kent has a wall full of charity receipts confirming the generosity of customers who have put coins in collecting devices there. The local pub features a picture of the labrador financed by local drinkers on behalf of Guide Dogs for the Blind (and a little chart showing how much they have raised for the next labrador). When you 'sponsor' an acre of rain forest with WWF UK you receive a certificate confirming your status as a donor. Be they ever so humble, such things confer status, however privately.

They must seem banal in such a sceptical age. But they work, even amongst people you might expect to be above such gewgaws.

I cannot think of a better example than the totally unlikely one of the Social Democratic Party, that comet that temporarily blazed across the British political skies in the 1980s. In its *annus mirabilis,* the year of its foundation, 1981, the SDP recruited nearly 90,000 signed-up members, many of them the famous 'political virgins' who had never before been involved in politics and who had clustered excitedly around a new political product that was suddenly fashionable. How could we persuade these fashion purchasers, to renew their membership for the second year when the fashion was waning?

Would you believe a certificate, nay a Founder Member's certificate? The SDP actually had very little money, no matter how much the media insisted otherwise. All we could afford was a four-page A4 piece, with two pages devoted to a message from the then Gang

Simple but effective: the famous SDP Founder Members mailing.

of Four (what fun it was to get copy approved by Jenkins, Owen, Williams and Rodgers), with the back half of the piece serving as the famous Founder Member's certificate, facsimile-signed by the aforesaid Gang of Four. We could not even afford to personalise it, humbly asking the members to write in their own name on the dotted line. They did, bless them, they did. Renewal rate as a result of this piece of heroic tat was not much less than 90 per cent.

And remember, these were sophisticates – professional folk, the chattering classes, those who could be expected to find such crude direct marketing techniques just slightly beneath their patrician dignity. I visited one of them in South London a little later – a considerable journalist of fiercely stated views. There, above the mantelpiece of the Georgian drawing room, was our little SDP certificate – not just dutifully signed by the master of the house but, even more dutifully, framed by him under glass.

And what is the Democratic National Committee offering supporters for a large gift to President Clinton's re-election campaign in 1996? Why, a print of a water-colour of the White House! It is probably destined to be framed throughout the Union.

The donor's need for some degree of recognition can therefore be met at a simple and indeed a positively vulgar level. Paper products are cheap: they add pence to the appeal and can add pounds to the average donation. Better than that, they serve as a reminder of the relationship between your organisation and the donor, a relationship that will thrive because you made that extra effort at gratitude.

Not that certificates and prints are always the answer. An invitation to a special meeting or reception, even without fundraising undertones, is always flattering. Greenpeace UK was astounded at the numbers of *Frontline* supporters who flocked to the briefing meetings it offered, where campaigners brought them up to date with the organisation's work. Open Days at the charity's office may be irritating but they are always worth the irritation. ActionAid used to hold weekend conferences for its child sponsors. They are all ways of saying 'thank you', however obliquely.

For it is a simple idea really. Give something and you want to hear someone saying thank you. That is why they remain the two most powerful words in the fundraising vocabulary. But we too often leave them as words on a reply form. We should continue to look for ways to give them more meaning. For the donor, however apparently reticent, wants to hear them not just said but said out loud.

When Guy Stringer was director of Oxfam, he had a Friday evening ritual whereby he used to ring a dozen or so donors picked at random from that week's postbag. He just said thank you, and the sound of Guy's voice saying thank you must make one of the most warm and endearing phone calls you will ever receive. I wonder what was the eventual financial return on this tiny piece of communications investment?

So, what do donors want? They want an assuagement of guilt, they want a sense of achievement and of belonging, they want a sense of historic mission and they want some public or private recording of their giving.

Not all of them, I grant you. There are donors whose altruism is utterly worldly, who know that the world will never really change, who want to keep the charity at arm's length, who require no reward for their philanthropy for it is sceptically given. They do not dream, these donors.

Most of us do, though. Which is why fundraisers need to concentrate more on what donors want and less on what we want to tell them. For there is becoming a terrible cleavage here. The next chapter tries to articulate it.

BUT WHAT DOES THE DONOR GET?

Charities increasingly use the wrong word to describe people who give them money. They call them 'supporters', a comforting noun that suggests knowing commitment on the part of the donor. Sadly, it is often an over-statement of what has actually happened.

We need the word as a generic description of the many varieties of giving – members, donors, standing-order donors, covenantors and the like – but it deludes us, for it suggests *continuing* affiliation to our respective causes. We are faced with statistics that demonstrate just how thin a thesis that is – some people now calculate that as many as 62 per cent of donors never give again to that organisation and that less than 50 per cent of the minority who do give again will *ever* give beyond a second donation, no matter how vigorous or frequent the process of follow-up. We have invented another fancy word for this fall-off factor – we call it 'attrition'. Again, it suggests a relationship that probably never existed in the first place.

I have already tumbled into direct marketing language and I should make the point that I am talking about the process of donor recruitment that is achieved by direct marketing techniques – direct mail, press advertising and the telephone. These have become the staple means of new donor recruitment, at least throughout most of the Western world and the direct marketing budgets of many senior British charities now run into millions of pounds. The initial success and later foundering of these techniques are themes I will return to later. Right now, I should like to explore the dangerous tunnel vision that has come with the growth of database marketing in the charity field.

Very many donations are spontaneous. People respond to something they see in the media – a natural disaster, a Bosnia, a Rwanda. Or they respond to a revealed need closer to their normal lives – a cancer or MS diagnosis in the family. Or they feel obliged to do something at special times – Christmas remains the prime example. This spontaneity can be provoked by the direct marketer but the direct marketer should not presume on much more than the spontaneity. Too often they see that one response as a declaration of abiding support. It rarely is.

You see the phenomenon most clearly with disaster appeals, where the public will respond massively and quickly to press ads and broadcast appeals. But they are often giving to the subject area and not to the specific charity brand. There must have been six or eight direct response ads for charities in the British press in the days when the full horror of Rwanda was revealed on our television screens. They will all have done well, but the key word in the headlines was not Oxfam or Red Cross or UNICEF – it was Rwanda. It was a reflex act of generosity that did not leave these donors as supporters of the respective organisations – the vast majority of people will have said, 'I have sent money to Rwanda', not 'I have become a supporter of the Red Cross'.

This lack of brand awareness is amplified by every broadcast telethon. For here the appeal is at its most general and vacuous. People are giving to the event and only by derivation to an organisation. What exactly *is* Comic Relief or Children in Need? I do not wish to disparage these utterly successful and totally honourable appeals, which raise tens of millions of pounds every year, I just use them to underline the point that many donations are less than brand-specific. Run a piece of awareness research on specific charity brands and you will evoke lots of responses that say, 'I give to children's charities', or 'I give to cancer', before respondents start mentioning individual charities. Some of our most famous and heavily advertised charities will attain a spontaneous recall factor of no more than five per cent.

Yet we address letters to millions of people that begin 'Dear Supporter'. Which is a bit like addressing a list of buyers of a washing-up liquid seized from the supermarket shelf as 'Dear Fairy Liquid Buyer'. It is at best a harmless conceit, but at worst it suggests a certain presumption that could offend. And it certainly insulates us from thought. We need to explore the difference between two statements. One says 'We have 200,000 supporters.' The other says 'In the last 18 months 200,000 have given to us'. The second statement is fact, the first is bluster.

For, if you respond to a direct mail appeal, you will then receive other direct mail appeals, probably lots of them. You will increasingly receive telemarketing calls. The tone of voice of all these appeals will be the same, and the message continuous, 'you have given once, now give again'. It is probably the only area of human communication where a message so raw, so presumptuous, so insensitive is repeated so very often.

See it from the donors' point of view. They give a donation and they are asked to repeat it four times a year, six times a year, 12 times a year. Worse, you may have traded their names and addresses with another charity – more appeals, more irritation.

The fundraiser can hide behind the tradecraft. Mail enough appeals, accept the given percentage of predictive response and you are raising funds. Add in the marginal revenue from reciprocal rentals (which, incidentally, is a practice I endorse) and you have a vigorous direct marketing programme. Spend a million, gross three million, net two million – it is a conventional and practical achievement for such a programme.

But what is the true cost? Very few house mailings ever achieve a 25 per cent response – most are in the range five per cent to 15 per cent. Which means that the vast majority of 'supporters' deny us their support when asked. In fact, many charities I know turn out to have more 'lapsed' donors than they have 'active' donors. Is this a sign of organisational health? A fmcg company that had more former buyers than current buyers would probably withdraw that product from the market.

I pursue this theme because I genuinely believe that a charity donation is more important than the purchase of a supermarket product, an insurance policy, or a mail-order windscreen for the car. This probably makes me a sentimental old fluff, but I shall carry on insisting that a relationship with 'good' is, at best, more profound than a relationship with an artefact.

So, in worrying about the insensitivity of many fundraising direct marketing programmes, I am trying to occupy some higher moral ground in the belief that we are not always best served by the inevitable logistics of direct marketing. It cannot be a good thing that charities and causes become seen as mere junk mailers. And the equations over which we preside are becoming ever more difficult to explain to the donor.

THE EQUATIONS OVER WHICH WE PRESIDE ARE BECOMING EVER MORE DIFFICULT TO EXPLAIN TO THE DONOR.

Take a reasonable model of current practice. It starts with a recruitment package at perhaps £400 per thousand – 40p a unit. Response may be at one per cent, which means that 10 people in a thousand will reply and go on to our donor file. And maybe one of those 10 will reply to a further appeal. You can move these figures around marginally but they are neither unfair nor atypical. And millions of fundraising pounds are deployed in pursuit of such figures, for in volume terms they aggregate to apparently successful fundraising.

But, think about it from the donor's point of view. Let's saddle ourselves with some pretty bleak derivatives of the same arithmetic. Let's look at it like this.

1. We spend 40 pence to talk to one person with a mailshot.

2. We persuade maybe one person in a hundred to give.

3. We therefore spend £40 in finding a new donor, less whatever they send by way of a first donation.

4. We acknowledge that most of these donors will never give again.

Try explaining this to the average donor. Try saying that a £20 donation will promptly be used to buy another 50 mailshots geared to achieve the results described above. The donor would want his or her money back.

Of course, I over-simplify to make a point. I know that cold mailings can produce three per cent response rates. I know that it is possible to recruit at apparent break even. But I also know that such instances are the exceptions and that what I have offered above is nearer the fundraising norm. We should not be so dazzled by volume statistics, that we refuse to examine the raw and difficult equation over which we begin to preside.

For the donor would be troubled by it. And the donor is certainly troubled by the avalanche of appeal mailings that can now stem from that original donation. The failure to respond, the silence, the inaction of that donor is eloquent. All the evidence suggests that the donor is not getting what he or she wants.

THE FAILURE TO RESPOND, THE SILENCE, THE INACTION OF THAT DONOR IS ELOQUENT.

Imagine that you had given a pound to one of those young homeless people in the doorways of the Strand. Imagine that every night you passed them on your way to the station and every night they made the same request for a pound in the same tone of voice. Your original benevolence would be diffused as the days passed. By the end of the week you would probably have moved into outright hostility. Is it too much to suggest that you might have given this young person £5 during the week if the request had been varied, if it had been surrounded by friendly conversation, if you had been presented with convincing gratitude, with a more reasoned depiction of the need, with a *relationship* between the two of you?

Sometimes it is profitable to see fundraising for what it truly is – people asking other people for money.

Some of this may sound apocalyptic. It really isn't meant to be. I'd just like fundraisers to think better and more profoundly about what they are doing. Direct marketing will go on and it will increase. I am merely looking for ways in which it can be made more profitable – not just for the fundraisers but also for the donors. All the evidence suggests that the two ambitions go together.

The irritation threshold

I am staring at a mailing that arrived this very morning. It contains a plastic spoon. I have never knowledgeably given to the charity who sent me this mailing, but I know of them and what I know is good. But they have sent me a spoon.

The spoon is explained in a strong letter of 200 words, which tells me that they want to fill such spoons with sugar and salt, an oral rehydration therapy that will stop young children dying of dehydration. A treatment costs just 10 pence. With a £15 donation, therefore, I can save 150 children's lives.

This is probably the most important thing I shall be asked to do today. A charity appeal can have no more persuasive message than this one. So why am I still looking at this mailing? Why am I not rushing a donation into an envelope?

Sadly, because I am annoyed by it. It is a perfectly good example of direct mail tradecraft, produced cheaply and apparently sponsored by a salt company. It tells me no apparent lies, gives me a dutiful amount of information about the charity's work, makes its simple case with force and vigour. *But it's another bloody appeal mailing!*

So I don't like it. I don't like the message on the envelope, I don't like the mock-typewritten letter, I don't like the reply form with its tick boxes for respective donations, I don't like the reply envelope. And I certainly don't like the spoon.

And, because I resent this communication, I rationalise my irritation with darker thoughts. I begin not to believe the charity. Will it really spend my donation on its oral rehydration programme? Will 150 children really be saved with my £15? Does it really spend less than 11 pence in every pound on administration and fundraising?

These, I should point out, are considered reactions, those of someone who has actually opened the envelope and persuaded himself to articulate his feelings. If it had been addressed to my wife it would not have got this far – it would already be nestling in the waste-paper basket. *Another bloody appeal mailing!*

It is all horribly unfair. The charity has produced a communication of apparent integrity and considerable technique. It has made a simple request for a small donation that will save children's lives. And I, like the vast majority of people who receive it, look like refusing its request. This is the price we pay for the medium in which we convey the message. I know why this communication takes the shape it does, why it uses the tone of voice it does, even why it contains a plastic spoon. But I know precisely, too precisely, what will happen just as soon as I see the envelope on the doormat. I know that the envelope will contain a letter, a donation form, a reply envelope and a request for £15. I know that my name and address will be labelled on to the reply form, that its right-hand side will contain credit card details, that there will be tick boxes and the news that the Government applies GiftAid tax paybacks on a gift of more than £250.

Do I know these things because I am a practitioner of the same trade as the author, a keen-eyed spectator of fundraising mailings?

No, I know these things because I've already received eight such appeals this month. With tick boxes, credit card details on the right-hand side, news about GiftAid and a request for £15. I've been asked to help old people, to protect forests, to save endangered species, to fight AIDS and, now, to help rehydrate infant children. I am in favour of all these charities, I am rich enough to support most of them.

But my cheque-writing hand has stayed immobile. Because I have been *bored* into inaction. The predictable is rarely entertaining and hardly ever provocative. The constant, thoughtless repetition of the charity message in the same technical mode, using the same tricks, the same language, the same envelopes and the same tradecraft arouses boredom. It crosses an individual's irritation threshold. For the practitioner's earnestly applied tradecraft is simply the consumer's junk mail.

And there is one other reason why I am negative about this morning's appeal. It is the sure knowledge that, if I send £15, I will be added to the charity's 'supporters' file and will be sent lots of other appeals with tick boxes and credit card details on the right-hand side. Someone might phone me. The charity might continue to bore me in different ways. This prospect is truly chastening.

But, in the interests of professional probity, I shall now subject myself to this likely scenario. It is Valentine's Day, 1996 and I have just sent £15. Further reports are promised. I can keep the spoon. The letter tells me so.

What do we want people to buy?

I have tried to explain my own beliefs about why people give and what they expect of the charities to whom they give. And I have been distinctly peevish about what I see charities giving in return. It is time to explore this strange cleavage in understanding.

Not for the first time, it helps to take a close look at the words involved. Fundraisers tend to ask for 'donations,' or (particularly in the United States) 'gifts'. Occasionally you might see 'contribution' and for another kind of organisation it could be 'subscription'. But mostly it's 'donation'. Which clearly makes donors donors. Indeed, the totally unnecessary word 'donate' is now creeping into our vocabularies – a report in my files is solemnly titled 'Issues to which supporters might donate'.

But only the most pompous people actually use the word 'donation' in everyday speech. Indeed, it almost needs pompous epithets and excess verbal baggage as in 'I have made a considerable donation', or 'We are pleased to enclose a donation'.

Ordinary people do not talk like this. They say 'I've given money to...', or 'I support...', or 'I'm helping....', or even 'I contribute to'. Not that they particularly look for a verb to describe an act that they would prefer to see as a private one. The donor/donate/donation litany is that of the practitioner not of the customer. And this verbal dysfunction gets worse as the fundraising vocabulary expands to reflect the growing technique involved. The fundraiser talks of major donors, a form of words that the people involved would never apply to themselves, even if they knew where they sit on the database. Then you have committed donors, regular donors and that most shameful of categories, that lost tribe, the 'lapseds'.

All this heavy nomenclature is inevitable if we are to communicate with intelligence and precision. But we should acknowledge that we are deploying a different language, that we are using terms to describe people that they do not apply to themselves. For the language of segmentation can easily begin to infest the communication itself – I have seen letters whose salutation is the absurd 'Dear Major Donor', which sounds like it was mis-addressed to a fictional character out of *Catch 22*.

But unthinking allegiance to the language of the database infers something else. It suggests that our only language is fiscal, that the only measure of worth and activity is the recency, frequency and size of the donation, the response to an upgrading programme, the tick boxes ticked. It has to be an arid language, this constant repetition of percentages and ratios. True, we are stuck with it as the only final expression of our worth as fundraisers. But it can also make us myopic, for it correlates only in part to the donor's true instincts, needs and desires. How much is 'the donation' really the expression of those instincts, needs and desires?

Let me take that last example, the spoon mailing. It asks for a £15 donation and gives me tick boxes wherein I can vary that predictive donation. But it is actually communicating something far more dramatic, the apparent ability to save children's lives with oral rehydration therapy. This therapy, and the programme that doubtless sustains it, is the product, the fact. The donation is the device, the metaphor. I want to buy the product but I am forced to buy the metaphor. Bear in mind that this organisation is new to me. I have not asked for this mailing. I may know nothing about the charity that sent it to me. Yet it wants me to make *it* a donation. I suspect that it would be better off trying to sell me the product, the programme, the oral rehydration therapy. I am happy to accept it as agent for the process.

By now I am being distinctly unkind about this perfectly innocuous mailing. It commits no sins of taste, no professional heresies. I just suspect that it could profitably have said that 300 children in Somalia were due to get this treatment next month. At which point it could have asked £30 of me to pay for that event. I could not have a more pleasant dream.

The donor wants to buy something, however dream-like. That something can fairly if crudely be called a product. It is a product that should meet the donor's needs. Fundraisers rarely think in terms of product development, but they certainly should. And, given the pressure of competition in our market-place, they are probably going to have to.

Study your weekly shopping to see the analogy. My need is to wash up. My favoured brand for the process is Fairy Liquid. So I buy Fairy Liquid to do the washing up. I do not walk up and down the supermarket aisles wanting to make a contribution to the general well-being of Procter and Gamble who make Fairy Liquid. This may come as a rude surprise to the folk at P and G but it's only fair that they know the harsh truth. I think they are men enough to take it.

Actually, I suspect that they know it anyway. Charities need to know it as well, to see themselves as marketers of products and meeters of need. That traditional £15 donation may not be a good enough product for many people.

Life-enhancing products

There's something glum about the average £15 donation to a charity. It may leave you with a sense of duty discharged, but it rarely leaves you with either a sense of mission accomplished or dream enacted.

The products we need to create to meet donors' needs should set out to be life enhancing, thrilling, imaginative. It is possible, even in such a sceptical age as ours.

Some charities and causes are lucky enough to be able to offer these products by the very nature of their activity. They have donors who can say things like,

- I am paying for this child's education.
- I am supporting this project.
- I am sponsoring this exhibition.
- I am building this swimming pool.

Most charities cannot offer these simplicities. Their programmes are properly diverse and their managers properly inhibited at seeming to offer simplicities. Even a successful child-sponsorship organisation like ActionAid is keen to educate its supporters away from the wide-eyed belief that all the sponsor's money is simply spent on the one child. Quite right too.

But the donor's need to believe that his or hers is a distinctive contribution is not entirely dismissable. And the need can be met in other ways than formal earmarking of donations or project-specific appeals. It may seem paradoxical, but one of those ways is to ask for more money, lots more money.

Greenpeace UK famously did this with its *Frontline* scheme in the early 1990s. It took a deep breath and asked people to commit to giving £20 a month, an astounding request for an organisation believed to be supported by indigent hippies and tree-huggers. Surprise, surprise! Greenpeace turned out to have thousands of supporters willing to give at that level. I shall return to *Frontline* later for I regard it as one of those rare fundraising campaigns that promises to change the known rules of our business. But, at this point, I just want to record its apparent life-enhancing qualities, its obvious meeting of the needs of Greenpeace supporters..

Greenpeace invited the first generation of *Frontline* supporters to a meeting at headquarters where campaigners would bring them up to date with the organisation's latest research and actions. The event was utterly successful within those terms of reference, but it achieved almost mystical significance when supporters found their way across Greenpeace's little yard and into the warehouse at the back.

For there are stored the artefacts of Greenpeace's campaigns – the wet suits, the banners, above all those famous inflatables that we have all seen, bravely skimming the waves, confronting the whalers, out-manoeuvring the authorities. *Frontline* supporters were awestruck and visibly moved to be in the presence of these familiar tools of the Greenpeace trade. They beamed at them. Some eyes were distinctly moist. And, then a few brave souls reached out and touched the inflatables. It was as near a religious observance as a charity is likely to get. Touching the inflatables, it sounds like a line from a *Carry On* film, but it's a wonderful example of the strange and tender things that are in our supporters' minds.

FRONTLINE *SUPPORTERS WERE AWESTRUCK AND VISIBLY MOVED TO BE IN THE PRESENCE OF THESE FAMILIAR TOOLS OF THE GREENPEACE TRADE.*

Some life-enhancing products can be altogether more orthodox. 'Clubs' for larger donors may be anathema to some purists but they work.

They can be literal, as in the case of the NSPCC's Benjamin Waugh Foundation, or NCH Action for Children's George Thomas Society, offering get-togethers and special events for those willing to pay more for entry into a social network that may occasionally be enriched by the great and the equally good. The Labour Party now has a 500 Club where a commitment of £500 enables you to spend even more money on attending fundraising events and the chance to glimpse party luminaries. The British Red Cross Society launched a 125 Society, asking for a £1,000 opening donation. Such élite groups are probably the most important fixture in American political fundraising. There is no point in sneering at the base motives that may fuel this élitism – they make people feel good by giving more. And giving more because they feel better.

And 'clubs' can be more metaphorical than literal. You can surround a high-level appeal with the apparent glitz of an élite group and saddle yourself with no greater responsibility than that of further communication. In 1994 WWF UK launched a Guardians scheme to its most loyal donors (though not its absolutely top donors). The letter was from the director, the stationery was high class and the reply element took the

acceptance

form of an 'acceptance certificate'. It asked for a cool £1,000 to help fund the charity's work for tigers and promised only to keep Guardians in touch with the deployment of their subscription during the year of the appeal.

As soon as I saw the visuals at Smith Bundy, I knew it would work. It was authoritative, it was important, it was distinctive, it was special. And it raised over £150,000 – a sum that was repeated in 1995 when we made the same request on behalf of WWF's rhino preservation programme. Some segments of the carefully chosen list responded at nearly 12 per cent and subsequent telephone research has demonstrated how honestly pleased these donors were to be asked. Many of them have since eschewed any interest in how WWF spends the money (conspicuously few ever took up the offer we made of being able to phone a campaigner direct and discuss the projects). They take the charity totally on trust, a tribute to the relationship they enjoy with WWF.

But the biggest revelation of WWF Guardians was a technical one. The acceptance certificate did the decent thing in giving donors the ability to give their £1,000 in monthly stages – a less-forbidding £83 a month. Just three people took the option. The rest just stuffed a cheque for £1,000 in the envelope.

But there was also another element of the WWF Guardians appeal that undoubtedly fuelled its success. The newly appointed director of WWF, the signatory of the letter, himself pledged to give £1,000. This is clearly not a tactic that can be repeated too

To the Office of Dr Robin Pellew, Director, World Wide Fund For Nature, FREEPOST, Panda House, Godalming, Surrey GU7 1BR.

I wish to accept your

invitation

to become a WWF guardian for the calendar year of 1994.

Here is my donation of £ _____(minimum £1,000).
I understand that it will be used for WWF's Tiger Projects and that you will keep me regularly informed about the precise use of money donated by The guardians.

☐ *I enclose a cheque made payable to WWF UK.*

OR

☐ *I wish to pay by credit card, therefore please debit my Access/Visa Card (please delete as appropriate).*

Card
Number ☐☐☐☐ ☐☐☐☐ ☐☐☐☐ ☐☐☐☐

Credit Card Expiry Date _____/_____

Signature _____ Date _____

A single donation of £1,000 or more means that if you are a tax payer you qualify for Gift Aid.
☐ *The relevant information will be sent to you by return. Please tick this box if you do not pay income tax.*

☐ *I propose to pay by monthly direct debit in instalments of £ _____ and have completed the instructions to my bank or building society opposite.*

☐ *I would like to give by Covenant. Please send me the appropriate forms by return.*

OR *continued opposite...*

PLEASE DO NOT DETACH

Asking for a large donation demands an extra degree of authority and ceremony. It may just be a reply form but the use of words like 'Invitation' and 'Acceptance' elevate the proposition in the reader's mind. Note the careful use of typography throughout.

often lest charity directors descend into personal penury. But there is an American fundraising axiom that says 'The one who asks must first give'. Even on a mailed appeal like this, it may make sense to try to incorporate such integrity. Who else can get you into a club except an existing club member? Elitism is worth having in fundraising if the élitism is justified by giving.

Or, as Socrates said, 'Let him that would move the world first move himself'. And, with pleasing historic resonance, Socrates was a member of the Senate of Five Hundred. Which has to be a great name for a major donor club.

Everything I have described in this section is a product, a life-enhancing product, a product that your most loyal and committed supporters will want to buy. The success of products like these and, particularly of committed giving schemes around the world, underlines yet again the power of that great fundraising aphorism, 'You don't get what you don't ask for'.

It is a line I often use in seminars. Every time I do, half the audience look at me with knowing smiles. They are dwelling on budgets that are a fraction of those spent by some of the organisations I have just mentioned. They are thinking that they have a list of supporters in the low thousands. They are reflecting on those knowing trustees who insist that all supporters are just like them. And they conclude that what I am saying is a noise from a distant planet. There is a great dumb, useless form of words in a balloon above their heads. It says 'It's all right for them'.

I like to think that some of the founding fathers of Oxfam said that when they sat down to the inaugural meeting of the Oxford Committee for Famine Relief in 1942. How on earth could you persuade the British people at the very depths of the Second World War to send relief to Greece? History provides the simple answer: by asking properly.

People and fundraising geometry

Let's get another fundraising aphorism out of the way. It's the one that says that 'people give to people'. In other words, people don't give to institutions, or projects, or even charities. They give to people.

But you knew that already and I'm not going to labour the point. What I will try to do is to examine the weird science that we have now piled on that truism. Oddly, it seems always to take a geometric form.

Enter the dear old donor pyramid. I reproduce it here for the hundredth time. As you will see it offers a developing donor relationship. Someone enquires about the charity, some of the enquirers respond, some of the responders give a donation, some of the donors become committed donors, some of the committed donors get to be major donors and, lastly, a happy few make a legacy bequest. The numbers involved get smaller all the time as the pyramid approaches its peak.

Nothing wrong with that, it seems to me. Nor with the donor trapezium or, Lord help us, the donor wedge with which Ken Burnett develops the process in *Relationship Fundraising*. I shall suppress the instinct to unleash a donor parallelogram on a thirsting world.

But all such models trouble me. For they suggest a relationship *that is inevitably sequential*. By inference at least, they say that *only* donors become committed donors and

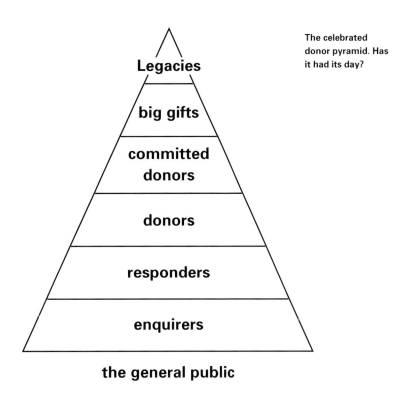

Legacies

big gifts

committed donors

donors

responders

enquirers

the general public

The celebrated donor pyramid. Has it had its day?

that large gifts are *only* to be had from committed donors. There is enough usable truth here to be generally applicable, but it is a defensive truth, one that again gives us tunnel vision. It suggests that the natural first stage to a relationship with a charity is a small donation and that the assiduous tradecraft of upgrading will be applied over the years to inch donors up the pyramid. It is also – as Ken points out in *Relationship Fundraising* – a pretty negative model, assuming as it does the gradual decrease in donor numbers as the pyramid is climbed.

It is the unthinking allegiance to the model of the donor pyramid throughout the world of fundraising that has persuaded us to preside over the cruel financial formulae I mentioned on page 49. In other words, it makes sense to use volume direct marketing because it produces enough names to occupy the first stage of the pyramid so as to feed the later stages of the programme. A regular appeals programme will winnow those numbers profitably, will turn a minority into committed givers, a minority of a minority into major donors and the true survivors of the barrage over the years will leave a legacy. It is fair to say that two legacies produced from every 1,000 names induced into the pyramid might well be a sensible return on the process.

I just worry about the dead relationships on the way to this statistical Valhalla. It has only just occurred to me that the donor pyramid is pretty well the shape of an old-fashioned kiln, the furnace-based oven wherein you shovelled fuel at the bottom and let the hot air rise. I will deny myself a cheap analogy.

For my main point is a positive one. Why do we presume that the fundraising process is sequential, one stage following the other? Why do we assume that donors start off poor and end up rich?

Again, examine our inbred language. We call all this donor development. Does it ever occur to us that donors might not want to be developed? Does it ever cross our seminar-fevered minds that they might just want to give us more money and be asked for it in more civilised ways? Who says that a committed giving scheme is the prerogative of the regular donor?

WE CALL ALL THIS DONOR DEVELOPMENT. DOES IT EVER OCCUR TO US THAT DONORS MIGHT NOT WANT TO BE DEVELOPED?

Fundraisers are a strangely defensive bunch. That is why I can provide no current examples that justify my restlessness with the donor kiln. Its regular application has made it a self-fulfilling prophesy. I can offer just the one example of how much promise there is in an alternative theology. It is the simple and well-known fact that most legacies are still left to charities by people *totally unknown* to the organisation concerned. How dare they be so generous when they have not served their time on the donor pyramid?

We are simply not confined to our databases. We need to build giving products into a portfolio and present that portfolio to everyone *simultaneously*. How would you feel if your favourite beer only came in half pints, if its drinking was restricted to previous buyers and if you had to buy four half pints before being allowed a pint?

Lies, half-truths and demographics

It is easy to score theatrical points with the most absurd excesses of database marketing. On one platform I offered up a demographic description of my own household. I then lived in an inner suburb of London whose postcode clearly indicated that I was probably a council tenant, probably in low-wage employment, probably in receipt of supplementary benefit and quite likely a member of a racial minority. In fact, I was probably the only resident of our well-heeled street who did not appear regularly on television. I scored another modest *coup de théatre* by offering a demographically precise description of HM The Queen, that indigent pensioner with an unemployed husband and four children away from home, who again sweats it out in a part of inner London where credit facilities are hard to come by.

Cheap jokes, I grant you, but they do demonstrate the dangers of parcelling up whole swathes of the population and mis-labelling them. All macro-statistics of masses of people tend to throw up caricatures and the fundraiser is too often blinded by the apparent science in the search for more cost-effective targeting.

The British company ICD holds a database of 5.2 million individuals who have chosen to answer 1,500 questions about themselves, their families, their income, their homes and their hobbies (enthusiasm for replying to such questionnaires already makes for a warped sample, it seems to me). A massive profiling operation on these names enables the company to make the following claims about charity supporters.

> *Between 70 per cent and 80 per cent of them take holidays in the UK. Only 40 to 50 per cent*
> *take holidays in Europe.*
> *The cars they run are Fords, Vauxhalls and Rovers.*
> *Swimming is the favourite sport among donors.*
> *Thirty-nine per cent of charity supporters live in homes valued at less than £60,000.*

Doubtless, this has been an exercise of total statistical integrity. It reports that the average donor is, and I quote the report, 'A responsible, considerate citizen... living in a mortgaged home... ordinary working folks...' In other words, charity donors are real people. I do not propose to swoon in the face of this revelation.

But it is the solemnity of all such macro-statistics and the deference shown to them that concerns me. For years charities told me that their 'average donor' was a little old lady leaving near Tunbridge Wells: an anecdotal stereotype. Latterly, charities have begun to say that their 'average supporters' are ABC, university educated, 35 to 55 in age, readers of broadsheet newspapers: a demographic stereotype.

But, yes, of course they are. Anyone who has ever put a fundraising ad in the *Guardian* knows that it will outpull an ad in the *Sun*. Everyone knows that a house-to-house collection in a leafy lane will do better than on a council estate. Do we really need regular statistical evidence to justify the glum but eternal truth that *giving to charity is a middle-class preoccupation?*

George Orwell divided the British middle class into upper, upper middle, middle middle and lower middle. But he was writing 60 years ago, when the indices of these extraordinarily fine social distinctions were clear and well understood – servants in the house, private education, the very garb that the master of the house wore. Thankfully we now live in a more pluralist age. Bus drivers save up to pay for private education. Advertising men go to work in jeans. Everyone coincides at the garden centre.

For, this is the joy of being a fundraiser in contemporary society – if giving to charity is a middle-class preoccupation, we are blessed to practise fundraising in a society *where the vast majority of people think they are middle class*. Well, we are, aren't we? I'm middle class, you are middle class and practically all your friends are middle class. I am doubtless being presumptuous, but it seems a safe kind of presumption.

And I am not sure that there is any more to be said about 'the average donor'. He or she is middle class. Which makes him or her deeply ordinary. Which makes him or her a statistical majority among our fellow citizens. Exciting, isn't it?

This benign revelation that the average donor is most people can be tempered only by a few equally banal qualifications. These are the ones I have learned to think of as immutable.

1. More women give than men.
2. Younger people have lots of money but lots of financial commitments.
3. Older people have lots of money but fewer financial commitments.
4. Younger people turn into older people.
5. Most people are quite nice, really.

I have now exhausted my statistical overview of donor typology

It looks like I've stumbled into a 'point of view'. It suggests that we can subdue much of this keen-eyed targeting science (I say 'subdue' and not 'dismiss') and widen our eyes to the amazing potential of the human emotions over which we preside.

It is an optimistic point of view. It insists that many people can give more and that many of them want *to give more. It suggests that our fundraising tradecraft has managed to find ways to occlude this happy vision.*

For we need to find more ways for people to give, build more products around the process, stop taking people for granted. Which, ironically and tragically, is what we do with so much of that tradecraft.

You can fault this thesis. You can be sceptical about it, find every worldly reason why it is indeed wide-eyed, measure its undoubted naivety against your recent failures.

But I think you will be a better fundraiser if you start to accept it.

We can now begin to look at the ways in which such dreams can be communicated.

FUNDRAISING CREATIVITY

'That which is creative must create itself.'
Letter from John Keats to James Hessey, 1818

WHAT REALLY MATTERS CREATIVELY

We live in a deferential society. We have elevated words like 'education' and 'training' beyond their true level of service, for we have accepted in our bewilderment at the world we live in, not just that everything can be taught but that everything should be taught. Thus, everything you seek to learn is the result of someone or something in didactic mode. Our politicians are forever telling us that we must invest in training lest we fall behind our competitors.

But we live in an extraordinarily well-trained world. Britain is full of well-trained unemployed engineers. Hundreds of thousands of young people have been trained in 'computer skills' yet lack employment because those skills were imparted a computer generation ago. English football teams are doubtless superbly trained but never seem to win anything. Training is clearly not a passport to success. And education is clearly not a mark of prowess.

It is good to learn. But learning is an enabling process, not a defining one. If you think of all the things you have learned in your life – speech, the rules of chess, playing the piano, driving a car, a foreign language – it should be clear that the learning process at best gave you the confidence to do all these things better and *in your own terms.* You will have been taught the names of the chess pieces, the use of the clutch, the notes and the scales… and out of this familiarity with the mechanics of the process

you will have moved on to develop your own version of the respective skill.

But adults seem to lack that confidence these days. They want to hear precisely how everything works and precisely how everything should be done. These didactic certainties may be appropriate to brain surgery or spot welding but they are rarely appropriate to any process that is half-way creative. It is one of the penalties of professionalisation that we often pretend otherwise. In both the direct marketing and fundraising fields over the last 20 years, I have watched the growth of an 'audience culture', a strange act of ritual obeisance that has 100 people in a seminar room listening to one person who is supposed to be cleverer than they are.

It is years since I complained in print about the dangers of this deference. Indeed, I said that those of us who were privileged to have been around for some time and who were already beginning to haunt a conference circuit were being accorded the status of gurus. The use of the word was meant to be pejorative, reflecting my belief that experience was being taken for wisdom, that common sense was being elevated to Holy Writ. Pity the poor iconoclast! We all became gurus overnight. People clearly need them.

The 'audience culture' is dangerous in fundraising. It suggests that everything is known, everything is on a list, everything is reproducible. Do it this way, is the inference, and untold riches will be yours. Follow these rules and you will be successful. Such simplicities demean us all.

And they certainly lead to creative formulae rather than creative thinking. For too much fundraising communication is formulaic, predictable and dismissable. Which is why it gets dismissed.

Those of us who have given seminars over the years should be raddled with guilt for we failed to anticipate the deference of our audiences, the need for guru-dom. Those of us who had written successfully were hauled into conference rooms and told to teach. What we did was all we could do – tell people how we did it. Little did we appreciate how religious would be the observance of such humble remarks. Soon a whole theology was spawned. Letters could be four pages long, the PS was vital, the second para could be indented, you could use second colour, you could use a rhetorical question on the envelope to get it opened. And so on.

I kiss away all these points in a sentence, though I am as capable as the next guru of turning them into an hour-long seminar. And I kiss them goodbye with relief. For their regular restatement bred a generation of dreary look-alike letters and a slavish adherence to a formula that was never actually a formula. Such is the thirst for knowledge, the myth of training, the ludicrous quest for conventional wisdom.

For it has led to fundraising communication that *only exists as fundraising communication*. Who else writes you four-page letters with second para indents, a PS and a rhetorical question on the envelope? Who else calls you a supporter when you've given just that first, spontaneous donation?

We have become inbred in our communication. We have developed yet another tribal patois. We have ceased to communicate. And, because we are trying to communicate something a little more important than a magazine subscription or a supermarket promotion, I think that this is a minor social tragedy.

I give you two conference anecdotes.

I was at the NSFRE convention in Atlanta a few years back, following a track in which three teams of creative honchos were given an assignment as exercise – a mailing for a local symphony orchestra, as I remember. They returned at the end of the convention with their creative recommendations – three mailing packs that looked exactly the same, said exactly the same things and made exactly the same offer. The irony of this extraordinary creative symmetry seemed to pass the audience by. Indeed, the convenor warbled over the fact, 'great minds obviously think alike' he said. The conventional wisdom was reinforced – three top creative honchos had, after all, reached the same creative conclusion. And everyone was happy. No one seemed to mind that the packs were crap, doomed by their own familiar mediocrity. And the sceptical Brit in the audience sure wasn't going to spoil the party.

And I tried to say some of this at the International Fund Raising Workshop later that year. I offered my own pragmatic experience that the old model of long, four-page letters was beginning to founder on the basis that it had become a jaded formula and that maybe, just maybe, people couldn't be bothered to read them any more – a thesis that was thankfully endorsed by the sainted Jennie Thompson from the United States.

Up jumped a dour Dutchman. 'But George', he said, 'this is a complete contradiction of what you were telling us five years ago.' I struggled to make the point about a changing world, readers' boredom thresholds and all that. I struggled and I failed. The Dutchman's face spoke of savage disappointment at such whimsicality. He made a big note on his pad. I fancy it said, 'George Smith is a contradictory prat'. In Dutch, of course. Who needs contradictory gurus?

So, if anyone asks me these days if four-page letters outpull two-page letters, or if red is the best choice of second colour, or whether you should have a photograph on the outer envelope, I offer an answer far more valuable than the ones I used to offer. It goes as follows, 'I don't know'.

And it's true. It seems to me that we have paid a large enough price for deference, for accepting too listlessly the experience of others. We need again to widen our eyes and stop looking for the 'nine points' that will make up a creative Holy Grail. People should start thinking for themselves – surely the genuine aim of all genuine teaching.

Or are we happy that most people we talk to never respond to us? Me, I'm outraged by such rudeness. Which means that I spend every working day in a mood of outrage. I recommend it as therapy.

What follows is therefore no more than the best I currently know about creativity in fundraising in the first half of 1996. This is not a false humility, the greater wisdom of a super-guru who has learned that the 'truth' is never quite attainable. It is rather the honest reflection of a journeyman who has learned just how quickly the world changes and how very quickly last year's conventional wisdom turns into this year's thoughtless mantra.

For these chapters will give you the grammar of creativity, the building blocks with which you can construct your own language, your own message and find your own voice. And, if they persuade you to question everything you have ever heard from a platform, or challenge everything you ever read in a book (including this one), then we shall have engaged in a true learning process and not a list-making ritual.

With a thrilling lack of self-consciousness, I shall in fact start with a list. It is time to get conventional.

The seven point checklist

These are the seven things that should be in the back of your mind every time you prepare a piece of fundraising communication.
1. Who am I talking to?
2. What precisely am I asking them to do?
3. Why?

4. Have I made the message sound important (or evocative, passionate, crucial, urgent... select your own epithets but you'll need most of them).
5. Have I made the point as simply or as powerfully as possible?
6. Have I made it as simple as possible to respond to what I am saying?
7. Have I done something that has never quite been done before?

Of these, only the seventh is a luxury. The rest are fundamental demands on your communication, though often more honoured in the breach than the observance. Which is why we need to spend a little time with them.

1. Who am I talking to?

In *How to Write Sales Letters that Sell,* Drayton Bird says 'Write to somebody not everybody'. It is the sort of advice we all nod through. Common sense is rarely stimulating.

Ideally, all communication should be one to one. The personal conversation will always be the most effective way of asking for money. The telephone call is probably the most effective substitute. But, for most of the time, we are stuck with mass communication – the ad, the mailing, the insert, the door-drop leaflet, the radio or television appeal. We are communicating with thousands, hundreds of thousands, perhaps millions of unknown people.

It is still worth trying to picture them in your mind's eye. How old are they? What gender are they? What do they eat? What television programmes do they watch? Do they listen to Scarlatti or Oasis?

Frankly, picturing your audience is no more than a creative device. Your chances of sociological accuracy are minute except on those rare occasions when you can be totally presumptuous of the bond you share with the audience. The Oasis Fan Club would be easy. So would the Scarlatti Society.

But personification of the audience must help make for better communication. It is vital that you peel away those lazy words that we use to describe an audience and expose a real, breathing human being underneath. The average written brief gives you only a dull litany of categories – ABC1s, regular donors, lapsed donors, *New Internationalist* subscribers, female investors, ACORN category B21, listeners to Classic FM, *Guardian* readers. But every one of the people with whom you are trying to communicate is an individual. Try and get a fix on that individual. You are talking to a real person not a list.

As I say, you need not worry too much about the pinpoint accuracy of the picture you draw in your mind's eye. What matters is having a picture, any picture. Try Mrs Jones, aged 45. She is worried about her weight and how to transport her 15-year-old daughter back from the disco on Saturday. She wants to plant those shrubs she just bought and finish the latest Catherine Cookson lent to her by a friend. She is furious with her husband who wants to go back to Majorca for the umpteenth time this summer. She thinks John Major is rather unfairly treated and has a secret thing about Paul Newman still.

I can see her now. Can't you? She's the lady over there, wearing leggings and a jumper from Next. We shall communicate better because we have drawn this entirely notional picture of her.

For we would probably not shout at Mrs Jones. We would not seek to alarm her unduly. We would not confuse her with our own long words. Picturing her gives us the language we would use if we were privileged to be talking to her direct. Do you use the same words to your mum as you would use to your friends in the pub?

Maybe you should think of your mum every time you write a piece of fundraising communication. She is probably the likeliest model of the average donor you will ever meet.

2. What *precisely* am I asking them to do?

Give money is your puzzled answer. But anyone bemused by my listing of such an obvious question would be well advised to spread out a collection of charity ads or mailings on the desk. For they will often be asking for money in strange ways, ways that the potential donor will have to decode more often than you think.

Take those infamous tick boxes that signify successive donation levels. They have become a rather tiresome cliché of the fundraising trade, but my point here is a different one. Does it really pay to offer donors alternative donation levels?

The classic reply form. It's efficient. But it's also a cliché.

We never say no to a call for help – please don't say no to ours.

To Jane Gomersall,
I enclose my donation to help in your fight against cruelty. Use it however you think is best.

£100 ☐ £50 ☐ £20 ☐ £15 ☐ £10 ☐ £6 ☐ Other £ _____

Name _____
(Mr/Mrs/Miss)

Address _____

_____
_____ Postcode _____

Enclose your cheque or postal order (made payable to RSPCA) with this donation slip in the Freepost envelope provided. **Freepost means you don't need a stamp, but if you use one then even more of your donation will go to prevent cruelty to animals.**
We are only sending receipts out on request, so please accept our sincere thanks now.

I wish to make my donation by Access/Visa Card

Number [_____]

Signature _____
Please send me details of how a regular gift can help even more. ☐

Thank You. **RSPCA**

3

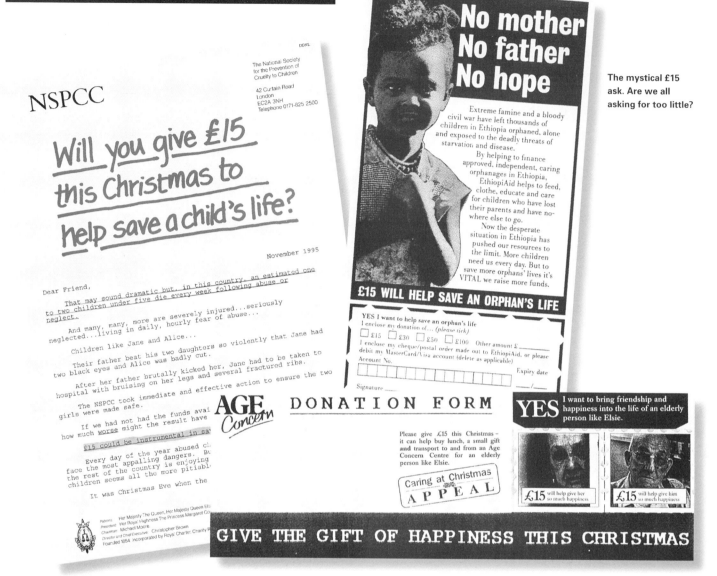

The mystical £15 ask. Are we all asking for too little?

I ask in all innocence. I ask as someone who helped invent the technique in the first place. I ask as someone who has participated in many a technical discussion about these tick boxes. Should the highest donation level be first? Should the figures be rounded off into pounds, or quoted in meticulous pounds-and-pence detail so as to offer greater authenticity?

All experience says that most donors will sensibly tick the lowest tick box. But what is the proper minimum? Among the material I am looking at, the RSPCA's minimum appears to be £8, Sight Savers' £12, the Mental Health Foundation's a cool £20. The topmost donation in each case is £20, £125 and

£100 respectively and in a mailing from Voluntary Service Overseas an utterly mysterious £252.

This is quite a spread of fiscal ambition. And even when a committed giving scheme is being communicated the same tactics are sometimes used. An insert from the RSPCA bids you to become a Friend of the RSPCA through a monthly standing order. The minimum payment is £3 a month, the quoted maximum £10 a month and you can enrol your partner and 'up to two children (under 17 only)' for an extra £1 a month. The enrolment form asks for details of the second adult, the first child and the second child. It is a large enrolment form.

I fancy that these complications are caused by the RSPCA's membership structure, for the scheme bestows automatic membership of the organisation with full voting rights and all that. And perhaps it has been nervous in the promotion of the Friends Scheme – would animal lovers be happy with £5 or £8 a month? My own experience says that they certainly would. And my own suspicion is that many donors would have been confused into inaction by the prolixity of the offer.

The size of the NSPCC's recruitment programme probably winnows out such corporate self-doubt. Having decided that the £15 donation is par for every conceivable course, they simply ask for it – in ads, broadcast appeals, mailings and inserts. 'Will you give £15 to help save a child's life?' is doubtless a braw and crude form of words but it does simplify the nature of the donor's reactions. You don't get what you don't ask for. Yet again.

On this NSPCC piece there is just one alternative to the £15 tick box. It is that familiar option 'Other amount'. I always feel sorry for people who have to tick this box. There is something brutish about it. Are you man enough to use it to announce that you are a cheapskate, incapable of making the minimum donation and enclosing a woebegone £5? I always use it to enclose a really daffy donation like £10.87. It is a small personal revenge on the data entry clerks.

The vast majority of appeals make a request for a single donation. Sometimes the response device will include jaded forms of words talking of GiftAid or covenants, usually in six-point type, usually abbreviated to the point of incoherence. It is a tribute to the puritanical school of fundraising creativity, the one that demands that every square millimetre of space be used for afterthoughts. But afterthoughts confuse the primary thought. And that naughty white space can be used to make the primary thought more powerful.

I yearn to see a fundraising appeal that has the courage of its convictions, that is prepared to say something like, 'Why you will feel better if you can give us £250' and which follows such brio with a hard-headed case for the larger donation. Count up the words in an average appeal. The vast majority will be about the organisation's work. A small minority will be about the nature of the product on offer – usually the single donation. And hardly any will be about the needs of the donor – the ones I have tried to summarise in an earlier chapter.

It could be time to shift these percentages around a little. It would refresh the average appeal. It might tell the reader more precisely what we want them to do. Which is to give more for better reasons.

3. Why?

No one buys newspapers to read your ad. No one listens to the radio to hear your appeal. No one pants at the doormat waiting for your direct mail. In asking for money in these ways we are being intrusive, whether we choose to admit it or not.

So why are we intruding on them like this? Again, we need to brush aside our obvious professional justification for what we are paid to do and see the communication from the customer's point of view. Why exactly are we asking people for money? What precisely is the point?

Your own rationalisation for the communication is rarely good enough. What to you is a Christmas appeal, or an Easter appeal, or a May mailing is just another bloody appeal mailing to the customer. Likewise your twenty-fifth anniversary, your change of name from the Bewildered Fund to DAZE, your big new raffle, or your next sponsored domino contest. Talk about your organisation too much and you risk shrugged shoulders, even among those apparently committed supporters.

I repeat: why are you intruding on these people? Why on earth should they give to you? What motive spawned this communication other than the need to flesh out an appeal programme? Your readers deserve to know.

Sometimes there is an easy and a valid answer. In the summer of 1995 Greenpeace mounted a hugely successful and high-profile campaign against Shell's dumping of the Brent Spar oil rig. The mailing that came within a week of the campaign's astonishing success was simply a letter from a weary-sounding executive director, itemising the costs of the action and asking supporters to help pay for it.

Few charity appeals can be as vivid or as easily understood as that. But it is essential to depict as specific and as urgent a need as possible. Charity managers will always resist this instinct of the fundraiser to offer up specific projects or specific parts of the organisation's programme – the earmarked donation is always more troublesome than the one that vanishes happily into general funds. But the power of the specific need is greater than the attraction of the organisation reporting it – as every disaster appeal shows us. If I were running a charity I would make at least all postal appeals project-specific and go for general funding elsewhere. I would sooner have the occasionally over-endowed project rather than low-level response to more general appeals.

But that battle will rarely be won in most charities I know. The horrid fact is that most fundraisers are raising money – at least outside capital appeals – for reasons that they would have difficulty in articulating with precision. We ask because that's what we do.

There is a way around this familiar impasse, the one that denies fundraisers the drama of the specific need. Time and again we see the value of news coverage in fundraising. Greenpeace lives on it. The development agencies live in its shadow. Even a hitherto fusty organisation like the RSPCA can make media noise on a large scale and successfully raise funds on the back of it.

Not every organisation has such clout or such resources. But every organisation can create its own news, even though its dissemination may be restricted to its appeal programmes. Often the news is bad – which is probably good for fundraising. Maybe the old

people's home has been refused a fire certificate. Maybe vandals smashed up the Family Centre over the weekend. Maybe a grant from a trust is coming to an end.

Sharing these intimate little details of your organisation's work does two things. It articulates the need and dramatises it. If the old people's home needs £30,000 spent on fire precaution equipment, if the Family Centre needs redecorating to the tune of £20,000, if the charity is going to be short of £50,000 a year as of next January, then the donor is being offered a context in which to give. Ironically, it is a lesson often applied in humbler levels of fundraising. When there was an appeal in my village for our little village hall it was the floor that was the subject of the appeal, for too much rowdy dancing had rendered it unsafe. And a little corner of the new flooring is forever mine, £10 worth as I remember.

But sharing your tribulations and making news of them does something else. It makes you sound human. It gives you the language of one friend to another, the quiet honesty of everyday speech. And the stories themselves are no weaker for being everyday events. Can't you imagine those vandalised children's toys at the Family Centre? Can't you picture the old folk who will have to be moved from their rooms? I could certainly picture my neighbours falling through the floor at the village hall. Not all need is melodramatic. Indeed, humble events can often have greater credibility.

A couple of years ago the AIDS organisation the Terrence Higgins Trust ran its most successful appeal on the basis that the Government had slashed its financial commitment to the AIDS sector. Few supporters would have known unless the Trust had told them. I had the privilege of looking through some of the thousands of letters that accompanied the donations. They expressed outrage at the Government's action, which was perhaps predictable. But they also thanked the Trust for telling them what had happened. Many of them went on to take out standing orders and Paul Gambaccini was sufficiently moved to mount a brilliant major donor drive among his show business contacts. Bad news can be good fundraising. But only if you share it.

And you can offer a specific need in the most unlikely areas. In 1995 Charter 88 needed to retool its computer set-up, on which it is unusually reliant. We needed £15,000 and the only space in which we could ask was a tiny panel in the Charter's quarterly newspaper, *Citizens*. I showed a diagram of the optimum network that would be created by the new investment, listed the new kit, talked about the delights of being able to fax press releases direct from the PC, warbled about the Internet and a few other words given to me by their chief boffin.

And, yes, it raised slightly better than £15,000. I know for a fact that some of the respondents knew as little about the subject as I did. But they gave. Because it sounded real and urgent and because the need was expressed in quiet, restrained and slightly matey terms.

Above all, we had answered the question 'why?'

4. Have I made the message sound important?

Giving money is rarely a human routine. It only usually happens when it is provoked. And people are provoked when they think something is important.

Watch the way in which people read newspapers. They scan the front-page headlines and then they turn to the pages that most interest them. For men it will often be the sports pages, where they make a further selection between the important and the less important. For women it might be the fashion pages or, increasingly, the pages that reflect their professional interest – the education pages of newspapers quickly disappear in my household because my wife is a teacher.

No one is interested in everything. People make choices and the choices are subjective ones made in deference to personal relevance, interest, or passion.

Most sports fans will check on the football results in the Premiership, the state of play in the Test Match, who beat who at Wimbledon. Far fewer people will check out Fulham versus Barnet, or Derbyshire against Durham. Hardly anyone will go looking for the korfball results – though they are often there.

This hierarchy of presumed importance applies throughout every aspect of human affairs and it sometimes works in very sophisticated ways. More than 70 per cent of us will vote at the next general election – twice the proportion that will vote at a local election, an event that arguably has more effect on everyday living. But, if that local election is fought in a marginal ward with the political parties evenly balanced, turnout will mysteriously go above the 50 per cent mark. The added importance of voting in a marginal ward seems to be appreciated by the local electorate. They perform accordingly.

Where does this leave fundraising? Frankly, nowhere very prominent. People may leap out of bed in the morning to scan the news or catch up on last night's football results. They may even pick up their post with enthusiasm. But no one starts the day with the intention of making a charity donation. And no one says to their partner, 'Honey, the appeal mailings have arrived'.

A charity appeal has to fight its way through this familiar torpor. It actually has a harder task than ordinary product advertising, where the advertiser can make a reasonable assumption that the reader or viewer is in weekly need of cereals, seasonal need of things for the garden and perhaps an annual need for a new car. Fundraisers cannot presume on this perceived importance. They have to create it.

News headlines, as we have already seen, often create the importance for us. But we cannot rely on them, though we can increasingly provoke them through the media. How can a routine charity appeal create the same 'sense of event'?

It is a phrase I have used for years now. When I do, people tend to skitter off into the most literal directions. A 'sense of event' suggests an event. Thus, the anniversaries, the birthdays, the launch of a multmillion pound appeal. These things may help but their importance is the fundraiser's not the reader's. They still leave you with the task of persuasion.

A sense of event can be simply personal. Today I have agreed to sponsor a whale. Today I have made a contribution to the local hospice. Today I have committed myself to helping political prisoners in Paraguay. These are the things we want people to do. We can persuade them to do by elevating their importance. Giving should be memorable not dutiful. The mailing pack produced by WWAV Rapp Collins for a committed giving scheme for the animal charity Blue Cross actually asks you to sign a pledge – a series of affirmations that the donor truly believes in animal welfare.

Good creative work often contrives the sense of event by sheer power. That is why it is worth asking yourself a series of really dumb questions while you are producing it.

- Is it evocative?
- Is it passionate?
- Does the need sound crucial?
- Have I made it sound urgent?

Answer an honest yes to all these questions and it is likely that you will indeed have created the importance of the appeal, provoked that sense of event. But, do not delude yourself that you achieve it with routine language, or familiar visuals, or last month's clichés. An appeal gains little sense of urgency by being labelled with the wan word 'urgent'. A message does not acquire importance by being solemnly labelled 'important'. The constant deployment of these two words has rendered them practically meaningless.

In producing creative work that asks for money, it is usually worth bolting into your head a melodramatic description of the reaction you are trying to evoke in your reader's mind. I offer you a very lurid version.

Unless I give £20 to this appeal today, people will die and suffer things I have never suffered. I can stop these things happening tomorrow. I shall not miss the £20 and I know what marvellous things it can achieve in other hands. I will have done something remarkable today by sending this donation.

Too strong, too simple-minded? I wonder. You can temper these words, you can adapt them to become more appropriate to your organisation. But you should not pretend that the reader has any higher instinct than rising to the rhetorical challenge that they depict.

They make giving sound important and distinctive. Sadly, many charity appeals fail both tests.

5. Have I made the point as simply or as powerfully as possible?

Think of the last three times you gave money to charity. Statistically it is likely that at least two were the result of a face-to-face solicitation – the knock on the door for a house-to-house collection, the flag day at the station, the collecting tins in the local shopping centre. How many words were exchanged before you parted with your money?

Very few, I suggest. When the good Doctor Wood next trundles up my path collecting for Help the Aged, he will say, 'Good morning, I'm collecting for Help the Aged'. He is not a man whose collector's badge I would demand to see.

And he is certainly not a man who will enlighten me with the statistics of ageing, belabour me with thoughts on heating allowances, or confuse me with a list of how many projects Help the Aged has on the go. But he goes away with a donation. Similarly, with the street collections – I do not demand polemic from the people asking me for money.

So, why are we so keen to do it in charity appeals? Why do we presume that a donation can only be provoked by a four-page letter, or 200 words in a press ad? Who do we think is listening or reading?

We have created yet another bad practice in fundraising, another cliché. It is called prolixity.

Doctor Wood's request for Help the Aged was obviously an easy one. I know him, I know the organisation, I know the cause. Both parties can afford to be presumptuous. So can the street collectors, for putting money in collecting tins is a ritual response indulged by many ordinary people walking those streets. Communicating with large numbers of people you cannot see and whom you do not know is a totally different proposition.

But, is the difference to be measured by the number of words employed in the same process? For there is plenty of evidence that verbosity suppresses simplicity. And that a simple case can be made complex by too detailed an argument.

There is a wonderful old acronym in direct marketing. It is called the KISS formula and stands for Keep it Simple, Stupid. I have never wavered from my allegiance to it. (Though I have to tell you that I was once approached for some comment on the KISS formula by a business academic at the University of Leiden in Holland. Unfortunately it has lost something in translation – my Dutch professor insisted that the acronym stood for *Keep it Simple and Stupid.*)

Try applying the KISS formula to your creative work in fundraising. For simplicity lies at the heart of what we want to achieve, the simplicity of giving. And simplicity is powerful and universal. Don't be diverted from it!

I know how easy it is to be diverted. The social workers are nervous of your crude monosyllables and want the copy rewritten in jargon familiar to them. The campaigners demand room to report every nuance of their work. The director thinks the style should defer more to the new mission statement. All in all, the approval structure of the average charity has much to answer for.

But, know this. If someone criticises an appeal and says 'This is a gross simplification of the issues', he has just awarded you the highest prize. Quote

Winston Churchill at him or her. The great man was famous for demanding brevity of communication from his generals and ministers. And he left us the best of aphorisms for fundraising appeals.

Out of intense complexities, intense simplicities emerge.

Thank heaven no one was allowed to amend Churchill's speeches. Otherwise, this form of words may have appeared in Hansard on May 13th 1941.

What we are predicting is further entirely regrettable loss of life, very considerable amounts of hard work for everyone involved in the process, the inevitable suffering that always applies in this situation and increasing application on behalf of all the parties concerned.

You can almost hear John Major saying it. What his predecessor said on his first day in office was altogether more memorable.

I have nothing to offer but blood, toil, tears and sweat.

I am perfectly willing to believe that my country survived the Second World War because its Prime Minister regularly said complex things with great simplicity.

6. Have I made it as easy as possible to respond to what I am saying?

Dick Hodgson is a direct marketing guru. He always makes a lot of sense. I give you one of his precepts that we should all apply in fundraising. 'If there's one absolute rule for direct mail copywriting, it is: always write the order form first.'

There is a sort of mock heroic about this sound advice. No one likes writing order forms or response devices. Indeed, they often go unwritten. To suggest that you apply your opening creative zest to such a humble piece of paper is to suggest a sort of knightly vigil, a rite of passage. Few creative people can be bothered with such ritual. Which is how response devices get to be produced by administrators and not creative people. Which shows.

Again, we have developed another cliché in fundraising. I can track its progress. In the dark ages of fundraising, round about 1965, there probably was no response device at all. Ads, in particular, were averagely without coupons for the very excellent reason that coupons diminished response (they probably still do). But direct mail grew and response devices grew. To which we added the reply envelope. To which reply envelope we added the Freepost address and that wonderful form of words that says you don't need a stamp but it saves money if you do – I don't think any sentence I ever wrote has lasted so long, been used so widely and changed so little.

By now Ken Burnett had invented the self-reply press insert at ActionAid, causing an early-eighties revolution in origami. And by now the Cheshire label had become the conventional addressing medium for direct mail. Logic and economy suggested that it went on the response form. Which meant that the reply form became that new thing, the address carrier. Which meant that the outer envelope became a window envelope. As DL envelopes conventionally come with windows on the left, the name and address will therefore always be on the left of the reply form/address carrier. Which means that the newly important credit card details will always be on the right.

Thus did one stage of technology and tradecraft beget the next. The current orthodox reply form is a perfectly logical beast, the result of diligent begetting and true natural selection. Only the coupon in charity press ads has withstood this logical process. It has fallen into the hands of fashionable art directors. It is often a sliver of a rectangle, doomed only to be completed by people with keen eyesight and pens with a very narrow nib.

Which does, of course, defeat the first demand on any kind of response device – to make it user-friendly. How many older people are inhibited by those tight dotted lines we give them? The vast majority of people over the age of 50 wear glasses and plenty more below that age. Yet, the more complicated the reply form we offer, the more we try to squeeze it into the same traditional space. Direct debit and bankers order forms have become a particular nightmare for many would-be donors.

I am all for the known economies of paper sizes. I am all for the apparent money-saving integrity of the reply form that occupies the bottom third of an A4 letter. But economy and integrity may sometimes be achieved at the risk of demeaning the one part of the communication that is physically shared with your reader – the response device. Remember: we want this communication to be seen as important. Is importance conveyed by grubby rectangles filled with familiar clichés, prompt boxes, dotted lines and five-point afterthoughts? We have moved too near the stern, joyless communication of the banks or the tax authorities.

Try making the response device bigger. See what happens if you devote an A4 sheet to the process of reply. See what happens if you make sensible use of a second colour or a tint of black (a simple art apparently known to too few charities). You can probably do all these things with flourish and excitement.

1. Tell the reader what you want them to do.
2. Tell the reader how to complete the form.
3. Remind them of what they are achieving with their donation.
4. Give them user-friendly panels and lines in which to write.
5. Say thank you properly. By which I do not just mean the ritual words set in italic.
6. Make the form an integral part of the appeal.

A reply device like this must pay dividends. For it has a greater status. It suggests that greater importance.

It suggests the 'sense of event'. A donation is worth surrounding with a little ceremony.

If I offered that brief to a classroom of creative trainees, the most amazing work would be produced. Reply forms would emerge the like of which we would never have seen before and, while some of them might be completely scatty, others might be revelatory in their brilliance. How odd that charities and their suppliers never get set this task. Response devices offer as much creative potential as any other part of the communication. Only our dangerous weariness denies us that obvious perception.

7. Have I done something that has never quite been done before?

As I said at the beginning of this section, this is a luxury item among a list of essentials. But it is an ambition still worth conjuring out of an apparently commonplace brief. So much fundraising communication is now formulaic that the merest adventure, the smallest piece of pioneering will stand out from the crowd.

'All great truths start as blasphemies', said George Bernard Shaw. Fundraising creativity now needs its blasphemers.

I think of the creativity that had Burnett Associates using the name field on the laser to put a personalised direct debit request in a speech bubble above the head of a Greenpeace campaigner. I think of the YMCA campaign that stuck a penny on a card. I think of the WWF legacy

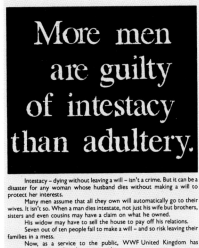

An ad from Chapter One Direct that has now run for about 15 years. Someone must have jibbed at the use of words like 'intestacy' and 'adultery'. And they must have been overruled – wisely so.

campaign that majored on the little-known word 'intestacy'. I think of the first charity that wrote a four-page letter and the first charity that just sent a compliments slip. They must all have been blasphemies in the face of contemporary truth.

Someone will always say 'you can't do that'. They are almost always wrong. Novelty is not always a virtue. But innovation is a constant necessity.

The four leverage points. Or is it five?

Whether fundraisers like it or not, their increasing concentration on direct marketing technique makes them heirs to a lot of direct marketing truisms. It is deceptive to think that fundraising exists on a higher moral plane than commercial direct marketing. To the consumer it seems to enjoy much of the same technique and, sadly perhaps, derives a similar response.

The figures prove it. A good house list for a commercial product or a catalogue will perform at a response rate close to the percentage achieved by a charity donor file. And the miserably low percentage return on a cold piece of donor recruitment will be matched by a similar mailing from a credit card company or an insurance company. The consumer does not separate the commercial mail from the fundraising mail and save the latter for more earnest consideration. Junk mail is junk mail, no matter how diverse the motives of the mailer.

More successful rule-breaking – a combination of clever technology and saucy language makes a direct debit application come alive.

THREE GOOD REASONS WHY YOU SHOULD FILL IN THE SIMPLE (IF RATHER DULL) REPLY FORM ENCLOSED:

(1) it won't cost you a penny, will save you hassle, will save Greenpeace administrative costs and frankly, if you don't fill it in, we'll have to write to you again because it's that important.

(2) Er...

(3) ... that's it. Thank you.

So, it is profitable to glean a few lessons from direct marketing tradecraft, a field far more chronicled than our own. It is ripe with rules and lists, dos and don'ts, snappy acronyms and simplistic instruction. It is also, like fundraising itself, subject to fashion and counter-fashion, to theology and heresy as one 'expert' mounts a point of view and another 'expert' challenges it. Axes grind here as elsewhere.

GREENPEACE

'If Mr Sample fills in a Direct Debit it won't cost a penny and I'll be able to block off even more of these bloody pipes!'

A Greenpeace campaigner seals one of the 11,000 discharge pipes spewing deadly toxic waste into the seas around our shores as part of our campaign to turn off the tap on marine pollution.

THE DULL (but very important) FORM

This is your current payment to Greenpeace ▶ £99.00 per year

Mr Sample
99 Anystreet
Anytown
Anydistrict
Anycounty
ZZ9 9ZZ

Supporter No. ⅃⅃⅃⅃⅃⅃⅃
HN034

GREENPEACE

Why not spread your annual donation over 12 monthly instalments? Greenpeace is totally reliant on supporters for funding, and knowing how much we can expect to receive each month helps us to plan ahead and avoid 'lean periods'.

My new payment to Greenpeace is
£✗_____ per month/year*
*Please delete as appropriate

To save you trouble, we have filled in much of this form for you and marked the sections you need to fill in with a green cross. But please check that all the information it contains is correct, and that you have filled in the section above telling us how much you want to give. Then return this whole sheet to Greenpeace, FREEPOST ND944, Northampton NN3 6AZ, not your Bank, in the envelope provided. Thank you.

Instruction to your Bank or Building Society to pay Direct Debits

If we are holding the wrong bank details, please accept our apologies, alter them and initial the changes. Doing this will help make sure it never happens again. Thank you.

1. Name and full postal address of your Bank or Building Society branch
(Please note that not all Building Society branches have their own discrete sort code, in which case the name and address of your society's regional head office may appear on the form.)

To: The Manager   Anybank   (Bank name)

Bank address   99 Anystreet Anytown

Anydistrict Anycounty

ZZ9 9ZZ   Postcode

2. Name(s) of account holder(s)   Mr Sample

3. Branch sort code   123456

4. Bank or Building Society account number
12345678

⬤ DIRECT Debit

Originator's identification number 9 7 2 2 4 8

5. Payment date
I/We* wish to pay monthly/annually * starting on the
✗ ☐ 1st ☐ 15th ☐ 28th of_____ (month)
or shortly after this date (*please delete as appropriate)
(Please note that no money will be taken from your account until at least four weeks after we receive this form.)

6. Instruction to your Bank or Building Society
Please pay Greenpeace Ltd Direct Debits from the account detailed on this instruction subject to the safeguards assured by the Direct Debit Guarantee.

Signature(s) ✗

Date ✗

Banks and Building Societies may not accept Direct Debit instructions for some types of account.
NOTE TO BANK: This Direct Debit supersedes all existing payments to Greenpeace Ltd.

Standing order cancellation

To: The Manager   Anybank   (Bank name)

Bank address   99 Anystreet Anytown

Anydistrict Anycounty

ZZ9 9ZZ   Postcode

Please cancel, with immediate effect, the standing order to Greenpeace Ltd under:

Account holder(s)   Mr Sample

Account number   12345678
Branch sort code   123456

Signature ✗
Date ✗
Supporter number   ⅃⅃⅃⅃⅃⅃⅃

When you have completed these forms and checked that all of the information they contain is correct, please return them to Greenpeace, FREEPOST ND944, Northampton NN3 6AZ – not your bank. Thank you.

But it seems to me that the older truisms are the more useful ones. They are the ones that have created vast mail order businesses and still sustain much of the direct marketing activity that you see. A book club ad in the UK or in the USA still looks the same as it did 30 years ago. *Reader's Digest* still promotes itself successfully with techniques that should founder in our more sophisticated age. The newer wave of direct-selling insurance companies have taken the old mail order techniques successfully on to television, merely replacing a coupon with a telephone number. The fact that our Consumer's Association, that key purchase of the informed middle classes, recruits so very powerfully with sweepstakes should give us all pause. The educated buyer, like the educated donor, seems not quite to have surfaced on any scale.

So, it is worth listening to the best of the older truisms. In some dim sense they seem to be workable. And they are certainly pertinent to fundraising as much as to direct marketing.

Roger Millington is a polymath in direct marketing, a representative of a slightly endangered species. He has written books on crosswords and computers and joined me in writing a few of the trivia quiz books that were fashionable a decade or more ago. He still writes copy by the metre for clients as diverse as Amnesty and Time Life and clumps around the world with entertaining presentations that tell people how to write. It was once said that he has more ideas while falling over in drink (only very occasionally, that) than most writers have in a year. All I know is that he has a great gift for summarising the true nature of direct marketing. His famous four leverage points are well worth recording.

Like all great teaching, the leverage points sound simple. They reduce the search for direct marketing success down to four factors of varying importance. They are not always welcome in a world that wants greater sophistication and a greater celebration of what the practitioner wants to practise rather than what the consumer wants to hear. Which is why they are particularly valuable.

Millington's four leverage points are Audience, Offer, Format and Creative. To each of them he attaches a value by which the performance of a direct marketing piece can be improved.

Audience is clearly the nature of the mailing list, the newspaper, magazine, or broadcast channel selected.

The Offer is what it says – the answer to the time-honoured direct marketing question 'what's in it for me?' In commercial terms, this could be a price reduction, a free gift or a 10-day trial period. In fundraising terms it could be any combination of those donor needs that I summarised a while back.

Format covers the means of reproduction. Is it an ad? Is it a full-page ad, or a classified? Is it a full-colour mailing, or a simple letter?

And Creativity is what's left – the words and pictures that we use to communicate the message.

Few would argue with this reduction of direct marketing down to its essential components. And, though some might argue with the values that Roger attaches to each of them, it is worth recording that they are the distillation of tests and campaigns from around the world conducted over a decade or more.

We all know, at least if prompted, that Audience is the most important leverage point. In other words, an ad in the *Guardian* will always have more provenance than one in the *Sun,* and the Campaign for Nuclear Disarmament would be wasting its time mailing members of the Conservative Party. In fact, Millington gives Audience a leverage factor of 200 per cent, saying that the best of a well-chosen array of mailing lists will usually outperform the worst by a factor of three to one.

The Offer ranks second in this hierarchy of values. Any direct marketer will know its importance for he or she will have tested discounts, carriage clocks, calculators and free product trials. For the fundraiser, this somewhat glum list seems irrelevant. But is it? Roger gives the Offer a leverage factor of 100 per cent, reporting that one offer can outpull another by a factor of two to one. We would do well to acknowledge the lesson and look for ways in which we can find our own ethical equivalents to the carriage clock.

Format is given a Millington leverage factor of 50 per cent. Again, it is a judgment that checks out with fundraising practice for it says that a change in physical format can affect response by a factor of 25 per cent to 50 per cent. Not always, of course, and not always in predictable ways. Size, famously, is not everything and it is common for a smaller ad to outpull a larger ad, not just in terms of cost per reply but in terms of net replies. And there is no evidence whatsoever that response to a mailing increases with the size of the pack or the number of pages in the letter. But it is still worth identifying the role of format and the boost that change can give to response.

Which leaves Creativity, the words and the pictures to which Roger ascribes a miserly 25 per cent leverage factor. The exceptions, he says, prove the rule – the very occasional time when one headline outpulls another by three or four to one, or when a change in second colour produces a breath-taking difference in response. Not for the first time, we creatives are chastened into a new state of proper humility by all this. Those words we slave over, those photographs we commission so expensively, that typography we ordain so carefully are all less important than things like lists, offers and things that print buyers do.

Well, of course they are. Any creative-wallah working in fundraising needs this sense of proper perspective, this understanding that there are things more important than the writer's choice of adverb, or an art director's affection for quarter-tones or

Garamond. You can cavil at Roger Millington's percentages for his leverage points but you cannot challenge their common-sense depiction of what is important and what is less important – in fundraising as much as in direct marketing. Like hanging, they concentrate the mind wonderfully.

And that greater concentration should teach all of us to take a wider view of the creative process, to stop limiting ourselves to words and pictures, to assume responsibility for all the other things that make fundraising work. Millington's four leverage points give us a menu over which we should slaver. *Everything* is creative if we want it to be.

I will leave Roger Millington at this point by quoting him directly, for I am not sure that there will be a more valuable sentence in this whole book.

Rather than waste a day searching fruitlessly for a new creative approach, it is easier and much more profitable to spend 15 minutes devising a bright new offer. (If the offer is a good one, then the headline magically writes itself!)

One last footnote on the leverage points. I think there is probably a fifth leverage point in fundraising. It is timing. We have already seen how crucial it is in terms of an emergency appeal, but it is a factor worth listing in everyday fundraising as well. Does it really make sense to mail an appeal at the height of the holiday season, when a good percentage of the post is going to lie unseen for two weeks, or more? Does it really make sense to launch a committed giving scheme three days before Christmas? Both of these two pained sentences stem from experiences of mine in the last year, when highly promising and meticu-lously planned propositions were sacrificed to the daft demands of an unthinking mailing programme.

Only experience will define the perfect timing for your fundraising – it is not always obvious and it is not always logical. I know many charities whose prime fundraising season is the week or so *after*

Christmas. And I can certainly remember the furore we caused when we started to distribute Oxfam Trading's Christmas catalogue after the August Bank Holiday. We were right, though – people do start thinking about their Christmas presents at the back end of the cricket season. And a mail order catalogue certainly needs 12 to 14 weeks of sales to optimise sales and smooth out the logistical problems of delivery and fulfilment.

Timing is probably of more importance to the fundraiser than to the commercial direct marketer. So maybe we have five leverage points and not four. But let's take a look at the leverage point least reported in orthodox fundraising – the offer.

The primacy of the offer

For decades now, anyone on a marketing course or attending a sales seminar has been confronted by a picture of a bull-headed, middle-aged businessman who is growling the question that every sales person has to answer. 'What's in it for me?'

It is a crude American expression for an attitude that is universal. The prospect is the prospect, the salesperson is the salesperson and the sale is only ever closed when Old Bull-Head is given a satisfactory answer to his question.

Fundraisers would have an attack of the vapours if they were subjected to such base language. But they should not be quite so delicate. The would-be donor is asking the same sort of question, though it might be posed in a slightly more elegant form. Only slightly though – try 'Why the hell should I give you money?' Few of my fellow Brits would ever descend to even that crude form of words, but it remains an unspoken mind-set, one that is worth attacking.

I have already tried to dismiss the warm glow theory of fundraising, the belief that what we do is somehow charmed and ethereal, a graceful meeting of minds and decencies. Donors want something in return for their donation or support. It matters little

that the something is often cerebral or spiritual rather than acquisitive or material: the something is still worth defining.

So, what is your offer? And how does it match the needs of the donor that I outlined in a previous chapter? Remember them? The assuagement of guilt, the need to belong or to achieve something, the desire to stop or start something, the demand to be seen to do good. Few of us think of trying to meet these needs with what Roger Millington would call an offer.

But what else is WWF's proven practice of sending out a panda window sticker with each and every cold recruitment mailing? The device has been tested to destruction – it simply increases response to any list.

Defenders of Wildlife in Washington DC send you sticky address labels and a wolf decal and promise a Wolf Adoption Kit that contains a wolf photograph, a wolf guide and an 'adoption certificate'.

For years Greenpeace UK successfully offered a map of Antarctica for a better-than-minimum subscription. Even now, WWF will send you a set of colour prints if you give within 15 days. All these things are offers.

They are also simple, universally proven, incentives that every charity could deploy if they lacked the sense of patrician disdain that denies them such obvious techniques. The dread phrase, 'our donors don't like that sort of thing' combines both hauteur and ignorance and should be inscribed on a headstone for many unsuccessful fundraising campaigns.

Offers are all around us if we think about it. The apparent ability to sponsor a child, a dog, whale, or wolf is no more than a pleasant packaging of the charity's message. It can be attacked as over-simplification, but so can your next general election vote. We take out a sponsorship in exactly the same way as we vote – we know it is a metaphor for how we feel, but it is a metaphor that makes us feel better because we understand it. It is an offer.

So is the plastic membership card issued by the International Fund for Animal Welfare a few years back. Why do so many charities eschew these obvious and conventional means of enabling supporters to signify their support? I can see nothing wrong with badges, cards, pin-stickers, or any other device that suggests affiliation to a cause.

But, perhaps the offer should indeed be more cerebral. At least twice a year I get to write a 'matching funds offer'. A third party has offered the charity or cause a handsome sum if that sum can be matched by its own supporters. With WWF it is the Government's Overseas Development Administration that offers a block grant if the sum can be matched. We have both an event and an offer with this appeal. It should surprise no one that the two things combine to make a perennially successful fundraising campaign. How often, after all, can you be as directive as this?

> *Trying to find £2.1 million, as we have to to match the ODA grant, is a tough job at a time like this. But, the ODA challenge to WWF supporters carries with it a thrilling idea, one that I think will make you want to give. It is this...*
>
> *That, every pound you give will be matched by the Government.*
>
> *That, every £20 you give will become £40.*
>
> *That, your donation, whatever its size, will immediately be doubled in value.*
>
> *If ever there was a time to give an additional or a larger donation to WWF, it is obviously now. The ODA money is there for the taking. The quicker we can match that £2.1 million, the quicker we can release those Government funds and get on with our conservation work.*

The matching grant is a superb example of the truism that there is nothing new in fundraising. In 1750 Benjamin Franklin lobbied the Pennsylvania Assembly to give £2,000 to his favourite project, the Pennsylvania Hospital. The assemblymen agreed to appropriate that £2,000 if Franklin's volunteers raised £2,000 themselves. Franklin's autobiography offers a pat rationalisation of the process.

> *The members of the Assembly now conceiv'd they might be charitable without the expense... and then in soliciting subscriptions among the people, we urg'd the conditional promise of the law as an additional motive to give, since every man's donation would be doubled; thus the clause work'd both ways.*

It is almost worth trying to convene a matching grants situation so that you can produce this offer for your readers. For its power is not restricted to Government-supported causes or large charities. The Joseph Rowntree Reform Trust gave a life-saving grant to Charter 88 in 1992 on exactly the same basis. The appeal I wrote made exactly the same offer – except that we insisted on the extra commitment of standing orders to raise the necessary £250,000. We raised it – in months!

There can, of course, be quieter and less melodramatic offers. The feeling that you are an explicit part of an explicit programme is sometimes a good enough reward, even at the higher giving levels. WWF Guardians give £1,000 a year and receive regular letters from the director updating them on the deployment of the Guardians' Fund. Supporters of Greenpeace's *Frontline* receive press releases and even memos from the notice board to strengthen their feeling that they occupy a special sense of intimacy with the organisation.

For it could be argued that the best offer of all is that special sense of an important relationship between the charity and the supporter. Intelligence is a commodity rarely to be seen in direct marketing. When it is used, it rarely fails. I can think of no more intelligent offer than the one you get when you give a donation to Botton Village, a community for mentally handicapped adults in Yorkshire.

It gives you the chance to ordain the whole post-donation cycle of communication. Do you want newsletters, appeal mailings, or both? Do you want us to write just at Christmas?

A lot of people say yes to that last option. They go into a very special file, one that is restricted to just the one appeal a year. And one that responds at better than 50 per cent.

We need to think about the offer as regularly as our direct marketing cousins. But there are clearly other ways of meeting donor needs than with carriage clocks and calculators.

Let's pause right here. Have you thought through what it is you are communicating? Have you considered how you propose to meet the donor's needs? Have you pictured the donor in your mind's eye? Have you articulated an offer? Above all, why precisely are you producing this piece of fundraising communication?

List all the questions I have raised so far and it makes creativity sound like a parade-ground drill. By the right, picture the donor, by the left, construct the offer. Good creative thinking rarely stems from such literalness. But they do matter, these questions, for you are about to communicate as one human being to another. You are about to do that devilishly difficult thing, asking for money. That is why I urge you not to put a word in place before you have had some sort of debate about these primary questions. Have the debate with yourself, for it is quicker and cheaper. But have it. And, when you've had it, start writing.

WRITING FUNDRAISING COPY

Parody is sometimes helpful. Let me start with a bit. In fact, let me start with a letter I just dreamed up, the sort of letter that you might get from one of your children who is away at university.

Dear Dad,

It was so good to hear you and mum over the phone. I've made a lot of new friends here at college and I'm not short of things to do. But I do miss home — especially Mum's cooking.

Can I come straight to the point? I need a new computer. The old Amstrad has had its day. It's slow, it's not printing properly and I'm wasting hours shouting at the damned thing. More seriously, it's getting in the way of my course work — I've got a 10,000-word thesis on Jack Kerouac to turn in by the end of term and, at this rate, I'm not going to make it. Worse, anything I produce on it looks crap compared with the professional-looking work that other students are producing. I know you've already spent a small fortune on getting me here — all I can say is that another couple of hundred quid will make a heck of a difference for the next three years.

I've seen a secondhand PC advertised in the college magazine. It's not quite state of the art but it does have Windows 3.0 and a decent printer and it's all I need to see me through to my finals. The bloke wants £300 and I think I can knock him down

to £250 if I move fast. I think I can contribute £50 from what I've got in the bank.

So, I'm asking if you can spare another £200. I know it's a lot to ask and I think you know that I wouldn't ask unless it was genuinely important and urgent. If you can't afford it, then I'll shut up and soldier on with the Amstrad. But if you can, then it really is going to improve everything I do here. What do you say?

I really need to call this bloke before the weekend (I'm sweating that nobody else has made him an offer in the meantime). So, if could call me or, better still, just put a cheque for £200 in first-class post, then you'll make my week.

Sorry to be such a pest. All I can offer if you say yes is a beautifully presented, well-worded thesis on Kerouac that I'll happily show you at Christmas and which will make your paternal heart swell with pride.

I can't tell you how much I'm looking forward to Christmas. College is great but there's nothing like family. So, give my love to Mum and to Jenny.
Adam

Great fundraising or what? Heaven forfend that one's son should ever produce such a crafty piece of asking. It's got punch, urgency, personality, warmth and even humour. The need is articulated and given documentary reality. There's even a whiff of an offer in the Kerouac thesis. Above all, this letter sounds true. It sounds like the plea of an impoverished student desperate to do a little better. It sounds like one human being talking to another.

Apply some of the rules of direct mail letter-writing, though, and it might come out like this,

Dear Dad

Your kind gift of £700 has been safely received and is already at work in buying course text books and enabling me to enjoy a full part in the social life of the college. I cannot tell you how grateful I am for your continuing support.

I just cannot continue with this clapped-out Amstrad

A decent PC is vital for today's student. When lessons are over, we typically go back to our rooms and write up our notes. Failure to do so can lead to poor marks, slippage in course work and – all too often – the derision of our fellows. 25 per cent of students fail to complete a degree here. The cause is often an inadequate computer.

I am one such student.

I labour nightly on an Amstrad which is a positive impediment to my chances of academic success.

I ask you to imagine this computer.

It is slow.

Its printer is trouble-prone.

It will not interface with any other known machine.

In short, I risk severe under-achieving. I have to tell you that I just cannot continue with this clapped-out Amstrad.

Just £200 will make the difference!

Yes, a secondhand PC of the required quality can be procured for just £200. Can you find it in your heart to make such a gift? You have proved yourself such a dutiful parent that I am sure you will want to make this extra investment in the academic future of your first-born son. But, please, give NOW... every

day counts when it comes to vital word-processing. I can only buy the computer with YOUR help.

Yours sincerely

Adam

PS. Why not phone through your response – the need is truly URGENT.

PPS. I cannot tell you how much this gift would mean to me!!!

Okay, this is an over-ripe parody. If my son wrote me a letter like this, I would presume him to be overly dependent on strange chemicals. But the parody helps me to hammer home my central point – that much direct mail communication is already parodic. Charities do ask for money in this strange, over-inflated style, with its underlinings, its circumlocutions, its thumping use of upper case and its total lack of warm, human language. It is a form of communication *only* used in charity appeals. For all our apparent science, all our years of testing, all our slavish application of formulae... all these things have merely combined to produce yet another example of inbred, predictable gibberish.

These pages are devoted to the difference between such gibberish and language that is genuinely sensitive, genuinely moving and altogether genuine.

Here's one of the best fundraising letters I have seen in recent years. It is on one sheet of paper, it is dated April 30th 1993 and it comes from the United Farm Workers in the United States, a union in perennial dispute with a vicious breed of landowners and bosses. So vicious that the leader of the UFW, a Mexican immigrant called Cesar Chavez who had done much to publicise the plight of the farmworkers, had been murdered.

I buried my husband this afternoon.

Yesterday, thousands of us walked in funeral procession through Delano, the same little town where so many years ago it was only Cesar, only Cesar and a faithful few walking door to door with a dream.

I never stopped being amazed by Cesar. Somehow, from those first lonely days in Delano, he managed to plant his dream into many, many caring hearts. He was the kind cultivator, the compassionate sower, the gentle field worker, working in rocky soil where few believed justice could ever bear fruit.

I suppose I was the toughest one to organise. With eight children and only a beat-up '53 Mercury wagon, I wondered how far a dream would take us. But, with Cesar, if something was not worth giving your life for it was not worth doing. And in the end, he gave his last ounce of life to his beloved cause.

People say Cesar is with God now, but to me Cesar has always walked with God. He led us from fields of sorrow to the edge of the Promised Land.

I know that, truly, Cesar would not have left us without knowing that one day, working together, we will reap a safe and just harvest.

The work of the Union has now been given to farm workers who first learned that their voice could command change. This work has been passed on to our many friends who helped build our Union with unfailing generosity. And it has been entrusted to the Union's leadership who worked daily with Cesar and learned that action and commitment are the ultimate signs of love.

I ask you now, as we begin to look forward, to continue to help sow and harvest that dream that has brought us together. It is what Cesar wanted for the Union.

You can send gifts, in Cesar's memory, to the Cesar E. Chavez Non-Violent Action Fund.

Thank you
Helen Chavez.

I do not think that Mrs Chavez wrote this letter. I think it is the work of a consummate professional, prepared to arouse a sense of hope and inspiration from a man's death. It has integrity, dignity and warmth. It is prepared to deploy touching personal details – that sentence about the children and the beat-up Mercury wagon. It is prepared to parade fine thoughts with fine language – 'learned that action and commitment are the ultimate signs of love'. And it has an opening sentence to which no reader can possibly be immune.

It is also, of course, rhetoric. It sounds like a funeral oration, which is an entirely fitting style to adopt. But, check it out against my list of donor needs and see how well it fits. It has, inevitably, that 'sense of event' of which I wrote. But it also conveys hope, the continuation of the struggle. It has the courage to talk of 'the dream'. Above all, it lacks any hint of apparent 'technique' – Mrs Chavez's message would barely be enhanced by underlinings and indented paragraphs.

We can acknowledge a paradox. The only technique you need in fundraising creativity is the freedom from technique.

Blah, blah, blah

In other hands, this remarkable letter would presumably have been longer. But, to what point? Does anyone seriously believe that this terse, moving, message could possibly be improved by more words?

Again, we bump into the fashion cycle of creativity. Fundraising letters used to be short. Then David Ogilvy reported to the fundraising constituency that long letters always outpulled short letters in the commercial direct response field. The four-page fundraising letter was born, honed to perfection in the United States, slavishly copied elsewhere. Eight pages were sometimes sighted and legend tells of the occasional 12-pager, but the four-page letter became a norm. Indeed the norm began to be positively eccentric.

It began to have 'call-outs', or marginal notations – handwritten messages in the wide-spaced margins. It began to have photographs interspersing the text. It certainly had subheads to help the reader through the text. The solemn and desperate instruction 'please turn over', or 'please read on' began to appear on the bottom of the first page. And, because someone said that readers go straight to the PS, it always had a PS. And sometimes a PPS. A terrible oddity was born.

These letters only exist in fund-raising. No one else ever writes letters to you like these. This is why hardly anyone ever reads them. Another triumph of inbred, predictable gibberish!

It gets worse. For we surround that all-important letter with a leaflet or a brochure as a further act of deference to the norm. Maybe we include a second letter by way of third-party endorsement. We certainly include that response device whose formality I scorned earlier – and we will probably write some copy on the back of it. Before we take stock, we have already used up perhaps 1,500 to 2,000 words to make our case. It is a tribute to the energy of the copywriter, but such verbosity should not be confused with good communication.

An obstinately held opinion, then. *We write too many words.* We spend endless time debating the provenance of these words. And we miss the only point that matters. It is terribly

sad but increasingly true. People do not read all these words we write so carefully. Indeed, they are bored witless at the very sight of them.

Remember the KISS formula – keep it simple, stupid. Apply it, whatever the medium you are working in. I once wrote an ad for Sight Savers whose headline was 'Sight: £15' and managed to tell the story that a cataract operation cost just that in about 100 words. I shall never write a better ad, nor a more successful one.

O Orwell, you shouldst be living at this hour!

No one ever felt more keenly about the English language than George Orwell. He was an enemy of cant in any form and particularly waspish about the abuse of English by politicians, bureaucrats and those in power generally. No one has ever rivalled the glittering common sense he offers us in *Politics and the English Language,* an essay written as long ago as 1946. I am happy to quote from it extensively for its value outstrips any specialist contemporary text.

He offered as instruction a list of six questions that every writer should ask of himself or herself.

GIVE SIGHT £15

That's how much it costs for a cataract operation to restore the sight of a child needlessly blind in the world's developing countries.

Sight Savers works to prevent and cure blindness in over 40 countries. We restore sight to over 250,000 needlessly blind each year. We have now completed over 3,000,000 successful cataract operations. We help the incurably blind too by providing education and training that helps them get the most out of life.

Please help us do more. Was there ever a better use of your generosity?

SIGHT SAVERS

Restores the sight of 250,000 needlessly blind people every year

Sight Savers, FREEPOST, Haywards Heath, West Sussex RH16 3ZA
Telephone: (0444) 412424 Registered Charity Number: 207544

YES, I WOULD LIKE TO HELP RESTORE THE SIGHT OF NEEDLESSLY BLIND CHILDREN.

My gift is: £ _____ to restore the sight of _____ children.

Please make your cheque payable to Sight Savers, or if you wish to pay by Access or Visa, enter your cardholder no. in the boxes below.

Card expiry date _____ Cardholder's signature _____

Name Mr/Mrs/Miss/Ms _____
Please use BLOCK CAPITALS

Address _____

_____ Postcode _____

Simplicity triumphs again. Why write more words than are necessary?

1. What am I trying to say?
2. What words will express it?
3. What image or idiom will make it clearer?
4. Is the image fresh enough to make the effect?
5. Could I put it more shortly?
6. Have I said anything that is avoidably ugly?
   And he also offered an even more challenging list.
1. Never use a metaphor, simile, or other figure of speech that you are used to seeing in print.
2. Never use a long word where a short one will do.
3. If it is possible to cut a word out, always cut it out.
4. Never use the passive voice when you can use the active voice.
5. Never use a foreign phrase, a scientific word, or a jargon word if you can think of an everyday English equivalent.
6. Break any of these rules sooner than say anything outright barbarous.

In other words, Orwell was a demanding old cuss. How on earth can you avoid totally any figure of speech that you are used to seeing in print? But it is amusing to consider how he would react to the shoddy, useless, lazy language with which we are surrounded 50 years later. For his verdict on modern writing has never been bettered.

Modern writing at its worst does not consist of picking out words for the sake of their meaning and inventing images to make the meaning clearer. It consists of gumming together long strips of words, which have already been set in order by someone else, and making the results presentable by sheer humbug.

The chilling thing about these two sentences is that they were written 50 years ago. Yet they echo passionately and accurately down the years, challenging us all to use the language better. How much fundraising copy is just as Orwell describes, long strips of words, which have already been set in order by someone else… Does *your* copy pass the Orwell test? I think the Cesar Chavez letter does.

When you quote homilies like those of Orwell to a contemporary audience you stand accused of would-be donnishness, of a certain pretentious posing. It is as if you were dragging hard-bitten professionals back to their schoolroom days, when they were forced to read hated texts and learn dumb rules about English grammar. They resist what I see as total relevance.

So, it might help to quote Orwell on grammar rather than language. Here's what he said in 1950.

Correct grammar and syntax are of no importance as long as one makes one's meaning clear.

And, just to cheer you up with more apparent heresy about grammar, let me report what the Government's Board of Education said when Gladstone was still Prime Minister.

There is no such thing as English grammar in the sense which used to be attached to the term.

Use these stately quotations the next time someone complains about a sentence ending with a preposition, about a split infinitive, or about a sentence beginning with 'And'. Indeed, tell them that 30 of the first 31 sentences in the King James Bible start with 'And'. And (see, it's easy) that what's good enough for God is good enough for you.

Grammar matters less than style, content matters more than syntax. In fundraising copy, what matters most is the power that the language gives us to convey emotion and need. I speak as a man who was taught about adverbial clauses of concession. There are not many of us left but I have no urge to form a preservation society.

The practice of writing

I have listed what Orwell told us about writing in general. It is now time to get closer to our own particular demands in writing fundraising copy. Another list, then. If it checks out with Orwell from time to time do not be surprised, for it is my strongly held belief that fundraising communication does not need its own specially fabricated language.

Use Saxon words and not Latin ones

Ninety-five per cent of words in the English language come from either Saxon or Latin roots. The former are shorter and therefore better. They have more force. If you don't believe me, try swearing with Latin-based oaths.

Use vivid words and not hackneyed ones

Sounds obvious, doesn't it? But I suggest that you challenge your next piece of fundraising in these terms. Start with the reply device, then look at the body copy of an ad, or the text of a letter. How many times could you have used a substitute word to greater point?

Use short sentences and vary the lengths

The full stop is there for a reason. It helps people understand what you are saying by chopping your text into bite-size pieces called sentences. Remember: nothing else matters except meaning. A sentence does not need a verb. Not at all. It need not be long, need not defer to the Johnsonian tradition of the periodic sentence that ran to perhaps 200 words complete with subclauses and the full complement of colons and semi-colons to separate the various constructs; a tradition that continues to this day in the hands of writers such as Bernard Levin, a journalist who rarely deploys 20 words when 200 can fulfil his sense of personal grandeur, a quality that some may admire but which most would resist on the basis that there are only so many hours a day in which one can read a newspaper.

Did you fall asleep during that last sentence? Good, I have made my point. A long sentence is not just damned hard work, it also provokes the language of pomposity and self-regard. Short sentences are more appropriate to fundraising. Like

this. But not always. Boredom sets in. Truly it does. Honestly. See what I mean?

And I play these games because the short and verb-free sentence has become just a little bit of a cliché in its own right. Sentence length should be varied. It helps the reader understand what you are trying to say. That's all.

Use short paragraphs and vary the lengths

A similar but separate point. You can create a powerful paragraph out of just one sentence. But if every paragraph – or succeeding paragraphs – is so leanly constructed then the power is lost and the ghost of professional technique begins to haunt your message.

Avoid the temptation to write snappy little paragraphs like these.

They can work. But not always.

In fact, they can be boring.

And I hope the three paragraphs above prove the point. The paragraph I am writing now is, ironically, much easier for you to read. It is also more courteous, for short sentences in short paragraphs have a habit of sounding like slogans.

Get to the point!

You are a charity. People expect you to be asking for money. So, do not delay this primary reason for communicating. Do not feel that you have to lead up to your vulgar request via 200 words of self-justification, for nothing is more tiresome than an overlong preamble to a predictable question. Would a tax demand be more acceptable if it offered a couple of paragraphs about the history of the Inland Revenue or an update on the trade deficit?

Use active verbs and not passive ones

A direct echo of Orwell, I know, but charities do have a habit of slipping into the passive voice – I suspect because they think it makes them sound somehow more corporate. Paradoxically, it achieves more or less the opposite, subtracting them from the equation and making everything sound like a bureaucratic memo. Compare and contrast,

Tents will be sent to Kurdistan as a matter of urgency

with,

We must send those tents to Kurdistan urgently.

Relate the story to the reader

It is possible more often than you might think. Remember those donor motivations I listed earlier, particularly the ones that define the donation as a 'thank offering'. Remember, too, that we are all surrounded by half-appreciated, semi-digested facts that we relegate to the backs of our minds. Good fundraising copy can promote them to the front. And it does no harm to be as personal as possible.

One in three of the population will suffer from cancer is a chastening and provocative sentence.
One in three of us will suffer from cancer is that much more challenging. But there is nothing ethically wrong with pushing the point to its logical and most personal extreme.

One in three of your friends and family will suffer from cancer.

It is, of course, equally and completely true.

Ask for money not support

We have all become self-conscious about the M word. Politicians have invented the word 'resources' to prevent them saying 'money' out loud and frightening the voters, for it sounds more mystical and less personally demanding. It goes without saying that charities have also begun to talk of resources. Indeed, I have already received a mailing that talks of nothing else but the charity's need for 'more resources'. I was tempted to offer a couple of old shirts and some faded typewriter ribbons.

The word is money. Not support, or help, or contribution, or commitment (though each of these words have their place in a fundraiser's vocabulary). And it is extraordinary how seldom it is used.

The only exceptions surround those occasional situations where we are indeed asking for something other than money – participation in a sponsored event, a raffle, or a demonstration. But even here the M word could make the occasional appearance.

Use 'I' and 'you'

Avoid the first person plural unless it is totally necessary – and it rarely is. This is a commonplace instruction for letter-writing on the obvious basis that letters should be seen to be completely individual communications between two human beings. But I am by no means sure that the I/you habit should be dropped from other parts of the communication. Why should an accompanying leaflet slip into a more formal and objective mode?

We are fortunate in English in using the pronoun 'you' in both singular and plural forms. But the plural can still make an accidental appearance, 'Dear Friends' is a terrible way to start a letter. And do watch out for that corporate royal 'we'. 'We at the National Westminster Bank' is an appalling piece of pomp-speak. But 'We at Oxfam', or 'We in the environmental movement' are even worse for they suggest good causes adopting the verbal mores of corporations – not what most donors want to hear.

Does it sound like someone talking? If not, why not?

This really is the summary of everything I have said so far. I have laboured the point on conference platforms for the last decade, embroidering the instruction by reading out random pieces of direct marketing or fundraising and trying to fit them into regular patterns of ordinary speech. A good audience will howl with laughter as they listen to the dislocation between the way we write and the way we speak.

Does it matter? I think it does, particularly in fundraising. We are now so bombarded with selling messages from every conceivable medium that we tune out those that are tiresome, or jaded, or boring, or just plain hysterical, either in content or in tone. We are aware of the verbal artifice and we react accordingly.

Fundraisers really have no excuse for communicating in any other than acceptable human speech. Great issues do not require hysteria to be seen as great issues; the perception of need is not strengthened by the shrill language of the marketplace. We need passion, we need honesty and conviction, we need emotion, authority and urgency. We should not need verbal tricks.

There is one true test of whether your fundraising copy is effective. Read it out loud – to a colleague, your partner, or whoever. If they burst out laughing, you have written parody copy. If they fall silent, you have made an effect. If they threaten to blub, you have hit the jackpot.

All fundraising copy should sound like someone talking. Accept that and you will find that it is easier to write than the inbred gibberish.

All right then, another acronym

It should be obvious by now that I hate formulae. I particularly hate formulae that lurk behind neat acronyms. But I have already promulgated the KISS formula and it would be entirely silly if I refused to report the longest lasting and most useful acronymed formula in the whole history of advertising.

For the AIDA formula will serve you well in any medium. It goes Attention, Interest, Desire and Action. And it could be argued that it applies, almost supernaturally, to every piece of successful advertising.

So, secure the customer's Attention. That's the job of a headline, the opening sentence in a letter or the beautiful shot with which you start a TV commercial.

Then, arouse the customer's Interest. Which is how you build on that attention you just gained. It's the point at which you develop the selling argument.

Then, cultivate the customer's Desire. This is where you switch from general product virtues to more personal application. 'What's in it for me?' is being answered.

Lastly, begin to close the sale with the Action. If it's a direct response ad, that means a coupon or a telephone number. If it's not, it's often a list of stockists or retail outlets.

Only the most sceptical of us will find the AIDA formula inappropriate to fundraising. Actually, I like to amend it slightly in our field, slipping in a P for Proof or C for Conviction, representing the occasional need of fundraisers to report third-party endorsements for their request – testimonials or case histories for example.

So it becomes the AIDCA or AIDPA formula. And it saves you being sued by Verdi's estate.

Five deadly sins of all direct marketing copy

Call this Curmudgeon's Corner. It enables me to list some of the dumb habits that copywriters in fundraising are falling into. So, it's cathartic. And I think I sense the ghost of Orwell beaming at me as I write.

1. Polysyllables
Why on earth do we think that a long word is more impressive than a short one? They combine to form a language that is bureaucratic rather than human, corporate rather than personal. Fundraisers should mark the difference between these pairs of words,

Approximately	–	About
Participate	–	Take part
Establish	–	Set up
Utilise	–	Use

Go looking for equivalent long words that have clambered into your own vocabulary and which have learned to nestle there comfortably. Smother them.

2. Tautology

An increasing amount of words we use are redundant. And sometimes positively contradictory. We grow used to tautologies through their sheer repetition. Thus,

A major nuclear disaster. So, what exactly is a minor nuclear disaster?

Said he had nothing further to add. The word 'further' is redundant.

Taking strike action. Workers used simply to strike.

First invented or discovered. How can you invent or discover something second?

Mutual agreement. Can an agreement be other than mutual?

Full and total support. The doubly adjectived noun is a particularly sinister form of tautology for it has begun to mean the precise opposite of what it says. A football manager who enjoys the 'full and total support' of his chairman is about to be fired. It is the very phrase used by Prime Minister Major of Norman Lamont before he dispatched him from the Cabinet.

Died of a fatal dose of heroin. The cause of death is usually fatal!

Eyes glaze when I use examples like these in seminars. I guess that quite a few people have to look up the word tautology these days and they certainly have to think hard to see what's wrong with phrases like these. This makes my point for me. Tautology is a particularly pernicious thing if you cannot spot it.

3. Jargon

The English language is in danger of breaking down into mutually discrete tribal patois, sub-languages that use a vocabulary that is rarely accessible to members of other tribes. This very book must contain numerous examples of such tribal language – its excuse being that it is indeed produced for a specialist tribal audience.

But charities have their own jargon and they are in increasing danger of inflicting it on their donors. What exactly is 'community development', or 'biodiversity', or 'skill sharing'? I have just found all three phrases in a handful of appeal mailings on my desk. They come from the language of project workers and programme officers and it is often a lazy and opaque language, even within the field that invented it. To transfer it idly into fundraising is to risk complete reader stupefaction.

4. 'Autoblag'

I invented this word to describe the copy that you could write on a sort of mental auto-pilot. Your mind is switched off, you are going through the motions, yet somehow acceptable words and sentences seem to have issued from your word processor.

I have begun to offer a deeply subversive homily about autoblag copy. It says 'If your boss or client is comfortable with the copy it is probably under-achieving'. Sheer provocation, I know, but for a reason. It really comes back to Orwell's point about 'gumming together long lists of words'. You can get away with doing just that in a lot of professional situations. It is always wrong.

A typical client brief these days offers only a ritual salaam to the process of thought. It may offer the mechanics of the appeal to be written but it will often tail off into a phrase like 'you know the sort of thing'. And indeed I do know the sort of thing. Indeed, I can produce work guaranteed to arouse the heartening reaction 'Yes, that's the sort of thing'. As a journeyman I can be satisfied by this reaction. As a writer I should be infinitely depressed. Words should be worth discussion. If they look right first time round, if they are indeed 'the sort of thing', then both parties are presiding over mediocrity. It may work, but it could have worked better.

Fundraising copy deserves better than comfort.

5. The handy cliché

Roger Millington used to have a presentation slide that said 'Avoid clichés like the plague'. Not too many people saw the irony.

Like tautology, clichés are pernicious – you need reminding that these easy constructs are indeed dull repetitions of words that have long since lost any power. Unfortunately we live in a society where much communication consists of stringing together cliché after cliché. People are forever 'moving goalposts', or asking for a 'level playing field'.

We are all guilty. For years I wrote copy for mail order catalogues, the sort that offered you apparently hi-tech gizmos – solar calculators that made the tea and changed colour with your mood swings (I exaggerate, but only a little). You rarely saw these products, for they were usually being run up in Taiwan as you were writing. So you were forced back on a curious vocabulary of adjectives and adverbs that covered your graces. Everything was 'elegant', or 'beautiful', or 'distinctive'. If you had no idea what a product looked like, it could be always be 'a conversation piece'. The joy of these desperate words was that you could move them around at will. Thus, something could be 'elegantly beautiful', or 'distinctively elegant'. *In extremis*, you would see the words 'a beautiful and elegant conversation piece that is truly distinctive'. Soon, clients began to look for these words in their copy and another odd set of clichés had been assembled. It is still in use.

Like much modern writing, it makes free use of the redundant adjective or adverb, the habit of bolting together an automatic epithet with a noun to make a cliché. Consider these, 'shocking fact', 'appalling truth', 'viciously attacked', 'prompt action', 'chilling accounts', 'savagely beaten', 'cruelly neglected', 'isolated case', 'appropriate action', 'urgent need'. Each of these bolt-on clichés is used in one short fundraising letter from a child-care organisation. Each of the powerful truths being reported in it could have been made more powerful by a greater attention to alternative words or alternative means of expression.

Why does just about every fundraising radio commercial end with the message 'We're waiting by the phones'? It is because charities assume that there is a verbal model for every kind of communication, one from which they depart at their peril. It is yet another example of clinging desperately to formulae, like shipwrecked mariners clinging to the wreckage in the belief that it is a life raft.

The first person imperative

Just about the most difficult letter I ever had to write for Greenpeace was about global warming. It is a terrifying subject, which trails lots of statistics and can easily create nothing more evocative than a sense of apocalyptic gloom. It is not the most fertile subject area for an appeal mailing.

Fortunately I was briefed by a young campaigner who had had his first child the previous year. Before he embarked on the statistics and the minutiae of Greenpeace's policy, he said a thrillingly human thing. I think I can remember it verbatim. 'When I read this stuff again, I'm just shit scared about what's going to happen to Joe.' We talked a little more and the very conversation became the lead-in to the letter.

> *I am writing this appeal on a hot July afternoon.*
> *My 11-month-old son is playing at my feet as I do so.*
> *I look at Joe and I look at the blazing heat outside on the Finsbury Park streets and I wonder how I can avoid talking about the Greenhouse Effect in nakedly personal terms.*
> *But why shouldn't I? Why shouldn't I tell you how much I fear for the world we're preparing for Joe…*

Some may find this a trifle mawkish and it is fair to record that some Greenpeace people thought it an unnecessarily sentimental depiction of a complex issue. The appeal was successful, though, and I choose to believe that the success stemmed from the use of the first person singular, from the fact that this awesome message has been put into the voice of a real person.

As so often, I must acknowledge that it is not always possible. But, again, it is probably more possible than you think. It always makes at least the letter sound more compelling. Here are some examples from the United States that start the letter in very first-person terms.

By now, my children are safe and warm at home, huddled around heaters or beneath their covers, free from winter's icy chill till morning.

Red Cloud Indian School.

I wish you could have known George. A kind, sensitive man, he weighed only 90 pounds when I met him last year…

AIDS Resource Centre.

One of my favourite tasks as president of Defenders of Wildlife is to read all the mail we receive from people all over the country who are concerned about America's wildlife and want to see it protected.

Defenders of Wildlife.

And this is a similar technique I applied on behalf of the Director of Y Care International in London.

I arrived back home from India just after the Gulf War broke out – jet-lagged obviously, irritated by the dogleg of a journey I'd had to make, thankful that I'd got back in one piece.

An Oxfam letter dating from 1987 is from Marcus Thompson, then their man in India. It takes familiar material and turns it into a brilliant plea.

Dear Supporter

Doesn't it upset you to walk among people who have lost everything? Doesn't it distress you to see small children dying in their mothers' arms?

I am often asked these questions when I return from a disaster zone. Quite frankly, it does and it doesn't….

It doesn't because I'm busy when I'm visiting the scene of a disaster. I don't feel the helplessness you

feel in front of your TV. Just the opposite, I have the privilege of being able to do something to ease the suffering.

But of course it hurts when someone you've got to know dies.

In the civil war in Uganda I was visiting camps for people fleeing the fighting. We picked up a very sick mother and her starving children to take them to hospital in Kampala. In the crowded jeep a little boy of five or six sat on my lap. We smiled at each other as the jeep bounced along the rough dirt roads. He died before we reached the hospital.

That evening I just dissolved into tears. I have a child about the same age.

This cannot possibly be anything other than an honest man talking. You have just read it – and I think you were moved. You may just be flicking away tears.

To lighten the mood, I will report a current example by one President Clinton. This is the start of the letter thanking Democratic Party donors with a print of the White House.

It's hard to believe it has been almost three years since that cold, January day when Hillary, Chelsea, Socks and I moved into this wonderful house.

These are the authentic cheesy tones of the leader of the Western World. Your toes may curl when you read that letter, but it sounds exactly like the President to me.

Remember my earlier question – does it sound like someone talking? The use of the first person singular makes it easier to answer in the affirmative.

Some under-used virtues

Let me try and round up this section with a few afterthoughts on the process of writing fundraising copy. For there are four creative virtues that go strangely under-reported in seminar rooms.

I. Candour

I have suggested already that charities should be prepared to share their experiences with their supporters, to be prepared to bring them bad news if bad news is a valid reason for an appeal.

But I think charities should be altogether more candid anyway in their fundraising. Too often the fundraiser hides the common sense of a piece of communication behind an artifice of technique and undue obeisance to that dreaded tradecraft. Consider for a moment that basic practice of sending regular appeals to people who have given you a donation. Why not give them the opportunity of *not* getting those appeals? Some British charities are beginning to follow the example of Botton Village that I reported earlier and profiting accordingly. But few would allow the writer to use truly no-nonsense prose.

Charter 88 allowed me to do just that a few years back. There was a traditional four-appeals-a-year programme aimed at conjuring an average of £25 a year from each supporter. So, why not just ask for the £25 in the first place and spare a few trees?

Thankfully, Charter 88 were new to the fundraising game and saw no reason why we should mask such a request with the traditional verbiage.

And please send us a contribution to help our work. It always pains us when we write to you that we have to conclude our reporting back with that time-honoured phrase about needing more money. We know full well that you will receive many such letters that ask you for financial support. And we know full well that it must get tiresome in the extreme.

Can we suggest a way to spare both of us this regular embarrassment? If you can send us a donation of £25 or more either by cheque or standing order in response to this letter, we promise not to ask you again during 1991. We will continue to keep you updated with information about the campaign, and we may even ask you to do other things to help us. But we will spare you the regular

begging. We may be the first cause group to talk to its supporters with this kind of honest maturity, but we're not going to be ashamed of that. We need the money badly but we hate the mendicant mode.

This simple mailing achieved Charter 88's best ever response in its early days. Was it because all our supporters were highly intelligent and worldly? Or was it because the language was refreshingly unorthodox? I shall never really know and it is tragic that so few people feel comfortable with the language of candour. Then again, I doubt that many people would feel comfortable with a phrase like 'the mendicant mode'.

2. Rhetoric

Why are we so afraid of eloquent or elegant writing? Again, we deceive ourselves by presuming that we must always express ourselves in the same lowest-common-denominator prose that disfigures so much of our contemporary culture. The current appeal of Jane Austen adaptations and Shakespearean films may lie to some extent in our love of pageant and beautiful costumes; for myself, I choose to believe that it reflects our need to be subjected, at least occasionally, to the thrill of fine language. I would advise any contemporary politician to suspend the dismal litany of soundbites and start imitating the verbal ambition of a Gladstone, a Churchill, or a Bevan. Votes, I suspect, would follow such ambition.

Rhetoric should be particularly relevant to fundraisers for rhetoric is, by definition, exciting, motivating, aspirational. Yet you rarely see it in fundraising communication. Only Greenpeace seems to be able to describe its case with eloquence. Consider this start to a letter from their Canadian office.

Great towering trees straining for the sky.
Their lush verdant canopies covering a moist and humid world playing host to a super abundance of life. Jaguars, toucans, orang utans, pythons, tigers

and giant sloths. In all, five million species of animals, birds, fish, reptiles, insects and plants. Fifty per cent of all living things. Such is the wonder of the rain forest.

The incessant whine of the chain saw and the deafening roar of the bulldozer threaten this cornucopia of life. Every minute of every hour of every day 100 acres of irreplaceable rain forest are destroyed or seriously damaged...

I could pick quite a few holes in these paragraphs for they smack just a little of a fifth form essay. But the general effect is what matters. Someone has been trying for poetry, someone has tried to describe a familiar issue with a certain passionate eloquence. You will read further into this letter because it tries so hard at the beginning to catch you at your thoughtful best. I understand from Steve Thomas in Toronto that it remains the control package for Greenpeace Canada's acquisition programme. I am not surprised.

More of us should suspend self-consciousness and see how our message sounds if it is communicated in higher-flown language. Rhetoric can work.

3. Brevity

'Brevity is the soul of wit', it says in Hamlet. I sometimes think it might be the soul of fundraising. In our search to say everything and to repeat most things, we create that strange verbosity I reported earlier. I repeat, we write too many words.

Consider this one-piece mailing from the Canadian Red Cross. Above this letter is the response device/address carrier. The reverse gives you basic statistics about the Red Cross in Ontario. And that's it!

Dear Friend,

DISASTER! It can strike anywhere, anytime.

And, when it does, the Red Cross Society knows how to help.

In a matter of moments – perhaps in the time it takes you to read this paragraph – disaster could be striking somewhere, even affecting the life of someone you love.

Please make sure the Red Cross is there ready to help. I urge you to take a moment now to write a generous cheque. A donation of $25 or more will qualify you as a Sustaining Member of the Society.

Thank you

Sincerely

John R Finley

President, Ontario Division

You could argue that such brevity is presumptuous, that the success of this letter (and it is another proven control package) relies on the universal appreciation of the Red Cross and its work. But I am still left wondering how much more successful we might be if we gave the reader less to read. There can certainly be no better exposition of the KISS formula than the above.

Why not try it? Test a standard four-page letter against an edited two-page version. Then, take a deep breath and edit it back to one page. I have an awful suspicion that your tests will show little variance.

4. Rewriting everything

Every now and again it makes sense to move the furniture around at home. The room looks totally different. You realise that the wing of an armchair has been blocking the television. You find things under cushions. You expose the awfulness of that painting you were given 10 years back. You always intended to do something about the room and you always half knew what was wrong with it.

The same applies with fundraising copy. We get used to it. In particular, we get used to those parts of it that seem never quite to need change – the semi-statutory paragraphs with which every piece of fundraising communication is inevitably studded. In the UK, this includes deathless phrases about the Data Protection Act, the ritual incantations about

GiftAid and covenants, and that time-honoured sentence about not needing a stamp but how the charity saves money if you use one (vintage 1971). All these things can be rewritten. And all these things should be rewritten on the simple basis that more people would then read them and react to them. Take that ugly apology we have sometimes to make when we are worried about mis-addressing or picking up an existing donor with a widespread cold appeal. Why not use plain English? Why not make it sound fresh and genuine? Why not turn it into a selling point?

Amnesty Canada did all these things. This copy sits on the back of an outer envelope of an acquisition pack.

> *Sometimes mistakes happen. You may receive more than one copy of the same letter from Amnesty, or you may already be a donor. We try hard to stop this happening, but sometimes the computer records contain two slightly different variations of your name and address. You can help us. If you receive a package with a mailing label that has an error in your name and/or address, please correct and send it back to us with your donation.*
>
> *If you receive more than one package, we suggest that you pass the extra one on to someone who is concerned about human rights violations.*

This succeeds in sounding totally honest and straight-forward. It shows how much more you can achieve when you continue to challenge every phrase you ever write, be it ever so humble. I just hope Amnesty has changed this wording since. The point about moving the furniture around is that you are never quite going to be satisfied. Nor should you be.

SIX

THINKING VISUALLY IN FUNDRAISING

Let's start with the cliché – a picture is worth 100 words. Or is it 1,000?

But, however you factor the power of the visual in fundraising, it is a strangely under-reported power. You will find textbooks galore that tell you how to string the words together; you will find little in print that even celebrates the visual, let alone offers you instruction on how to optimise it.

There is a simple explanation. Art directors don't write books. Writers write books. It is an imbalance that often extends to the power structure of an average creative team. Usually the writer is leader and convenor of the creative effort. The art director is secondary, too often there to make the writer's ideas fit. These days, with the Apple Mac replacing the drawing board, the art director's casting as a type-fitting mechanic is strengthened. It is a very great pity and a perceptible reason for that formulaic

No copywriter could have invented the Oxfamily box. It first saw the light of day 30-odd years ago, but it remains a testament to the very special power of the art director.

work of which I regularly complain. But the only way to change creative habit is to mandate the art directors to seize power, to produce a concept before the writer starts scribbling. This needs to happen far more often in fundraising. They would doubtless produce zany and unworkable ideas, these newly mandated art directors, but they would prompt more adventurous thinking. When, on occasion, it happens, the results can be extraordinary. I think of the Oxfamily box produced in the mid-sixties by an art director called Bob Williamson. I think of the Ryton Gardens pack produced at Burnett Associates 20 years later. Would a writer have produced these ideas?

There is a sort of ideology behind the *de facto* suppression of adventurous art direction in fundraising and it is worth exploring. For years we have taken as read the 'homespun' theory of how a fundraising appeal should look. It was said that

Another triumph of the art director. Ryton Gardens is the National Centre for Organic Gardening. The mailing piece was a single sheet of brown wrapping paper. So it could be recycled into seed pots, thus defusing members' known aversion to junk mail. It raised eight times its target.

donors would be troubled by 'slick professionalism' (odd how the two words came to be gummed together). An appeal therefore had to look as if it had been produced by two old ladies working from a backroom. It is a theory to which I dutifully subscribed for many a year. And it is a theory that still echoes around the world of fundraising. In January 1996, Hal Malchow of Malchow, Adams and Hussey in Washington told me that any package must be kept simple '…donors don't respond if they see the imprint of Madison Avenue'.

As I say, I have played a full part in proselytising this theology. I have argued for letters that use

typewriter faces (and still would). But I have also argued for the puritanical use of monotone, the relegation of purely visual devices and the overall supremacy of the integrity-packed word over the dangerously attractive graphics. Now that I shade away from this fundamentalism, my apostasy may be of greater interest.

The 'homespun' theory was probably always a little light in logic. Those members of the public given to complaint about wasting valuable charity money on that dreaded 'slick professionalism' tend to do so whether the appeal is in black and white or full colour – it is the fact of the appeal, not its aesthetics, that offend. They would even be right, for postage is likely to remain the biggest cost component of any mailing and space costs will always far outstrip creative and production costs.

But the shift away from the old visual puritanism is necessary for one big reason – the fact that we now live in a highly visual world. Ads and posters from the commercial sector now prioritise the visual image over the copy to an unprecedented extent. Compare press ads 30 years ago with press ads now. An ad for a breakfast cereal or a washing machine would then have had a headline and perhaps 100 words of body copy. If it was an ad inspired by masters such as David Ogilvy or Bill Bernbach copy would certainly have been king and the photograph its subject. Indeed, a headline from Ogilvy could often involve more words than an entire ad in the 1990s. Only direct response ads now keep the tradition of long copy alive.

And words are even more victimised in television and cinema advertising. It is now possible to see commercials with no dialogue and no voice-overs till the pack shot at the end. The product or service is increasingly communicated by ambience, atmosphere, brilliant photography and cinematic cutting. This fashion for demanding imagery, always visual imagery, has now trailed back into the older media. It is occupying the commanding heights of press and poster advertising throughout the world.

Don't ask me to worship it. I believe it to be increasingly narcissistic and self-referential, yet another of those tribal sub-languages I reported earlier. It relies on a presumed wit and aesthetic on the part of the audience that cannot possibly be universal. Put simply, many people do not understand it or cannot decode it – decoding being the quality now demanded of them. But the pictures are pleasant and the images well heeled; it is as if the virtues of the products and services involved are allowed to *waft* into your subconscious. These ads do not threaten you and they do not irritate you with stupid claims and over-the-top language and repetition. When you watch television in the United States, or in Australia you immediately step back into the older tradition of crudity. Presenters rant to camera, the language is shrill and production values are scant. Your heart sinks as you watch.

I report on this new tradition of advertising only to make the point that our audience is now surrounded by a new visual culture. It expects communications to be well designed and imaginative. Indeed, a part of the audience is happy to accept design as a prime part of lifestyle – how else to explain the fuss about 'designer' clothes, or the decor of a new restaurant? Even the haircuts of footballers are now seen as fashion statements.

None of this says that fundraising communication should ape the fashion of the commercial sector. But I record a new-found belief that there is no point any more in fundraising communication looking shabby – if only because it is competing for attention with the highest standard of design ever witnessed by the consumer. Indeed, there are dangers in clinging to the old 'homespun' tradition – it suggests an unworldliness, the solemnity of the religious tract rather than the power, authority and importance of a contemporary message. I think we should make better use of design at every point.

A session with Doctor Vogele

Old direct marketing hands used to attend the International Direct Marketing Symposium in Montreux every year. A regular star of the show was a German professor, Doctor Siegfried Vogele, who had researched with suitable teutonic thoroughness how a reader reads a mailing package.

He used eye cameras to trace the eye movements of readers of direct mail packs and studied their body and hand movements to check their emotional and physical responses to what they were seeing and reading. As always with such work, scientific research seems often to coincide with unscientific common sense. But sneering would be unfair. Vogele's work is the result of thousands, if not tens of thousands, of such tests. And the results are – as they say – indicative. I have only space to list a few of his observations, for they amount, even in précis, to a full-day seminar and a very heavy book in their own right. But these points may be helpful.

● The reader spends more time on the back of the envelope than on the front. Having said that, the entire envelope-reading process lasts seven seconds.
● The average time spent reviewing the contents of the mailing is just 11 seconds. During this time, readers' eyes are fixed only on pictures and headlines, never on body copy.
● There is a 20-second timespan during which the reader decides to read or dispose of the mailing piece.
● 50 per cent of readers read the letter first. They start at the top and tend to go straight to the bottom, looking for the signatory. More than 90 per cent read a PS before they read the rest of the letter.
● Large pictures will get attention before smaller pictures. Colour pictures will be noticed before black-and-white pictures. Portraits will gain attention before full length pictures of people. Eyes will be the first thing focused on. 80 per cent of readers will go to a vertical shape rather than a horizontal shape.
● Don't place an eye-grabbing illustration at the lower right side of any piece. It will draw the eyes immediately to the 'exit' position at which the reader turns the page.
● Handwriting will be noted before written text. Numbers are noted before longer words. Copy within a border will be read before open text.

I will stop there for I am already beginning to apply severe editorial selection to the good doctor's research. He says much about underlining, highlighting, fixation points and scanning patterns. It is not that I disagree with him. It's just that too many direct marketers have imbibed the research by the bottle and promptly rebottled it – Doctor Vogele is probably single-handedly responsible for the veneration of the PS in international direct marketing and fundraising. But, if you want to get further into his findings, the book is called *Das Verkaufgesprech fuer Brief und Antwortkarte*. You probably won't find it in W. H. Smith's.

The outer envelope

Controversy used to surround the vexed question of whether the outer envelope should have anything on it. Indeed, people wrote to the trade press quite a lot. The older generation used to argue for the dignity of the minimal – perhaps the quietism of 'Private and Confidential', or, indeed, 'Urgent' or 'Personal '. The younger Turks were all for snazzy graphics and a headline on the basis that such treatment would compel the reader to rip open the envelope and get inside.

This last argument has always struck me as baloney. Only a true misanthrope fails to open an envelope, whatever it says on the outside. Even those sombre buff envelopes from the tax authorities get opened in the belief that they may contain a rebate rather than a new demand, such is the power of human optimism. I have no evidence and no experience to suggest that readership of an average pack is changed one whit by the use of the outer envelope. I have plenty of evidence to suggest that the outer envelope can be one more repository of fundraising cliché. For, just as much copy has become the arena of the redundant adverb and the redundant adjective, so has the outer envelope become the arena for the redundant rhetorical question, or even the redundant answered rhetorical question. It is where you find phrases like 'How would you feel if you found a dog screaming in agony outside your window?'; or 'How could a mother abandon her newborn baby?'; or 'How much is a child's life worth?' And where you will find the ritual responses, 'To the children of Beirut, war is no joke'; or 'To Mr and Mrs Jones, living in bed and breakfast is no joke'.

Mark the symmetry of these last two envelope messages. They demonstrate how easy it is to fall into another special language, Outer Envelope Language. It is another mess of clichés with which we have surrounded ourselves. We do not need them. They serve only to flesh out a jaded brief, 'outer envelope,

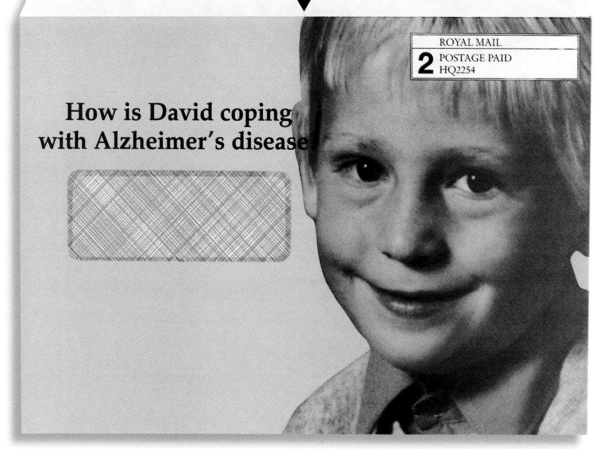

A benign example of Outer Envelope Language. The combination of words and photograph makes it intriguing and irresistible.

long letter plus leaflet, you know the sort of thing.' And so, 1,000 redundant sentences are born.

I refuse to take sides between the outer envelope minimalists and the outer envelope exhibitionists, though many claim to have to have secured an increased response with an outer envelope message. I will just quote one from each side that seem to me to do a creative job. The first, on a door-dropped communication, just says, 'From the office of the Director General of the Cancer Research Campaign'. The other shows a picture of a child with the wording 'How is David coping with Alzheimer's disease?' The piece from the cancer charity relies on authority and dignity. The piece from the Alzheimer's Disease Society relies on your sense of shock that a child can be affected by the disease. Both stimulate your attention because they apply different kinds of intelligence. Would either be improved by outer envelope language?

And would either be improved by verbosity? Another appeal on my desk manages all this on a small envelope,

> *John, 72, was found lying under his Christmas tree.*
> *Sheila, 64, froze to death in her garden.*
> *Douglas, 72, collapsed beside his unposted*
> *   Christmas cards.*
> *But, thankfully, we found Mary before it was too late.*

All the charity really needed to say was, 'This is a Christmas appeal from Age Concern'. I do not need to be depressed into subjection before giving to an old people's charity at Christmas.

The lift letter

This is a direct mail technique that I report with some inhibition for, yet again, it can become another of those tiresome and predictable clichés. But at best — which means at most relevant — it can add hugely to the perceived power of an appeal.

My nanny by David

My nanny was very happy and kind. She dansed and play the piano and smild a lot

We used to take her and grampy on holiday. Now she has Alshers, and we have to feed her and see her in a home cald the Albany.

She can't use her knife and fork

I wish somebody would make her better again. I am sad

grampy is left at his hous all alone and he feels sad as well.

we have to go to see her evry day so she won't forget us

She can't talk or rember.

Some day she mite sing a song with grampy

If you must have a lift letter, make it distinctive and make it powerful.

A lift letter or 'publishers letter', as it used to be known, is merely an additional letter written by someone other than the original signatory of the appeal. It is always shorter and seeks to reinforce the primary letter in a different tone of voice. Sometimes these lift letters go out with the signature of an eminent supporter or trustee. Sometimes they are written by a field or project worker. It is not unknown to have more than one.

If they are to work, they must be seen to be realistic. That means that they deserve the designer's attention and imagination, because if they look merely like a continuation of the primary letter by other means they become just another irritating enclosure.

You will often see memos of the 'From the desk of…' type. You will often see handwriting. You certainly should see a different letterhead. You should always see a different printing stock.

Without these simple differentials, the point of a lift letter is lost. It should offer a third-party endorsement from someone slightly unexpected. Technically, it may well be read before the main letter. It cannot afford to be predictable, either verbally or visually.

The temptation to make them a vehicle for those eminent supporters is always strong and usually worth resisting. Am I the only donor unimpressed by the fact that the chairman of a charity's board might seek to add his two penn'orth? Or, indeed, by the habit of some charities of unearthing a second division celebrity and sticking a 20-year old photograph of her (it's usually a her, I fear) atop the lift letter?

The device deserves better. I have never seen it used more powerfully than in an Alzheimer's Disease Society pack produced by Chapter One Direct. This is the one I referred to earlier, which has the enigmatic and provocative outer envelope message 'How is David coping with Alzheimer's disease'. Inside the pack, David's relationship with dementia is explained – his grandmother has gone into care. It is a story told in a lift letter that is a reproduction of a page taken from a school exercise book.

> *My nanny by David*
>   *My nanny was very happy and kind. She dansed and played the piano and smiled a lot.*
>   *We used to take her and grampy on holiday. Now she has Alshers and we have to feed her and see her in a home cald the Albany.*
>   *She can't use her knife and fork.*
>   *I wish somebody would make her better again. I am sad.*
>   *Grampy is left at his hous all alone and he feels sad as well.*

> *We have to go to see her evry day so She won't forget us.*
>   *She can't talk or rember.*
>   *Some day she might sing a song with grampy.*
>   (*Sic* throughout.)

David Strickland-Eales, who gave me this pack, tells me that it was a genuine school essay by the eight year old that was reproduced. I believe it.

Its efficacy proves several things. First, my repeated demand that all fundraising copy should sound like someone talking. Second, that eight year olds can write great copy (notice how spare this copy is, how visually colourful). Third, how very powerful a lift letter can be if it offers that second voice with integrity. Fourth, how design enhances the words.

For, there must have been a temptation to tidy up the spelling and typeset David's message. Another temptation well resisted. For the pack secured an average donation of £27.50. And lots of them.

Photographs and illustrations

The control recruitment package for the South African National Council for the Blind in October 1995 was produced by Downes Murray. It is a simple thing – a short letter, a reply form, a small format, all in black and white. But, nestling in the middle is a colour print of a little girl in a party dress smelling a flower. She is of course blind and, in fact, deaf. The copy on the back of the print just says 'Unable to see or hear, Elize finds pleasure in the scent of flowers and the warm touch of sunshine.'

The equivalent pack from Botton Village in the UK contains three such prints, genuine-looking 'snaps' that look as if they have just come back from the chemists. They are simply photographs of the residents of Botton and this time the messages on the reverse are the actual words of those residents, reproduced in their handwriting. Thus, 'Here I am chopping vegetables for lunch. I love helping to make

This is our family in the garden at Rowan house I am sitting on the bench in the middle with the children,

The message of Botton Village is brilliantly conveyed in simple, personal photographs.

the meals for everyone.' And 'This is me with Deborah. I am 41 and Deborah is 36. Botton is my home. I hope I can live here forever.'

How simple! How very evocative! And the evocative simplicity teaches us something. For a photograph is a known component of a successful appeal. It offers documentary veracity in a way that no other device can, and it does so in a form that is familiar to everyone. We all look at 'snaps'. We keep them in albums. We can't wait till they emerge from the photo-processors.

Isn't it odd, then, that our first thought with a photograph in fundraising communication is so often to *reproduce* it, to make it a component of a piece of print, to enlarge it or reduce it, to ensure that it fits

in the graphic scheme of things? Why not preserve it in its most telling form – the original photograph? These two packs thrive on the atmosphere created by this simplicity. That picture of little Elize would have been unremarkable if it were reproduced in other than its original form.

Photographs have power and you can build on that power. A famous pack produced by Chapter One Direct in the late eighties for the Royal Society for the Prevention of Cruelty to Animals offers a long letter, a lift letter in the form of an internal memo to the fundraising officer, a 'handwritten' note from that fundraising officer and an apparent extract from an RSPCA inspector's diary, detailing his day's work in chasing up animal cruelty reports. This is powerful

WARNING!

This envelope contains photographs of animals—victims of cruelty.

The RSPCA adds a touch of relevant drama to its photographs of the atrocities committed on animals.

reportage indeed, but it is capped by the use of four black-and-white photographs of cruelly treated animals rescued by the charity. They are harrowing. But their power is enhanced, not just by their simple reproduction and typewritten captions, but by the fact that they are enclosed in a small envelope with the blunt word 'Warning' on the outside. Few readers will resist the temptation to slit open this inner envelope for there is a voyeur in most of us. And very few readers will be unmoved by what they see. It is a superb example of making simple photographs the key element of an appeal.

But the choice of photographs is critical. Just as charity appeals often suffer from verbal prolixity, so do they run the risk of visual prolixity. In other words, we probably use too many photographs.

The Apple Mac revolution has undoubtedly led to a generation of designing-by-grid, with squares and rectangles offering neat symmetry but too little power. The copy width is adjusted and space left in the margin for three photographs of equal size and equal geometry. The photographs are fitted in and selected on their ability to be so fitted. It is all rather glum and schematic.

Far better, it seems to me, to acknowledge the power of the photograph at the outset and to make a selection based on that power. Which will probably mean using less of them and using them better.

The only photographs that matter are those that depict the object of the charity's appeal. Which mostly means people, fellow human beings, or at least fellow creatures if your cause is an animal-based one. The shot of the new research block or the onion store in an African village may enjoy a role in your annual report but it will rarely enjoy a role in your appeal. Photographs should be used to demonstrate the need for your work, however implicitly. ActionAid's advertising for the past decade has been built around the simplicity of one child looking straight to camera. The eye contact is irresistible.

In these days of automatic, idiot-proof cameras, anyone can produce photographs of the required quality. When Oxfam sent me to Africa in 1967 it armed me with a sophisticated Pentax and assigned me to produce usable photographs that the field staff were unable to supply. This should no longer be necessary. Nor should the hiring of professional photographers to do the job – you are as likely as Lord Lichfield to deliver the goods. Remember: your only aim is powerful documentary veracity. You can leave photographic artistry to the colour supplements.

Illustrations rather than photographs? Frankly, hardly ever. I have seen some compelling material produced by American wildlife organisations that used exquisite pencil or wash drawings and I once produced a pack for Greenpeace that deployed a dramatic linocut to tell the story about whaling. But, frankly, the latter was an indulgence, born of the fact that the whaling photographs we had would not have reproduced on the cheap printing stock we were then using.

The use of illustrations might well be a happy contribution to this new world of visual sophistication. But illustrations are always less evocative than photographs.

Brochures, fliers, leaflets and newsletters

Who needs them?

This may strike you as a somewhat braw declaration but it is a question rarely posed and seldom answered. The instinctive enclosure of

Newsletters would rarely win a creative award but they are often more welcome than aggressive direct mail.

Our Awesome Res

DRIFTNETTING ... Driftnets continue to cause havoc - not just with whales and other cetaceans such as porpoises and dolphins, but with seals, sea lions, turtles, sea birds and large fish of every kind. Despite their size and strength whales become entangled in the endless walls of mesh and drown. The IWC estimates that up to a million whales, dolphins and porpoises died in 1990 from driftnets cast in the Pacific and Indian Oceans and in the Mediterranean. WWF have been involved since 1991 in a highly effective awareness campaign throughout Europe to get governments to commit to whale and dolphin-safe driftnet policies.

Photo: WWF

MARINE POLLUTION ... We know frighteningly little about what is happening in the ocean depths. But we do know that organochlorines such as DDT and PCB's are used the world over and are extremely hazardous to the environment. Traces of DDT have even been found in Arctic ice and on penguin eggs. Some organochlorines are "synthetic hormones" which interfere with the natural hormonal systems. This marine pollution will be affecting not just whales but any sea creature, rendering them less able to produce offspring and less able to defend themselves from infection. WWF continues to research marine pollution on behalf of every species that depends on the ocean as their natural habitat.

Photo: WWF UK

CHEMICAL POLLUTION ... There has been a series of mass die-off's of marine mammals since the 1980's - almost certainly the result of industrial pesticides and chemicals getting into coastal waters. Many whales are coastal feeders and the endangered beluga whales of the St Lawrence estuary are now among the most contaminated creatures on earth. When they die, they are regarded as "toxic waste". WWF are campaigning vigorously for a sharp reduction in the level of toxic discharges entering St Lawrence.

WHALE-WATCHING ... WWF is actively promoting well-regulated whale-watching. 5.4 million people are believed to have gone whale-watching in 1994. The total revenue generated from this new leisure industry was over $500 million during that year. Hearteningly, it has become big business in Japan - former whale-hunters now serve as look-outs on the whale-watching boats. The first whale-watching venture was inspired by WWF research - now several other whale-watching enterprises exist around the coast of Japan.
Photo: WWF

WHALE-MEAT AS FOOD ... Fifty years ago whale-meat was a staple part of Japan's daily diet. Now it is a difficult-to-find luxury, selling for $200 per kilo in December, 1994. Such prices inevitably fuel an illegal trade in whale-meat and TRAFFIC - WWF's wildlife trade monitoring arm continues to track shipments of whale meat in the Far East. In 1993 a three and a half tonne shipment of "shrimps" at Oslo airport, labelled for South Korea and Japan, was found to consist of whale-meat, inexcusable from a country which had promised severe self-regulation of its whaling activity!

Photo: William Rossiter/

WWF IN ACTION THROUGHOUT THE WORLD ... Ou whale campaigns are worldwide. In South Africa we have suppo a monitoring programme since 1969. In Norway our research is helping cla the relationship between the orcas and the herring. In Canada we have helpe create a sanctuary for bowhead whales in Baffin Island. And we continue to lobby every international convention and gathering that can secure the future the whales and the seas on which they depend.

THE GENTLE GIANTS

Nine of the world's great whales

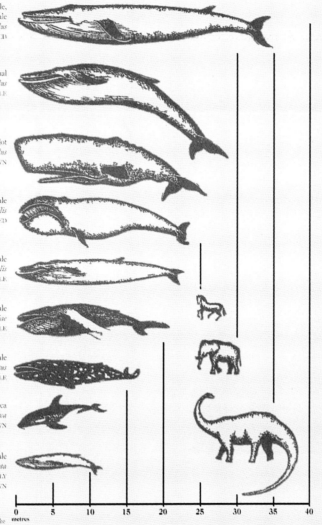

Blue whale,
or sulpher-bottom whale
Balaenoptera musculus
STATUS ENDANGERED

Fin whale, or common rorqual
Balaenoptera physalus
STATUS VULNERABLE

Sperm whale, or cachalot
Physeter macrocephalus
STATUS INSUFFICENTLY KNOWN

Northern right whale
Eubalaena glacialis
STATUS ENDANGERED

Sei whale
Balaenoptera borealis
STATUS VULNERABLE

Humpback whale
Megaptera novaeangliae
STATUS VULNERABLE

Gray whale
Eschrichtius robustus
STATUS VULNERABLE

Killer whale, or orca
Orcinus orca
STATUS INSUFFICIENTLY KNOWN

Minke whale
Balaenoptera acutirostrata
STATUS INSUFFICIENTLY
KNOWN

0   5   10   15   20   25   30   35   40
metres

All status categories are taken from the
IUCN Red Book.

another piece of print in an appeal pack is yet another convention that deserves toppling. For that leaflet will always be the costliest part of the pack and will likely demand the most creative time and greatest degree of debate. Be bold – is anyone reading it?

We know that the letter is almost always read. We even know to some extent how it is read. But we know very little about the attention given to other components of a pack. So I shall invade this information vacuum with a subjective opinion about that attention: I think it is often bugger all. A sad judgment from one who has written enough leaflets to paper the ceiling of the Sistine Chapel.

There are exceptions to my scepticism. Sometimes there is a sweep to a fundraising story that simply needs space to tell it. I think of the whale appeal that Smith Bundy produced for WWF in August 1995. The centrepiece was a massive fold-out leaflet, which enabled us to tell the full historical story of whaling and to demonstrate the size of these magnificent creatures. It was conceived almost as a wallchart in the knowledge that many younger WWF supporters would use it in just that mode. But, even here, I would have to be honest and admit to some scepticism about the return our client actually received on this brave creative investment.

But it was at least worth producing creatively. Too many appeal leaflets lack not just power but purpose. They are inevitably restricted physically by the outer envelope that contains them. But they are often restricted cerebrally – what are they adding to the appeal apart from more words and a few pictures?

If you have something left to say or to explain, it is worth considering whether the traditional leaflet or flier is the way to say it. That RSPCA campaign that I quoted in the last section would not have been enhanced if the photographs of animal atrocities had been depicted in leaflet form. It must make sense to produce materials that we know are going to secure attention.

A piece of print *can* secure that attention. But it does it by either communicating something remarkable, or by communicating in a remarkable way and ideally by doing both. If it is just a tired adjunct to the mailing process, if it is just a piece of A4 paper turned into six pages, if it is just a vehicle for repetitive writing and dull photographs… then it is probably not worth the effort of producing it.

I honour one total exception – the newsletter. Often they are as drab as drab can be, predictable in format, dull in execution. But they work. The reader sees them as different from a mailing appeal. There is almost comfort in the bland language, the happy photographs, the overall lack of appeal-type hysteria. Supporters are always willing to spend a little time with them, almost in a mood of duty. I read my local parish magazine in exactly the same way, as a sort of tribute to the people good enough to produce it and put it through my door. It is when we witness the power of the humble newsletter that we see just how crazed and wrongheaded many of our fundraising techniques are. For the newsletter is often technique-free. Yet it will often be the most valued communication a charity sends.

Downes Murray in South Africa runs simple newsletter programmes for many of its clients. It claims a regular six per cent to 10 per cent response rates from them. I believe it. I know of one charity in the UK that allows the supporters the privilege of only receiving the newsletters and not receiving appeals. It works.

People seem to like newsletters. They seem not to like direct mail appeals. Isn't it odd that we rarely acknowledge this fact and build communication and fundraising programmes accordingly?

People and testimonials

We live in a very personal age. There was a time when the great events of human history were reported as mere events, impersonal for the most part, unembellished by individual human opinion or reaction. The millions of combatants in the First World War would have known the names of perhaps six of the mighty fools who ordained the conflict – perhaps a Prime Minister, a Field Marshal, a couple of line commanders and a hate figure from the other side, probably the Kaiser. They may have heard the names, but they would probably not recognise their faces and they would never have heard their voices. And few would have heard the voices of the ordinary soldier save for his comrades and his friends and family.

Mass media has made the sound of other people's voices a familiar commentary on every issue of the day. Indeed, the 'vox pop' interview has become a cliché of news reporting, with the man or woman in the street allowed to opine to the microphone or camera on issues that range from European monetary union to the selection of England's hapless cricket teams. 'Phone-in' programmes throughout the world immortalise the views and prejudices of the ordinary man or woman. Politicians routinely subject themselves to the interrogation of a television or radio audience.

The process is rarely illuminating or culturally enhancing. But it does mean that we have become extraordinarily interested in what other people think. Or, at least, that much information we receive is already coloured by third-party opinions and judgment. Indeed, we have constructed entire media products around this acceptance that what other people say is somehow interesting and instructive. Think of all those chat shows, think of a personality based magazine like *Hello*. They are not about anything in the old-fashioned sense of provoking thought. They are just excuses for people to jabber at us.

Fundraisers seem to have missed the implications of this development. To an odd extent our communications are an unpeopled zone. The signatory to a letter is often faceless and while the people who are the subjects of the charity's cause will sometimes make an appearance it is often a curt and emblematic one. Open a pile of direct mail appeals – how many human faces do you see, how much personal speech?

It is one of the oldest proverbs in fundraising that 'people give to people'. I would expand that truism and say that 'people give to people because other people give to people'. In other words, we need in our creative work to reflect better some of those social instincts that I reported in an earlier chapter, particularly that need to belong, that need to identify somehow with fellow human beings in pursuit of 'good'.

Such is the nature of mass direct marketing recruitment that we may begin to say a troubling thing. Unless you are a member of a committee or physically involved in a charity's local work, *you are unlikely ever to meet a fellow supporter of that charity or cause. Your relationship with the organisation is a lonely one.*

Fundraising communication needs now to confront this phenomenon and to take advantage of this more personal age of ours. The supporters need to appear in the mailings as much as the recipients of the charity. So do the people who work for the charity. We need more real people to convey the message because most messages we hear are now conveyed by real people.

Why does Mrs Jones support Oxfam? How does Mr Jones support the Salvation Army? What goes through the mind of Jones Junior when he does a sponsored walk for WWF? Charities rarely try to capture these human instincts, these quiet passions of millions of individuals. They should, for they will always be evocative and they will quite often be inspirational. I think of the fact that in 1995 Greenpeace in Belgium had a 93-year-old supporter on its files. Can you imagine a more vivid or surprising testimonial for a cause group widely believed to be the province of the young than that of a nonagenarian?

A long and boring letter comes alive with the use of a news cutting. (But couldn't the letter have been shorter?)

Journal

FRANK RICH

The North Crusade

As Americans fixed their attention last weekend on the heroic military men who saved the world from Fascism, a tin soldier was leading a quiet coup back home. At a Richmond convention overflowing with zealots, Oliver North won the Republican nomination for the Senate in Virginia and in that instant gave the radical Christian right its most ominous victory yet in its stealthy pursuit of political power nationwide.

To appreciate how scary Mr. North and his movement are — and not just to moderate Virginians — consider this list of those on the *right* who have tacitly or actively opposed his Senate campaign: Ronald Reagan, The Wall Street Journal editorial page, George Will, Robert Bork and Edwin Meese. Virginia's Republican Senator, John Warner, will back an independent candidate rather than support Mr. North against the tarnished incumbent Democrat, Charles Robb. Bob Dole and Gerald Ford are wavering.

Why does Mr. North arouse such antipathy among his conservative confederates? The answer begins — but does not end — with the character issue. Not only is he a convicted liar for his Congressional testimony during the Iran-contra hearings, but he is a compulsive liar: among other self-aggrandizing tall tales, he invented an evening spent with Mr. Reagan watching television in the White House living quarters during the Grenada invasion. Even a conservative Republican nominally sympathetic to Mr. North, Senator Charles Grassley of Iowa, said last week: "Ollie North may be a nut. I don't know." Or as Colin McEnroe, a columnist with The Hartford Courant, aptly noted: "There's a Norman Bates sort of thing going on in his eyes."

Yet the gravest danger posed by Mr. North has less to do with him than with the radical forces he represents. His convention victory in Virginia was made possible by the legions of fundamentalists who are working tirelessly caucus by caucus, state by state to take control of the G.O.P. As Richard Berke has reported in The Times, the radical right has captured the party apparatus in six states besides Virginia — Texas, Minnesota, Oregon, Iowa, Washington and South Carolina — and is making major inroads in many others, including New York.

You don't have to look far to see why Republican leaders are alarmed by this spreading coup. It was the radical right's intolerant version of "family values" that soured the 1992 Houston convention, greasing the skids for George Bush's November

defeat. The more power the movement gets, the more it splinters the party, sabotaging the Republicans' chance to capture the Senate this year or the White House in '96.

What makes Mr. North's ascendancy inspire panic in his own party is the boost he gives to the insurgents, whether he ever gets to the Senate or not. An enormously telegenic national fund-raiser with a secular, derring-do public image, he is a far more salable front man for the radical right's agenda than the likes of Pat Robertson or Jerry Falwell.

For Democrats, a rising religious right dividing the Republican vote is an electoral dream, presaging a rerun of the G.O.P.'s Goldwater debacle of 1964. But for anyone of either party who cares about civil liberties, this fundamentalist crusade is a nightmare. Even without winning elections, the radical right can make life punishing at the state level for wom-

The radical right's march on Richmond.

en seeking abortions, homosexuals, racial and religious minorities.

Mr. North accepted his nomination in Richmond on a stage filled with white faces. As befits the radical right's push to bring anti-gay initiatives to nine state ballots this fall, he used his speech to rail against Clinton White House aides "with an earring and an ax to grind."

And there's more to worry about below the surface. Today in New York, the Anti-Defamation League will release a book-length study of the religious right, including such prominent North cheerleaders as the Virginia-based Christian Coalition, that will document both the movement's anti-Semitic rhetoric and the ferocity of its efforts to enforce its exclusionary orthodoxy on local governments and school systems.

Throughout his Bible-thumping campaign, Oliver North has been short on substance and long on military exhortations, referring to family values as a "battle cry" and even likening his Senate race to the Normandy invasion. For once he is not entirely lying. Whether he wins or loses, Virginia is only an early skirmish in what promises to be a protracted and ugly holy war. □

[Handwritten note on clipping:] ...and the rest of the country as well! Please join the ACLU today and help us stop them while there is still time. Thank you. I.G.

Let the supporters help you tell the story. They will tell it differently. And that in itself will be refreshing.

The power of news

Bad news, I have said, can make for good fundraising. The principle goes beyond the reports of major national disasters that automatically make the newspaper front pages, or the lead stories on television news. Sometimes the story that helps endorse your appeal is buried away on an inside page or in a little-seen magazine.

You still should want to report it. For, again, we can profit by the authority that third-party endorsement lends to our claim on people's cheque books. People defer to what they see in print. Reproducing news stories is an inexpensive but always persuasive visual gambit.

'A special message from Virginia' reads the outer envelope from the American Civil Liberties Union. It is an appeal for funds to counter the growing power of Pat Robertson's Christian Coalition. What makes it work is not the inevitable six-page letter. It is the reproduction of an article in the *New York Times* that reports the apparently insidious growth of the radical right in Virginia. It makes better reading than the letter and it offers a different language and perspective – I doubt that even the director of the ACLU would be prepared to say 'Ollie North may be a nut', or 'There's a Norman Bates thing going on in his eyes'. But a journalist can and the journalistic licence sits happily in an otherwise rather stately appeal. Just in case the reader misses the more mischievous paragraphs in the newspaper story the art director has taken a highlighter to them. It is all very simple, but it is all very effective.

A package from Stephen Thomas and Associates in Toronto does a similar job on behalf of a support group for the Canadian Broadcasting Corporation, a quality station under attack from its political opponents. This mailing, I am sure sensibly, manages to assail heights of jingoism rarely seen in fundraising. 'You can do something for your country today' says an outer envelope with the maple leaf flag rampant. 'Yes, I will stand up for Canada' says the response device. And the letter begins in similarly trenchant terms,

Dear Fellow Canadian,

Wrapping myself in the flag? You're darn right I am. Because I'm worried about the future of our country. And I'll bet you are too. But there's something you can do besides wring your hands. Read on.

This is obviously carefully calculated bluster, but it is also a proven control pack. Again, what justifies the bluster is the different tone of voice and authority given by three newspaper and magazine articles, reproduced on one piece of paper, that report the financial plight of CBC. These articles murmur the facts just as the letter shouts the slogans.

The third-party endorsement of the news coverage adds authority to the rhetoric of the appeal for CBC.

THE ARTS   The Globe and Mail, Saturday, September 23, 1995

CBC forecasts 3,800 in job reductions

Local and regional production centres projected as main targets of cuts, analysis says

Dear fellow Canadian,

You can do something for your country today.

Daily Mirror
FORWARD WITH THE PEOPLE
No. 12,905 ONE PENNY
Registered at G.P.O. as a Newspaper.

PEACE
JAPAN SURRENDERS
ALLIES CEASE FIRE

iccadilly, caught napping, woke up

Today and tomorrow V-da
"Enjoy yourselves" call
Attlee at midnight

Troops had to rescue the police

SHOW YOUR GRATITUDE TO OUR VJ DAY HEROES.

Who can resist reading old newspaper stories? And who could resist tagging their name to a balloon to celebrate VJ Day?

"I've remembered the bravery of those who fought for freedom with a gift to the Royal Star & Garter Home's VJ Day Anniversary Appeal."

Signed _____

Some charities obviously have it easier than others. Britain's Royal Star and Garter Home cares for men and women who have served in the British armed forces. As such, the fiftieth anniversary of VJ Day in September 1995 was a prime fundraising opportunity and the pack produced by Target Direct made full use of it. Here the front and the back of the outer envelope consists of extracts from the *Daily Mirror* from August 16th 1945. It makes compulsive and nostalgic reading and helps explains how a cold recruitment mailing of 112,000 managed to produce a return on investment of 1.48 to 1.

There was another reason though. It started with a 'sense of event' and built in a greater 'sense of event' by announcing the release of tens of thousands of commemorative balloons from a British warship to mark the VJ Day anniversary. With the reply form came a balloon tag. Sign it and your name would be attached to one of the commemorative balloons that would cross the English channel just as hundreds of thousands of British troops had 50 years before.

An involvement device, in other words. And a neat segue into the next section.

Involvement devices

Remember my plastic spoon? It was an involvement device. It will secure my greater attention to the message by enclosing something rather unexpected. That, at least, is the theory. And it works.

Many involvement devices are crass and predictable – personalised labels, personalised notepads, seals and the like. They are crass and predictable but they work. These things will always increase response. Some people claim that the response thus recruited is low quality. Frankly, I don't claim to know. But at least the equation is a simple one. An involvement device will increase your pack costs and increase your response. You find out the efficacy of the equation by testing a pack with an involvement device against one without. And that's all there is to be said.

Or is it? Personally, I am priggish about the damn things. I like an involvement device that does more than shovel up response. I like involvement devices that persuade the reader to think.

Mind you, crassness sets in here as well. A mailing for the South African National Council for the Blind actually contains a tiny white stick, a device that I fancy might offend politically correct sensibilities in the UK. But then the Republic seems to go in for involvement devices in a big way. A recent batch of mailings is found to contain, respectively, a fridge magnet, various vegetable and flower seeds and a small packet of peanuts – this last accompanied by the deathless phrase 'A small taste of what your support means'.

But, again it is pointless to sneer. I repeat – these things work.

An involvement device from Cancer Relief Macmillan Fund. Simple, inexpensive – and record response rates.

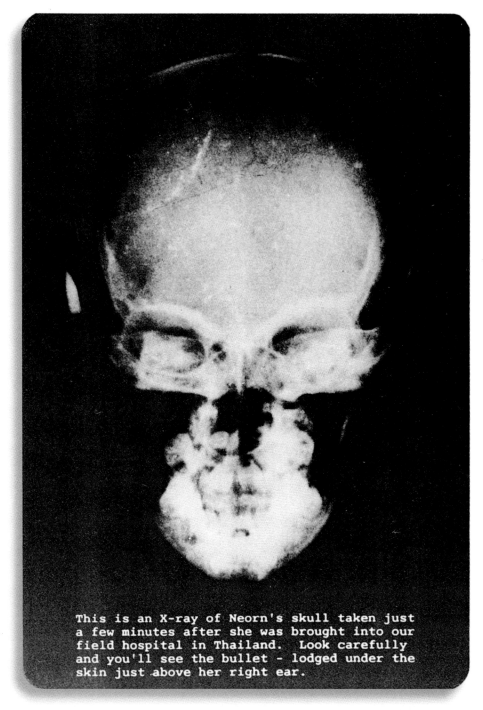

This is an X-ray of Neorn's skull taken just a few minutes after she was brought into our field hospital in Thailand. Look carefully and you'll see the bullet - lodged under the skin just above her right ear.

It is when you see an involvement device that is specifically relevant to the cause that your heart sings a little. Help the Aged has been doing this for years, simply enclosing a small piece of opaque plastic. Place it in front of your eyes, it says, and you know what it's like to have a cataract obscuring your vision. A winning package produced by Target Direct for the Cancer Relief Macmillan Fund contains a child's crayon, for the appeal is to do with children suffering from cancer. The PS is irresistible…

An anonymous donor kindly paid for the crayon I've enclosed. If you want to keep it you can. Or, if you prefer, you can return it to me with your gift and I will make sure it's passed on to one of our paediatric nurses with your best wishes.

WHAT YOU HOLD IN YOUR HANDS IS AN INSTRUMENT OF TORTURE

When the body of street child Catrachito Luis was found in Guatemala, his eyes had been gouged out, his ears and tongue cut off – treatment customarily meted out by police to informers. The police claim they were not involved.

GO ON Tear it off the page. Hold it in your hand. Feel the point. Think about it. Stretch your imagination. Because that's what torturers around the world do. They excel at it – using their imagination to fashion instruments of torture out of the most everyday things.

In Seoul, at the Korean Central Intelligence Agency, a 60-year-old man, Sok Tal-yun, was tortured with a **pen** like the one you are holding. His interrogators inserted the inner plastic ink tube into the urinary canal of his pen...

Police in Indon... into the eyes of... Ginting who w... They then use... **driver** to stab... a **hammer** to...

11-year-old Jos... mistakenly take... where police fl... him hold a **bri**... his head for mo...

Kim Hyon-cha... arrested in Sou... to balance a **pe**... arm. Try it you... you last. Every... Kim was beaten...

More relevant drama from Amnesty UK. The pen is no mere gimmick – it spurs the recipient into reading the horrifying copy.

IT'S ALSO AN INSTRUMENT OF CHANGE

In the right hands, the pen you are holding is a powerful instrument of change. In the right hands, it can make things happen. It can get justice.

Use it to sign up as a member of Amnesty International now. Use it to show that you believe in standing up for what you think is right. Use it to tell governments around the world that they can't get away with murder, torture and rape.

When you do, you'll be joining more than a million people in more than 150 countries who are prepared to stand up and be counted as people who won't look the other way.

The choice is yours. Put the pen down and you turn your back on people for whom you are the only chance of rescue or justice.

Or you can use your pen now to say, 'Enough is enough. I won't look the other way. Stop!' – by joining Amnesty International.

'When the first 200 letters came, the guards gave me back my clothes. Then the next 200 letters came and the prison director came to see me.... The letters kept coming: three thousand of them. The President was informed. The letters still kept arriving and the President called the prison and told them to let me go.'

Letter from a former prisoner of conscience in the Dominican Republic

You may want to become a member simply to show your support for Amnesty's work. Or you may like to join our letter-writing campaigns. It's entirely up to you how involved you get.

DON'T PUT THE PEN DOWN UNTIL YOU'VE MADE YOUR CHOICE

This pack recruited new supporters at a rate of five per cent on some cold lists.

And a Red Cross package produced by Chapter One Direct a few years back told the story of a Cambodian child with a bullet lodged in her skull. What better depiction of the story could there be than a reduced X-ray of the child's skull? Few could have resisted the temptation to hold the X-ray to the light and see where the bullet had lodged. It was tested against a package without the X-ray and came out the winner. Cost-effectively the winner, the extra production costs being compensated by massively increased response and higher average donation rates.

For these devices are not just gimmicks. They are true involvement devices. They provoke thought and action. They educate. They are, above all, relevant. When the Red Cross sends you an X-ray, or when the Cancer Relief Macmillan Fund sends you a child's crayon they are somehow sharing the tools of their trade with you. Your intelligence is not threatened by the process.

At best, the process can almost transcend the process of recruitment and fundraising and become an educational campaign discharged by direct mail. Burnett Associates' recruitment pack for Amnesty at the end of 1995 contained a small pen to make two points. 'What you hold in your hands is an instrument of torture' it said above the pen. And, overleaf and by the response device 'It's also an instrument of change', bidding you use it to make a donation. This would merely be a clever verbal idea if the first statement had not been totally justified by the accompanying story.

In Seoul, at the Korean Central Intelligence Agency, a 60-year-old man, Sok Tal-yun, was tortured with a pen like the one you are holding. His interrogators inserted the inner plastic ink tube into the urinary canal of his penis.

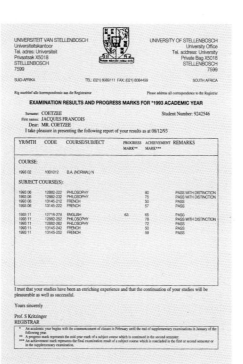

The involvement device at its simplest – and least expensive. A piece of printed paper can still be intriguing.

At the time of my writing, this pack is producing record response rates on some reciprocal lists. I am not surprised. It has power, it has intrigue, it has – above all – relevance to Amnesty's cause. I fancy that the organisation would not be as well served by personalised labels.

Let me end with an involvement device that's the cheapest yet. If you are worried about the cost of these gizmos, or if you have ethical qualms about using them, just consider what you can achieve with a simple piece of printed paper. The South African Blind Workers Fund runs a bursary scheme for blind students. It is obviously successful, for the simple involvement device in this mailing is a reproduction of the examination results and progress marks of Jacques François Coetzee, a blind student at the University of Stellenbosch. From it all donors can see the fruits of their support, as Mr Coetzee has passed with honours in philosophy and passed also in French and English. That university report is a true involvement device. For it dramatises both the need and the achievements of

Easter Seals help children with disabilities. Please use seals on your outgoing mail.

Les timbres de Pâques aident les enfants handicapés. S'il vous plaît, collez-les sur votre correspondance.

The appeal is for children. Why not let the children depict it graphically?

the fund with total integrity. And at a tiny cost. You can make involvement devices out of paper just as much as you can out of plastic. Remember the extract from the RSPCA inspector's diary? It was just ink on paper.

Make it pretty

Occasionally you see variants on the theme of visual austerity that marks most fundraising communication. Usually the charities concerned have a simpler job to discharge and that simplicity takes the form of cheerful, almost uplifting graphics.

The Easter seals campaign in Canada is a good example. The appeal is for children with disabilities, the device is the postage seal that is so popular in North America. Why spoil this familiar and happy offer with demanding visuals?

The household-drop devised by Stephen Thomas and Associates simply uses an Easter drawing produced by two little girls on the outer envelope. Another pack just uses a cheerful Easter egg theme. They have all the freshness of spring. Fundraising becomes a celebration as much as a duty.

We don't have to threaten all the time. It sometimes pays to cheer people up.

Keeping it simple again

In our endless quest for visual cleverness, we often miss the point that simplicity is still the most powerful mode in which to appeal, especially when words and graphics combine to give us that simplicity. Another example from Steve Thomas's agency in Toronto makes the point.

This control package for the Multiple Sclerosis Society of Canada amounts to a short letter and a reply form/address carrier. The letter folds twice, giving you these words on the first fold.

Red hot prickles gripped my feet. My dry tongue fumbled words. I pitched and and swayed across the room on numb legs. Fuzzy images taunted my eyes. Why was my body betraying me?

There is not a single graphic device in this mailing. Does there need to be, given the power of those words set simply in a little white space?

Let me close this chapter on the visual aspect of fundraising with a quote from a famous American art director, George Lois, who wrote a book called *The Art of Advertising.* It simply says that art is '… the defeat of habit by originality'.

Think about it.

CHAPTER SEVEN

MEANWHILE, BACK AT THE OFFER...

I talked earlier of the primacy of the offer, of the need to give better and more literal shape to that warm glow of giving. Too many fundraisers think themselves above this need – they fancy themselves in some superior world where duty, intellect and decency hold sway. They miss the point that even the dutiful, the intellectual and the decent among us need prompting. This is what an offer does. It presents a reward for giving, a reason for giving, an excuse (no matter how apparently superficial) for giving.

The Shakespeare Globe Trust seems to have been reconstructing the dramatist's Globe Theatre at London's Bankside for most of my adult lifetime. Finally it has taken splendid shape, a triumph of organisational will and a triumph of fundraising. And Friends of Shakespeare's Globe make you a whole series of fundraising offers that enable you to see your donation as part of the very fabric of this carefully reconstructed building. For instance, £10 'positions a bundle of roofing thatch', £50 'secures a mortice and tenon joint'. These are eclectic offers indeed.

But £300 buys you something quite remarkable. The piazza around the theatre is paved with York stone slabs. You are therefore asked to buy a flagstone. If you do, your name will be carved on it. Charlton Heston has already booked his and so have John Cleese and Anthony Hopkins. You will be in good company.

The one-to-one offer

No one should underestimate the power of personalising the offer in fundraising, of elevating the donation to the perceived level of a direct relationship between the donor and the cause in its most evocative form. Seeing your donation disappear into the maw of a large charity is one thing; seeing it as a direct subscription to something tangible is something else.

We are all willing to suspend a little belief when we are confronted with this agreeable fundraising conceit. The NSPCC regularly asks for £15 to 'help save a child's life'. Heaven knows how it can justify such a phrase but it would be almost impertinent to question the claim – we trust this fine organisation to mean it. Similarly, with the Globe appeal – few £10 donors will go looking for their bundle of roofing thatch. We are dealing here in acceptable metaphors.

The child-sponsorship agencies have cleverly covered the hinterland between the metaphor of the sponsored child and the reality of an overseas development programme. For the offer remains a one-to-one relationship between sponsor and child, though the charities concerned have gone to great lengths to explain that funds are used on a community basis. The donor is left with the dream of that old and somewhat incorrect 'postal parent' concept, but he or she can be under no doubt that their support is distributed beyond the needs of the individual child. This shift of emphasis has been handled with great integrity and surprising success. Child sponsorship agencies continue to thrive.

These days you can sponsor elephants, rhinos, whales and dolphins. No one seems to mind that this is a slightly fanciful fiction. Defenders of Wildlife in the States do not even seek to justify their 'adopt a wolf' offer. Despite the fact that the pack talks of 'wolf adoption' papers and offers you a 'wolf adoption' certificate, there is no pretence that a lupine beast is wandering Yellowstone Park with your name on it. It is just a metaphor and, again, a successful one. For it is this organisation's control pack, the subject of two and a half million mailings per programme.

Sometimes though, the metaphor comes close to actuality. The British are notorious for loving pets. Give them a chance to sponsor an individual dog and you have probably arranged the optimum fundraising relationship in Britain.

Non-British readers are allowed to suspend belief at this point.

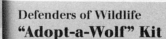

A classic American 'adoption' pack. But it still apparently needs the personalised stickers to succeed.

Defenders of Wildlife "Adopt-a-Wolf" Kit

1. Wolf photograph
2. "Wolves of America" guide
3. "Adoption" certificate
PLUS a one-year, free subscription to the award-winning **Defenders** magazine

Defenders of Wildlife
1101 Fourteenth Street, N.W., Room 1400
Washington, D.C. 20005

YES! **I wish to "adopt" a wolf.**

I know that the Yellowstone wolves — and all of America's wolves — need my help. **Please send me my Wolf Adoption Kit!**

Enclosed is my contribution of:
☐ $15

To help even more, I am enclosing:
☐ $20 ☐ $25 ☐ $35
☐ $50 ☐ $100 ☐ $500
☐ Other $_____

Please make your check payable to **Defenders of Wildlife** and return it with this form in the reply envelope provided.

Thanks for your caring and concern.

Your membership contribution, in excess of $10 allocated for **DEFENDERS** magazine, is fully tax-deductible.

A dog's life. But literally.

The National Canine Defence League has just over 100,000 supporters, half of them regular donors. In 1995 Burnett Associates helped NCDL to relaunch a committed giving scheme, based on individual sponsorship of a dog in its care. No more than 20 or 30 dogs were nominated, each of them named and described and the subject of an irresistible colour photograph. Thus, 'Sam the springer spaniel is an elderly gentleman. His owners had to move and, sadly, had to leave him behind.'

You can choose to sponsor Sam, or Trevor, or Captain, or indeed Beavis. You are asked for just £1 a week and it should be no surprise that the average pledge is for over £80 a year. You receive a sponsor's certificate, a photograph of your chosen dog and regular updates on the progress of your 'canine companion'. Better still, you can visit the dog, maybe even take it for a walk around the NCDL sanctuary.

It goes without saying that some of these dogs are already walked off their feet. For the number of their sponsors quickly rose over the 3,000 mark through a better than eight per cent response from the active donor file. The scheme is now recruiting successfully from off-the-page advertising and loose inserts are planned.

The point of this grand story is neither the efficacy of the one-to-one relationship nor the splendid eccentricity of the British. It is to celebrate how far we are willing to dispel cynicism in favour of enjoyable belief. For it takes no great mathematics to work out the amount now pledged to the individual dog – some of them must have more than 100 sponsors and an annual sponsorship fund greater than the income of many old age pensioners. No one minds. Nor should they.

For the one-to-one relationship confers enormous pleasure on the sponsor. They send you Christmas cards, these dogs. For Christmas 1995, a Burnett copywriter was tasked with writing 22 pieces of (hah!) doggerel for these Christmas cards. This is how Sweep offered seasonal greetings to his sponsor.

Because my legs are very long
I'd like to work for Santa Claus.
I'd gallop like the reindeer, with
The frosty snow beneath my paws.
This card's for you, dear sponsor,
I hope you like my rhyme,
It comes from Sweep for you to keep
This merry Christmas time.

Trevor, by the way, had told sponsors that what he really wanted was a frisbee to chase. His Valentine's day card to sponsors (I am not making this up) records that he now has more frisbees than any other dog in history.

He grabs them, tosses them into space and then
gallops around the field, barking merrily. As far as
treats go, though, enough is enough – Trevor's New
Year resolution is to watch his waistline.

If you think that NCDL might be going slightly over the top with this twee reportage, you can suspend your cynicism. For here are just a few of the many replies to that Valentine's day mailing.

Thank you so much for the Valentine card from Tulip.
I loved it! I received it on Valentine's day and will
keep it always as I have her Christmas card. Thank
you for a kind gesture which means so much to me.
I am so glad that Tulip is well and happy and
that she enjoyed her Christmas treats. I am enclosing
£15 for her.

Trevor sent me a lovely Valentine. Please give him a
hug from me and perhaps you will give him a little
something that he loves from the enclosed. It's the
first Valentine I have ever received at the age of 88!

Will you be our best friend?
NCDL Rescue Centre, Shoreham-by-Sea
Trevor, whom you met on the front cover, may not always recognise his sponsors immediately, but he certainly loves going for walks with them. He's even been on a camping trip with one sponsor.
NCDL Rescue Centre, Shoreham-by-Sea
JG is best buddies with Mayo – she taught him to play – and loves other dogs and people. Sadly, JG is incontinent and has a strange-shaped body, which means she's hard to re-home.
NCDL Rescue Centre, Shoreham-by-Sea
Tulip is a pit bull terrier who will be with us for the rest of her life. She is very outgoing, and genuinely loves people, although she is not so keen on other dogs.
NCDL Rescue Centre, Dumfries
Christopher, a lurcher, was found in a ditch in a terrible state, with no coat and unable to stand. He will probably never be re-homed because he is claustrophobic.
NCDL Rescue Centre, Ballymena
Glen the collie would make a great sheepdog. Unfortunately for his former owners, he tried to herd everything from cars to children! Great with people, Glen is a favourite at the rescue centre.
NCDL Rescue Centre, Ballymena
Poppy is a Doberman cross. When we found her, she was blind in one eye – we suspect she had been beaten. As a result of her hard life, she was terrified of people.
NCDL Rescue Centre, Shoreham-by-Sea
Mayo has only one problem – he always bites the hand that feeds him! Sadly, two attempts to re-home this lovable German shepherd have failed.
NCDL Rescue Centre, Shoreham-by-Sea
Phil is a failed racing greyhound whose owners abandoned him. He loves to run around and give chase in the grounds at the rescue centre.
NCDL Rescue Centre, Dumfries
Too old to race, Maggie the greyhound was abandoned in the countryside. When she arrived she seemed shy and fragile, but has since revealed a remarkable ability to sprint. She's lazy, gentle and very cuddly.
NCDL Rescue Centre, Dumfries
Rusty the sheltie loves children but can't be re-homed because of his tendency to defend all the houses he occupies – even against the owners!
NCDL Rescue Centre, Ballymena
Five years ago, Twiggy, a skinny, chocolate-brown lurcher was found as a stray in Belfast and brought to Ballymena Rescue Centre. Today, happily settled with us, Twiggy loves going for walks, but feels the cold terribly.
NCDL Rescue Centre, Ballymena
Sweep the lurcher came to us at three months old. Although friendly, he is so big that he's never been offered a home. He loves to be taken for walks.
NCDL Rescue Centre, Snetterton
Nipper the labrador cross has been a happy rescue centre resident for ten years. He hasn't been re-homed because of his possessive nature – he used to guard his master from the rest of the family!
Like Trevor, the 35 other dogs you are about to meet all need a best friend. Some have been abused, others neglected, others abandoned. They will probably all be with us for the rest of their lives.
If you care about dogs, why not be that friend, and sponsor one of them today. Your support will ensure that they, and the other dogs in our care, always get all the love and care they need to live a happy and fulfilling life. They have already been let down by other humans, please don't turn your back on them too.
NCDL Rescue Centre, Bridgend
Captain 2 is a border collie cross, and was abandoned on a motorway. He has a tendency to nip when he's nervous – but loves going for walks.
NCDL Rescue Centre, West Calder
Victor the Doberman cross simply loves life. He likes people, dogs, walks, games and edible treats. He once tried to climb into an oven to get at the food. He's a bit silly, but very lovable.
NCDL Rescue Centre, West Calder
When Prince the German shepherd cross arrived, his nasty eye infection gave him such a mean look that staff nicknamed him Bruiser. But once he recovered, he turned into a handsome Prince.
SPONSOR A DOG
NCDL Rescue Centre, Ilfracombe
Sheena 1, a German shepherd cross, loves rescue centre life so much that she will probably never settle as a family pet. Loving and gentle, she hates bathtime.
NCDL Rescue Centre, Ilfracombe
Meet Bobby – a black and tan German shepherd cross with a lovely, steady nature. Sadly, his tendency to guard 'his' territory makes him difficult to re-home. Bobby is a healthy dog who loves exercise.
NCDL Rescue Centre, Kenilworth
Laddie, a collie cross, was left alone for up to ten hours a day. As a result he developed behavioural problems which
NCDL Rescue Centre, Kenilworth
Velvet the greyhound was found as a stray – probably an abandoned ex-racer. Gentle, loving and
NCDL Rescue Centre, Leeds
Benji the pit bull cross was very withdrawn when he first arrived, but he's turned out to be a real character who loves having visitors. Sadly, his breed means he can't be re-homed.
NCDL Rescue Centre, Leeds
Max the spaniel was mistreated by his owner until he became confused and cantankerous. He becomes distressed when he is away from his friends at the rescue centre.
NCDL Rescue Centre, Evesham
A very pretty, white greyhound, Pearl is Evesham Rescue Centre's official 30th anniversary sponsor dog. Just four years old, she loves people (though not other animals) and adores going for walks.
NCDL Rescue Centre, Ilfracombe
Brought in as a stray, Specs was named after the distinctive white rings around his eyes. A fun-loving terrier, he's always ready for a game or a cuddle, but can be destructive.
And you can even visit your sponsored dog in person...
... walkies anyone?
Tess, a black retriever cross aged six, was found cruelly abandoned. Unfortunately, incontinence makes her difficult to re-home.
is thought to have been dumped by his owners when he stopped winning races. He enjoys a cuddle, and is rather partial to chocolate digestives.
For six long years, Samwell was kept tethered in a small yard. But when his owner died, neighbours rescued him. He loves the rescue centre – at long last he has warmth, walks, regular meals and cuddles.
NCDL Rescue Centre, Evesham
Jake the collie cross has lived with us for five years. He loves playing with children, but is less friendly to other dogs. Jake loves his home comforts – especially knitted rugs.
NCDL Rescue Centre, Evesham
Mac is a black labrador cross who came to us as a stray. Now ten and a distinguished elderly gentleman, he has never settled with new owners, but loves visitors.
NCDL Rescue Centre, Roden, Shropshire
Beavis the black labrador cross suffers from a pancreatic problem, which means he has to have a special diet. Still, he doesn't mind – he gets four meals a day instead of two.
He's an attractive and lovable dog, but incontinence makes him difficult to re-home.
NCDL Rescue Centre, Darlington
Martha the greyhound was found as a stray, probably abandoned. Gentle and sweet-natured, she loves to gallop around the rescue centre grounds and then curl up on a blanket to sleep.
NCDL Rescue Centre, Newbury
Gregor the greyhound is friendly and lively – but watch out for his constantly wagging tail, it cracks like a whip. He enjoys a walk and a crunchy biscuit.
NCDL Rescue Centre, Newbury
When Bridie the brindle greyhound first arrived as a stray, she was very timid. But her friendship with Gregor – another sponsored greyhound – brought her out of her shell. She loves people, but hates cats.
NCDL Rescue Centre, Newbury
Monty is a black and white collie cross retriever. He has quite wobbly back legs and likes short walks and playing with squeaky toys. He's prone to panic attacks, but lives happily in the kitchen at the rescue centre.
NCDL Rescue Centre, Roden, Shropshire
When Molly the collie cross arrived, she was suffering from a painful skin complaint. That's now cured, but this lovable dog still suffers a nerve disorder that makes her legs wobbly.

SHEENA 1

Sheena 1 is a German shepherd cross who was found as a stray. Despite her engaging personality, she has never settled as a family pet, but loves the rescue centre. Sheena is so reliable that she exercises herself in the field adjoining the kennels before going to bed.

SPONSOR A DOG

This is to certify that

_____

has sponsored

_____

of the NCDL Rescue Centre at

_____

and is helping to give their dog a loving home for life.

Signed for and on behalf of the National Canine Defence League

Clarissa Baldwin Date

Clarissa Baldwin, Chief Executive

NCDL
National Canine Defence League

Registered charity no. 227523

Who says a dog can't send you a Valentine's day or Christmas card? There's no point in sneering – this is consummate fundraising.

Valentine, you've made my day...

Merry Christmas

Dear Poppy

I was so moved by your Christmas note. And there was one for Valentine too. Poppy, you are daily in my thoughts. Am grateful, therefore, that you wrote!

PS Enclosed a little Easter treat.

These are letters written by real people as part of a real relationship. Half metaphorical and half literal, the NCDL dog sponsorship scheme is that most wonderful of fundraising ideas. For it is utterly successful, not just in fiscal terms but in terms of donor satisfaction. It is making people happy by allowing them to give.

When Trevor gets back from his frisbee-chasing, he'll probably woof his satisfaction as well.

How literal can you be?

You can just send a cheque to Feed the Children to support its work for Bosnian children. Or you can send a baby box, an idea that was actually suggested by an aid worker in the field. The baby box costs £25 or £30 to get to a Bosnian mother and every British parent will appreciate the literal value of its contents – 200 nappy liners, 10 nappies, two jars of baby cream and so on. At the height of the Bosnian crisis, the baby box was tested against an ordinary emergency ad. It performed better, despite asking for a donation much higher than the average.

The baby box doesn't just offer a literal and practical answer to the need of Bosnian children. It positions that need directly at the heart of our hopelessly guilty emotions about the crisis. The

The 'baby box' makes dreams real. It also increases the size of donations.

APPEAL FOR THE CHILDREN OF BOSNIA
Can you think of a better gift to send someone?

Disinfectant, nappies, washing materials – not the first things to spring to mind when you think about buying presents. But for mothers in Bosnia who have almost nothing left with which to care for their children, these basic essentials mean the world. And they can be found in each baby box sent with a donation in Britain to a despairing mother in Bosnia, via British charity Feed the Children.

As peace in Bosnia is trumpeted in the corridors of power, a young mother sheltering in a tractor cabin in north-west Bosnia knows what the really important issue is tonight: how to keep her shivering and vulnerable toddler safe from disease and infection in appalling conditions and biting cold.

She has been living on the edge of life since October, when she was forced to flee her home in Velika Kladusa – with only five minutes to pack a carrier bag – and huddle with 22,000 other people along five kilometres of road in Klupjensko valley.

She is one of 14,000 mothers in Bosnia and Croatia who have received baby boxes full of the basic essentials they need to help protect their children from the filthy conditions in which they are surviving: clean nappies and baby cream to soothe burning nappy rash, soap to wash urine-soaked babygros and dirty nappies, antiseptic for cuts, disinfectant for the muddy floors of their shelters...

you,'" explains Gaynor Jones, Volunteer Co-ordinator at Feed the Children. "They take it very personally."

So do the individuals who take up Feed the Children's invitation to send a message along with their £30 donation. "Seeing those mothers in Bosnia on the television, clinging to their children for dear

> **"I wanted to send some love with all the practical things in a baby box."**

life in appalling conditions, I wanted to do more than send a donation," says Karin Weatherup, who has sent a baby box. "I wanted to send a message. I wanted to say to the mother opening the box, 'You're doing an amazing job, and my family think about you every night'. Feed the Children enabled me to do that, for which I'm very grateful."

Julie Griffin was drawn to the idea of sending a baby box to Bosnia for the same reason. "I just wanted to send some love with all the practical things in a baby box. It was that personal involvement which really appealed to me."

Despite the Dayton peace initiative, mothers and young children in Bosnia trying to rebuild their lives need even the most basic essentials to succeed.

A message from you this Winter would mean so much to a Bosnian mother.

Does peace in Bosnia make a difference?

In many areas of Bosnia, peace simply means that the shooting has stopped. But the problem is that whole communities have been chased from their homes, and are either too afraid to return or will find only a scorched patch of earth or bombed-out shell where their home used to be.

"There are many truly lost people," says Stewart Crocker, Deputy Director at Feed the Children. "We must ensure they are not forgotten amidst the news of the Dayton peace initiative. Their needs are tremendous, especially those of the mothers and young children. They are trying to move forward, trying to rebuild their lives.

"People in Britain can take one major worry from these mothers by giving them what they need to care for their little ones – a Feed the Children baby box."

Children in Bosnia and Croatia have suffered enough. You can help them recover.

From me to you and your child

Inside each box, packed by volunteers at Feed the Children's aid supply centre in Reading, is a message from the person who made it possible. For the exhausted, often traumatised woman who receives it, it is a potent sign that somewhere, somebody is thinking of her, and her efforts to protect her child.

"It's like a voice breaking through the isolation and hopelessness surrounding these mothers and children, saying 'we know how hard it is for you, we care what happens to

▶▶▶
SENT WITH LOVE FROM A FRIEND

What's inside?
• 200 nappy liners
• 10 nappies
• 6 nappy pins
• 4 pairs of plastic pants
• baby powder
• 2 jars of baby cream
• baby lotion
• baby wipes
• 3 mild soaps
• sponge
• shampoo
• towel
• antiseptic disinfectant
• feeding cup with lid
• feeding bowl
• 2 spoons

It costs £30 to send a baby box to a Bosnian mother and baby. If you would like to send one – or more, please call 0990 600610 or complete and return the coupon below.
If you would also like to send a message to a Bosnian mother, please enclose it with your donation and Feed the Children will put it inside your baby box.

Call **0990 600610** now to tell us how many baby boxes you would like to send. **OR** please complete and return this form.

Please send _____ baby box(es) at £30 each on my behalf.

I enclose a cheque for £ _____ (total amount) made payable to Feed the Children.

OR Please debit £ _____ from my ☐ Visa ☐ Access ☐ Switch

Card number ☐☐☐☐ ☐☐☐☐ ☐☐☐☐ ☐☐☐☐

Last three digits of Switch card no. ☐☐☐ Switch issue no. ☐☐

Expiry date _____ / _____

Signature _____

Name (caps) _____

Address _____

Postcode _____

Telephone _____

If you would like to send a message to a Bosnian mother, please send it with this form and we will put it in your baby box. **Please send to:** Feed the Children, Dept. 431, FREEPOST, Reading RG1 1BR.

FEED THE CHILDREN
TAKING THE AID DIRECT
Registered charity no. 803236.

431

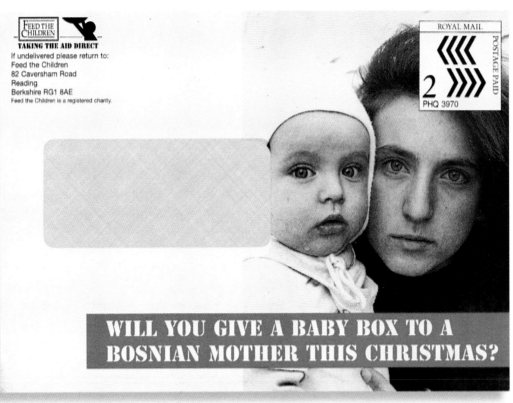

FEED THE
CHILDREN
TAKING THE AID DIRECT

If undelivered please return to:
Feed the Children
82 Caversham Road
Reading
Berkshire RG1 8AE
Feed the Children is a registered charity.

ROYAL MAIL
POSTAGE PAID
2
PHQ 3970

WILL YOU GIVE A BABY BOX TO A BOSNIAN MOTHER THIS CHRISTMAS?

Donors want to express themselves as well as give money. Why not give them the chance?

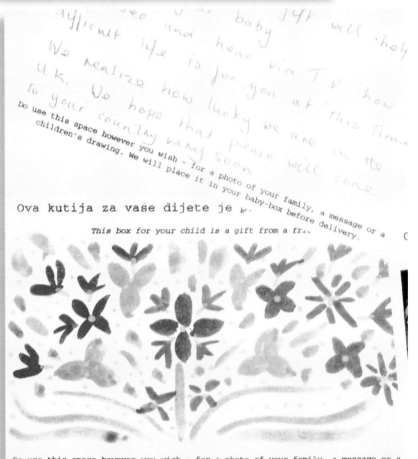

Ova kutija za vaše dijete je v▪

This box for your child is a gift from a fr▪

Do use this space however you wish – for a photo of your family, a message or a children's drawing. We will place it in your baby-box before delivery.

headline of a fact-packed ad reads 'Can you think of a better gift to send to someone?' And starts the body copy,

Disinfectant, nappies, washing materials — not the first things to spring to mind when you think about buying presents. But for mothers in Bosnia who have almost nothing left with which to care for their children, these basic essentials mean the world.

The juxtaposition of the 'give a present' idea with the 'needy recipient' idea is as old as the hills. But there is a new spin to Feed the Children's baby box. It offers you the simple device of a message card to be enclosed with your box — 'Do use this space however you wish', it says, 'for a photo of your family, a message, or a children's drawing.'

I am looking at a selection of completed baby box cards as I write. They do indeed have pictures of happy British families and children's drawings. And they have messages like, 'This is our new baby granddaughter. With our love to another less fortunate baby.' And 'We hope peace will come to your country soon.' And 'From one mother to another — if only your life was as secure as ours is here in England.'

If you can give people the ability to open their hearts like this, you are offering a rare privilege. If you can combine it with an artefact as powerful as the baby box, you are transcending fundraising tradecraft

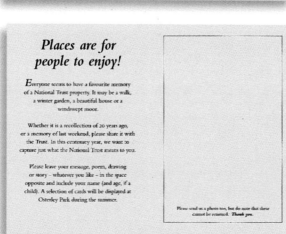

The National Trust's appeal for a £100 gift was humanised by allowing donors to commemorate their own memories of National Trust properties.

and offering an escape route for those finer emotions of love and altruism, which most of us harbour somewhere. Offering donors a greater apparent participation in the process of fundraising is a very great opportunity.

Let the donor speak

For we make a great mistake if we see the donor as merely the passive recipient of what we say to them. We have just seen with the National Canine Defence League and Feed the Children how eloquent the donor can be, how he or she can sometimes say things better than we can.

Invite that response and the results can be heartwarming, even in the least likely areas. In January 1995 Britain's National Trust launched a centenary appeal of fierce logic. That is to say, it asked donors for £100 to mark the Trust's 100 years of history. It was another triumph of 'getting what you ask for'.

Not just in fundraising terms either. For the suitably dignified appeal contained a little card that invited readers to record their own memories of National Trust properties. 'Tell us about your favourite garden, a walk along a coastal path, or getting involved as a volunteer.' A selection of cards were to be displayed at one of the Trust's flagship properties that summer.

Was it that promise of exhibition that spurred the thousands of responses? I think not. It just gave people a little space to celebrate their own enjoyment of what the Trust offers them. So they talked of taking their children to the country, of meeting their lifetime partner at a Trust property and, inevitably and sadly, of wives and husbands now departed but forever associated with love of the countryside.

Some respondents offered short poems; all of them offered the feelings of their hearts.

I fancy that the display of some of these cards must have been moving indeed. But I suspect that every donor who completed an 'acorn' card enjoyed the opportunity to participate verbally in the celebration of 100 years of National Trust history.

The appeal raised more than £1.5 million through a mailing and an insert, the former performing at an 11.30 per cent response. Remember – the request was for a no-nonsense £100. I choose to think that the 'acorn' card played a role in this extraordinary achievement. It allowed the donor to play a role in the appeal, however subliminal.

Asking for opinions

In the late eighties I discovered that Greenpeace USA was producing great results with what became known as 'survey packs'. The mailing asked respondents' opinions on how they felt about environmental matters in their community. Reader, I nicked the idea! I produced a similar device to be used by the British organisation for whom it survived in its recruitment repertoire till the mid-nineties. WWF produced one to great effect in the summer of 1995 as a door-drop. 'Survey packs' are now in danger of becoming another fundraising cliché.

The psychology is obvious. We all like to offer our views. It is flattering to be asked, especially on matters of weighty social concern. Recruiting new supporters through the survey or questionnaire technique slipstreams the practice of regularly published polls, which seek to solicit public opinion on everything from current political preference to the choice of England's football coach.

It is obviously a 'soft-sell' technique. The questions have to be put with seeming integrity and the fundraising appeal tacked on as afterthought. The WWF survey, which seeks to elicit a sort of hierarchy of anxieties from the public about the state of the countryside and their attitude to environmental matters, is solemnly titled 'What do people in Somerset think?' to give the survey a regional credibility (we were testing around the English shires). And I wrote this paragraph in the letter in an effort to bridge the dangerous gap between the solicitation of opinion and the solicitation of money.

Naturally, and because we are a charity, we are giving you the chance to make a donation to WWF or to join us as a member. But do let me make it quite clear that we want your answers to this survey whether or not you decide to support WWF.

The result was a mass of research information, which was by no means uninteresting and that was duly reported in WWF publications. But the door-drop was successful in orthodox recruitment terms. It seems to me that people are reasonably happy to

suspend a degree of belief when they are confronted with these survey packs. They can see the fundraising bones peeking out of the questionnaire but they are not totally outraged by the artifice. Perhaps again, the subliminal feeling of participation outweighs any danger of irritation.

But it is a delicate balance. A mailing for the Democratic National Committee in the States at the end of 1995 is solemnly titled a 'Re-election Survey'. Open it and you are confronted by a large, personalised headline, 'Do you, Mr Carlos M Sassoon, support President Clinton's re-election?' You even get yes/no stamps with which to indicate your reply. This is merely an orthodox piece of direct mail solicitation with the thinnest veneer of opinion-seeking.

1. Are you:
   ☐ Male ☐ Female
   ☐ under 40 ☐ 41-50
   ☐ 51-65 ☐ 66+

2. How would you describe your own eyesight, with glasses if you use them?
   ☐ Good ☐ Fair
   ☐ Poor ☐ Very poor

3. Do you personally know anyone who is blind or partially sighted?
   ☐ Yes ☐ No

   If YES, we may be able to help. Please see the leaflet enclosed.

Employment training ☐ ☐
Braille ☐ ☐

9. Would you personally be willing to help blind people, by making a donation to RNIB?
   ☐ Yes ☐ No

   If YES, you can make a donation using the form below. A gift of £15 could help pay for a day's schooling at an RNIB school.

   I'm enclosing the following donation to help blind and partially sighted people.

   £15 ☐ Other £ [   ]

   ☐ I enclose my cheque/postal order payable to: 'RNIB Charity'

ear gall bladders are used in and the species are poached and you think their use is justified?
   ☐
led
   ☐
   ☐

cerned with the protection of all k are the priorities?
   Preservation of the rainforests ☐
   Oceans and marine life ☐
   All these areas of life ☐

Survey packs work but we may be in danger of turning them into yet another direct marketing cliché.

l it back to WWF in the reply envelope bution to WWF's work.

ase tick this box ☐

the following items before you buy them
osols ☐ "Eco-friendly" deterg
gs ☐ Unleaded petrol
er Organically-grown
products/... liners ☐ fruit or vegetables
Cruelty-free cosmetics ☐

7. Do you try to recycle these items?
   Paper ☐ Bottles and glass ☐ Aluminium Cans ☐

8. Which national daily newspaper do you read?
   Guardian ☐ The Times ☐
   Daily Telegraph ☐ The Independent ☐
   Daily Mirror ☐ The Sun ☐
   Daily Star ☐ Today ☐
   Daily Express ☐ Daily Mail ☐
   None of them ☐

9. Is your age:
   Under 18 ☐ 18-25 ☐ 25-35 ☐
   35-50 ☐ 50-70 ☐ Over 70 ☐

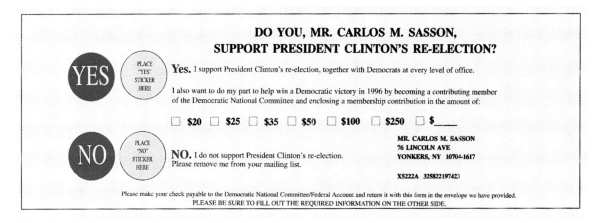

Worse, because it is trying so very hard, is a recent pack from Britain's Royal National Institute for the Blind. Significantly it is a mailing piece rather than a door-drop and its questions tail off far too soon into special pleading rather than objective information-seeking. Thus, 'Currently, anyone losing their sight does not automatically receive any training to help them live independently, or any free special aids, such as a white cane, that can make life easier. Do you consider this unfair?' And question nine is actually the ask, 'Would you personally be willing to help blind people, by making a donation to RNIB?'

This is surely a corruption of the survey technique. The enclosure of a free pen, '… so that you can reply quickly', marks a complete descent into the direct mail underworld. It is, I fear, a crass piece of communication for it insults the reader's intelligence. Who on earth is going to answer no to the first question I quoted? Hands up all the miserable gits who don't think blind people should have white canes! I understand that the package works, but it still troubles me.

Survey packs need a degree of integrity if they are to survive public scepticism and flourish as true fundraising communications. Sadly, all the signs are that we are killing the device by merely reproducing its format. It could be yet another victim of our dreadful ability to worship formulae rather than content.

Why not vary them in ways that are familiar to the reader? Why not build them into the sort of participative questionnaire that is common in newspapers and magazines? You know, 'How sexy are you really?' followed by alternative answers to questions that ask you how often you change your underwear, or whether you sweat while dancing. They are always compulsive as you add up your score. Switch the agenda to 'How good an environmentalist are you?' and you have a communication with inbuilt reader interest, a genuine participation device again. This is Derek Humphries', managing director at Burnett Associates, idea not mine. I shall doubtless claim otherwise in years to come.

The power of the cassette

Earlier I questioned our proclivity to produce printed materials that no one reads. Perhaps we need to consider the greater excitement of the audio or video cassette in communicating our message.

It is no longer a novelty. Cassettes have been in use in fundraising for at least 10 years. They are sometimes startlingly successful.

A word of curmudgeonly caution, though. When I was running Lambeth's libraries in the mid-seventies, I was assured by many of my more progressive librarians that books were a thing of the

Audio cassettes are now a conventional – and powerful – means of conveying the message.

rather than extinguishing previous choices. Newspapers are 250 years old, the telephone 100 years old, radio and television over 50 years old. They remain our prime methods of communication.

This is why I am distinctly sceptical about the much-reported future in which we will all communicate on the Internet. Technology produces its failures as well as its successes. Remember the eight track cartridge? Remember Betamax?

But the audio and video cassette are clearly not destined for the technological knackers yard. Household penetration of VCRs and audio cassette players is immense throughout the Western world. Many of those households now boast a whole collection of the things. Buy a child a television for the bedroom and the second VCR is already on the buying agenda. And is there a car left without a cassette deck?

We should still allow of a slight anxiety about older people. Ownership of VCRs and cassette players may be only slightly less than the rest of the population but familiarity with them is probably significantly less. We should not presume that our older supporters share our total zeal for forms of technology that, to them, are recent and troubling.

Having said that, the power of the cassette is obvious. Feed the Children makes dramatic use of audio cassettes, with the charity's director reporting on its work in Rwanda and a field worker offering similarly telling reportage from Bosnia. The combination of real voices telling the story is irresistible. A supporters mailing produced by Sheard

past. Children, in particular, were less and less interested in the printed word. They were interested only in messages that came to them through media to which they were more sympathetic – the television and the cassette recorder. Hence, we should stop supplying books and start offering cassettes.

Like a lot of fashionable theory at the time, it turned out to be eyewash. In the 20 years since, books – and particularly children's books – have enjoyed a renaissance, fuelled certainly by ever more adroit marketing. Look at the number of book retailers in the average High Street. They were supposed to disappear. Instead, they have thrived. For, one medium rarely replaces another — when technology develops it adds to the choice of media

Thomson Harris for the Royal National Institute for Deaf People contains a cassette that takes on a harder task, an educational one. The title 'Bringing Hearing Aid Technology into the 90s' is not exactly guaranteed to have you bounding toward the cassette deck. Nevertheless, this mailing achieved an entirely creditable 18.08 per cent response from the house list and a further three per cent from the follow-up. If the story had been told in traditional leaflet form, it could surely not have provoked such a successful response.

The cost of communication through audio or video cassette, both actual and perceived, is obviously a problem. It is conventional to have the production costs sponsored or, at least, part-sponsored, and to announce the fact so that donors are relatively untroubled by apparent wastage. It is also conventional to ask for the cassettes back so that they can be redistributed to other supporters. As to their real value in enhancing response (which cassettes will always do), you can only test as with any involvement device. Test packs with and without cassettes and calculate the payback on each.

Video cassettes cannot be idly distributed *en masse,* even to a donor file. They tend to be used as part of a two-stage promotion, the subject of a specific request, or the reward for a large commitment. The Royal National Lifeboat Institution now uses videos as part of its legacy campaign, with a short film that is of sufficient quality to be used, in extract, by television companies as news footage. Greenpeace reports back to its *Frontline* supporters with 20-minute videos compiled from coverage of its worldwide campaigns, topped and tailed by messages to camera by its director, Peter Melchett.

RNID

THE ROYAL NATIONAL INSTITUTE FOR DEAF PEOPLE

105 Gower Street London WC1E 6AH Telephone 0171 387 8033 Fax 0171 388 2346 Minicom 0171 383 3154

The RNID has funded 7 years of research to dramatically improve hearing aid technology. Please will you give £14 to fund our next vital step?

September 1995

Dear Supporter,

The tape I have enclosed with this letter tells you about some remarkable research being carried out by the RNID which is on course to change the lives of over **four million** hard of hearing people in the UK. The tape is introduced by actor David Swift, a keen supporter of the RNID, and the tape itself has been very generously donated by BASF. But before you take a few minutes to listen to it, let me tell you how you can play a valuable part in the success of this important project.

If you are a little hard of hearing or have a relative or friend who is, you will know that as well as finding it harder to pick up sounds, you also lose some of the ability to distinguish one type of sound from another. If you have ever tried a hearing aid, you will also know that most of them simply amplify all the sound they pick up. With the result that while all the sounds are louder, they are not necessarily any clearer.

Since 1988 our Science and Technology Unit has been working to find an effective alternative to this 'amplification' technology: one which reflects the many scientific advances that have taken place in recent years.

The idea behind our research is simple. We are working to develop a computer that can adjust the amplitude and frequencies of sound to make it easier for hard of hearing people to pick up. This would not only help them to hear the sound in the first place but also, for example, prevent ... h.

... ly be a social ... n over ...

Chief Executive Doug Alker

Bringing Hearing Aid Technology into the 90s

ACTION 95

THE ROYAL NATIONAL INSTITUTE FOR DEAF PEOPLE Reg Charity No. 207720

RNID

To save costs, please return this cassette for reuse in the freepost envelope provided

Even 'difficult' messages can be conveyed by audio cassette. The back of the envelope says 'thank you' in sign language – a nice touch.

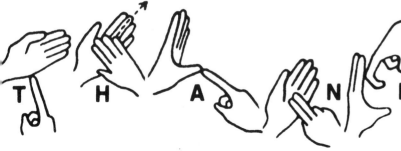

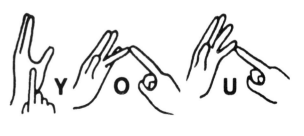

T H A N K Y O U

It is when you combine a video cassette with my sense of event that you probably achieve the best return on your investment. A superbly packaged video promotion produced by Target Direct for the Royal Star and Garter Home went to 5,000 major donors and celebrated the eightieth anniversary of the day when the Home opened its doors to the wounded of the First World War. Presented by Simon Weston, a veteran of a more recent war, it offered you a tour of the Home in its application for an £80 donation. It was phenomenally successful, producing a 22 per cent response, an average donation of £84 and a 12:1 payback on total costs.

And in 1994 UNICEF UK offered 3,500 higher-value donors the opportunity to receive a video of a visit to its Tanzanian projects by the charity's patron, The Duchess of Kent. The invitation practically suggests that you are invited to a royal cinema première rather than asking for a video to be sent (it also contains a lift letter from St James's Palace!). But the campaign, conceived and produced by Chapter One Direct, certainly worked. 22 per cent of those donors requested the video – and gave more than £5,000 at the point of request. 27 per cent of the video requesters then responded – with an average gift of £142. These figures obviously justify the investment, but I fancy that the video also did a great deal to enhance the relationship of these important donors with the charity. If they saw it as a reward rather than an appeal, it was probably still worth doing.

How long should your audio or video message be? There is an obvious danger in overstaying your welcome. Few donors will fail to play a cassette that they have requested, but the irritation threshold applies here as in print and I can imagine nothing more demeaning than the use of the 'off' button. Most of the material I have quoted here is around the 10-minute mark – it is usually quite enough to make your point, though the production values of the aforesaid RNLI video sustain viewer interest to the 16-minute mark.

Every charity should now begin to have a repertory of audio and video cassettes, just as they used to have a book list and a leaflet rack. The use of them will vary from public meetings to work in schools, from donor incentives to staff training. Their use in fundraising is now proven and awaits development. Who will produce the first interactive video, or the audio cassette to be used in conjunction with a piece of print? This is how foreign languages are taught; and it could be the way in which fundraising needs are transmitted. The cassettes we are producing in the mid-1990s will probably look and sound as dull and as unimaginative in a few years' time, as early television commercials do now. Don't get left behind.

The low ask

That £15 donation has become a mystical thing. Everyone asks for it. It can save a child, pay for an hour's research, pay for a day's education for a blind child and help run a bakery in Central Asia – and that's just the last four mailings I looked at. In the States it tends to be an equally mystical $15 or $20 – $30 there practically makes you a major donor.

These sums are based on nothing more than habit and self-fulfilling prophesy. They bear no relationship to what people can afford or feel disposed to give, and any hard research that may once have gone into the process is lost in the mists of time. I once tried to start a conversation about this with a senior British fundraiser. Her response was to tell me that the average donation to mailing programmes over a period of years was just a little over £15. Given that the charity had been asking for £15 for some 10 years, this struck me as unremarkable science. But £15 has become a formal index in the traditional fundraising formula, another of those clichés with which we surround ourselves.

Thankfully, some charities have become restless about it in the last few years. There is a sudden emergence of packs that ask not for more, but for less – for £5 or £6, certainly for less than £10. In January, 1996 Charles Orasin of Defenders of Wildlife in Washington told me of a similar ambition '... going downmarket, looking for the $5 donor'. The theory is obvious – lower the entry fee and multiply the number of respondents.

This certainly happens. I have heard response figures of eight per cent quoted for 'low ask' recruitment packs, though I have not been able to capture figures other than the anecdotal for this book. And it seems perfectly logical that more people will give you £5 than £15.

But I think the efficacy of these packs lies less in the fiscal request, more in the physical format of that request. In the specimen I am looking at – from NCH Action for Children – name and address is laser-printed on the reply form, the £6 sum is preprinted together with a requested date for the donation and the geographic location of the recipient is matched in at the top. Lastly, there is a tear-off stub on the left – just as there would be in your cheque book.

This is smart. For it jettisons the tiresome impedimenta of the traditional reply device and becomes a simple, assumptive receipt. Faced with

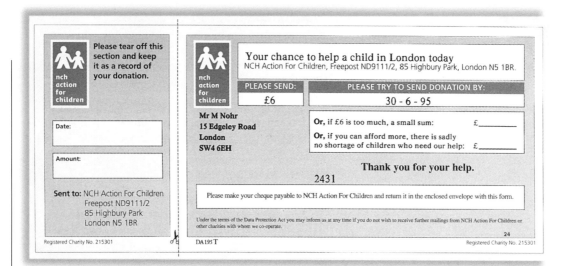

that presumption and simplicity, many people clearly do not resent a £6 donation. Indeed, the average donation was nearer £8.

What these donors will do in the future is another matter. While I do not accept that donors recruited in this way are inevitably poorer than most, it is likely that they will remain immune to any process that guides further donations upwards. Certainly Charles Orasin is going to have an interesting financial equation on his hands if he actually implements the search for the $5 donor – his organisation's current donor programme amounts to 10 appeals a year, eight renewal notices and a phone call; it is difficult to see an entry fee of $5 justifying such further appeals activity.

Frankly, no one knows whether the low ask strategy will pay off. But it is good to see someone trying to vary the cliché.

Postcards and petitions

To some supporters, the chance to campaign on your behalf is the natural mode of their support. Most progressive American cause groups – and plenty of the less progressive – offer a postcard to be sent to Congressmen and Senators to either demand or bewail forthcoming legislation. Some charities offer petition forms so that donors can collect signatures for the same reason.

I have had the privilege of seeing stacks of such things arrive in the offices of the fairly mighty. Sadly, they no longer carry convincing clout – any politician confronted with 10,000 identical postcards knows that they are the result of a direct marketing or advertising campaign and not a spontaneous outpouring of popular emotion. Even 1,000 handwritten letters on the same subject tend to be slight variants on a given theme of advocacy – usually from the animal rights or anti-abortion lobbies. We live in a cynical world.

It is, though, something different that you can ask your supporters to do and, as such, enjoys a listing in a chapter about fundraising offers. I actually won the DMA Gold Award in 1990 with a direct mail campaign for Greenpeace that asked supporters to ring up their Ford dealers and enquire about catalytic converters, then mail the Ford Motor Company with a rude postcard. We persuaded tens of thousands of Greenpeace supporters to do just that. We even persuaded Ford to introduce catalytic converters. But we didn't raise much money.

The moral is obvious. Give your supporters an alternative to giving you money and some will gratefully seize the opportunity. A postcard campaign may serve the campaigning zeal of a minority, for it is always a minority. It will only occasionally produce any political dividend. And it will almost always diminish financial response.

Give them something useful

The demarcation lines between incentives, involvement devices and premiums is a thin and wavering one. One charity's earlybird incentive is another charity's back-end premium. What dumb language we use in direct marketing!

Occasionally, perhaps too occasionally, you see something so very simple and successful in this area of giving things away that you want to beam at its authors. It is as if the heavy curtains of our frenzied tradecraft roll back and there on stage is an 'obvious good thing' with a spotlight on it.

A recruitment pack from the Samaritans includes a simple but usable telephone jotter pad – a perfect piece of symmetry with the fact that its volunteers do their invaluable job on the telephone.

The 1996 New Year communication from the World Society for the Protection of Animals, produced by Target Direct, is a one-piece A3 mailing, plastic-wrapped. Open it and it contains a letter, a reply device and a whole slew of information about what the organisation did in 1995 and proposes to do in 1996. Tear off the reply elements and you are left with a 1996 year planner, each month featuring an animal.

The diary that increased response by nearly 250 per cent.

At exactly the same time and on the other side of Gloucestershire, Chapter One Direct was preparing the Christmas mailing for UNICEF UK donors. In an otherwise humdrum pack, a simple pocket diary was tested. Like the WSPA calendar it is a humble enough thing, but quite good enough to be retained.

David Strickland-Eales shared the detailed response data with me in late March. You would expect an uplift where the diary was used as a give-away, but the scale of the uplift was breathtaking. The test was head to head – diary against no diary. Some segments saw a response of 9.55 per cent increasing to 22 per cent; another rose from 10 per cent to 24 per cent. Any fundraiser knows how rare such massive differentials are. It is a tribute to simplicity. For the diary merely offered a way to say 'thank you' to donors, explicitly or implicitly. Yet again we see the reward for being prepared to utter those fine words and give them meaning. The diary made UNICEF donors feel better about the charity. Feeling better, they gave more. Much more.

To call this an incentive device is to betray it. I prefer to think of it as a present from one friend to another. I don't mind being sentimental sometimes. Give me a 250 per cent increase in response and I'd be happy to be sentimental all the time.

Seven ways Botton can help you

Your support means a great deal to us and we want to help you in any way we can. Please complete the questions below if you wish to change a previous decision or would like additional information. Just tick the relevant boxes and we will keep in touch the way you want us to.

1 By letting you decide when you'd like to hear from us
We usually produce four issues a year of our newsletter, *Botton Village Life*, but you can choose one of the following options.

☐ *I would prefer to hear from you just once a year at Christmas.*
☐ *I would like you to keep me up to date with Botton's news through Botton Village Life, but I do not wish to receive appeals.*
At the moment I hear from you just once a year:
☐ *I would like to receive all four regular issues of* Botton Village Life.
☐ *I want to catch up on news at Botton with the past three issues of* Botton Village Life.

2 By sending you free advice
We produce *The Simple Guide to Making a Will*, which is full of useful, impartial information. Of course, if you do decide to remember Botton in your Will we would be very grateful.

Please send me my free copy of The Simple Guide to Making a Will, *currently only applicable to England and Wales.*
I would like the ☐ *standard print* ☐ *large print version.*

3 By showing you and your friends life in Botton
Our video, *Botton Village: A Very Special Place*, tells the story of our community through the lives of three villagers. It'll help you to get to know us better, especially if you haven't had the chance to visit us yet.

☐ *Please send me your video on a month's free loan.*
☐ *Please send me my own copy. I enclose £5 (see payment details overleaf).*

> Botton Village is part of The Camphill Village Trust, a non-profit-making company limited by guarantee 539694 England and registered as a charity, number 232402.

4 By inviting you to visit us
Visitors are always welcome at Botton. If you can, please give us a ring in advance on (01287) 661294. We can supply details of the opening times of our workshops and a guide to the best village walks.

☐ *Please send me your information for visitors.*

5 By giving you information on Botton's history
We have been producing our newsletter, *Botton Village Life*, for eleven years. Past issues feature lots of interesting stories from the Village's history.

☐ *Please send me a set of back issues (1–20), or issue(s) no(s) _____ (between 21 and 33).*

6 By respecting your wishes
From time to time we agree with other carefully selected charities to write to some of each other's supporters. This can be a very valuable way for us to find new friends.

☐ *I would prefer not to hear from any other organisations.*

7 By sending you information only if you want it
☐ *I would prefer you not to write to me again.*

Do let us know if you have moved to a new address, if we are sending you more than one copy of our newsletter by mistake, or if there is anything else you would like to tell us.

Let the donor own the relationship! Botton Village's astonishing response figures are underpinned by the startling honesty of the approach.

The greatest offer of all. Intelligence.

Let's stay a moment with truly mouth-watering response data.

I know of one charity with 68,000 donors who raised £732,000 gross and £630,000 net with its Christmas 1995 appeal. Response rate was 28.73 per cent, average donation £37.99. But, then, this is a charity that recruits at percentage responses of four per cent to nearly 10 per cent on a reciprocal list programme. Few will have heard of it.

Botton Village is a working community for people with mental handicap in North Yorkshire, 40 years old and thriving. It is also a jewel in the crown of Burnett Associates who has guided its fundraising for years now. Certainly its growth and fundraising achievements are a glittering exposition of Ken Burnett's theory of relationship fundraising and I must leave it to Ken to tell the full story elsewhere.

But Botton has always offered its supporters a rare degree of intelligence, underpinned – it has to be said – by a degree of database sophistication that larger charities would do well to envy. Its communications are the antithesis of flashy – they are averagely humble two-colour newsletters. Botton would win few awards for creativity – at least in the élitist terms with which that word is currently defined.

But they should win every award going for supporter care. In the reply form donors are given these options.

> *I would prefer to hear from you just once a year at Christmas.*

I would like you to keep me up to date with Botton's news, but I do not wish to receive appeals.

I would like to receive all four regular issues of Botton Village Life.

I want to catch up on news at Botton with the past three issues of Botton Village Life.

I would prefer you not to write to me again.

Can anyone doubt that the astonishing response data I have reported is rooted in the intelligence and sensitivity of this approach? For the donor is given ownership of the relationship, the power to ordain just how and when the two parties will communicate in the future. It is the antithesis of the mad pursuit of gross figures that we see elsewhere, a pursuit that must always involve colossal wastage and the loss of hundreds of thousands of potentially long-term relationships that have foundered in the face of insensitive and banal fundraising programmes.

Those Botton donors who asked only for a communication at Christmas responded to that appeal at more than 40 per cent. In 1995, 15,000 new donors were recruited – a figure that has persuaded the charity to stop recruiting for the immediate future.

How many other charities have reached this state of mature stability?

Botton Village offers fundraisers a model for the future. It makes an offer that is rarely seen. It is called intelligence.

Every story in this section is a story of a charity trying a little harder. Each has formulated an offer, a distinctive offer, so that their appeal is sharpened and made more evocative. Would the National Canine Defence League have raised as much money if it simply asked for unattributable donations? Would it have given such evident joy to its supporters? Would the otherwise routine appeals by the National Trust, Feed the Children, UNICEF and Royal Star and Garter Home have flourished without the

When you wish upon a star... A delightful Christmas device from Sense.

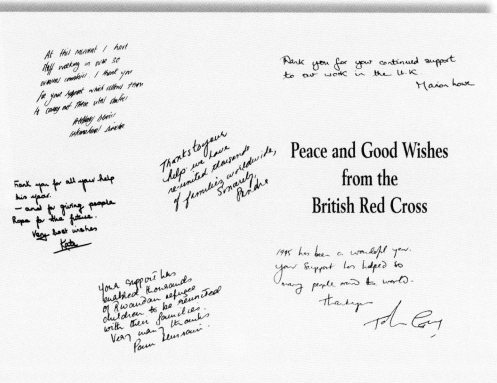

Peace and Good Wishes from the British Red Cross

Personal messages on a Christmas card from the British Red Cross. A large charity gets to sound more human.

small gestures they each made to the supporter?

Every charity can make a better offer than the simple request for donations. The Christmas mailing from the British Red Cross in 1995 sent a Christmas card with 'handwritten' messages from Red Cross staff. It also offered a prize draw by which a donor could win the chance to visit Red Cross projects in Africa and India. A WWF mailing offers a free print of a tiger for a completed direct debit form. Sense, the National Deafblind and Rubella Association, sent a little star on gold board, asking the donor to sign and return it so that it could be fixed to a Christmas tree at one of their family centres.

All these things are offers, the result of charities thinking just a little deeper about the process of motivation. Yet many appeals fail to apply that extra thought, fail to make an offer. They are increasingly presumptuous and increasingly they founder. No one should be surprised.

When you embark on any piece of fundraising — and particularly one discharged by direct marketing — you should be prepared to consider just what your offer is. A long time ago Samuel Johnson said 'Promise, promise is the soul of all advertisement'.

Fundraisers need to write that aphorism on the wall. Metaphorically, of course.

CHAPTER EIGHT

A POSTSCRIPT ON FUNDRAISING DIRECT MAIL

This book is about creativity and not about the whole panoply of direct mail technique. I am a humble hack, desperately aware of the dangers of posturing beyond my means. I am not the best man to ask about list profiling, merge-purging, or stratified samples and I am not going to pretend otherwise. But there are areas of this increasingly congested art where a man has to say what a man has to say.

So this is a round-up of opinion (mine) and fact (other people's) on issues that often affect the creative process.

Testing

I have seen more time wasted on testing than in any other part of fundraising. I am willing to accept that the greater volume mailings available in the USA justify the extraordinary sophistication applied to testing procedures there. But in the UK and in most European countries lists are so much smaller that the industrial-scale testing of everything that moves is quite often simply out of all proportion to the potential rewards from the process. I have seen a database of 100,000 split into 20 segments and subjected to a mind-boggling permutation of tests that included everything from the length of the letter to the nature of the premium to the message on the outer envelope. Three months later the client came back and waxed lyrical about how one cell produced 154 responses and another 173. Interesting, we all agreed, but hardly indicative. I can remember no single action that stemmed from this extraordinary process of statistical masturbation.

Sadly, direct marketing and fundraising have evolved a sub-genus of database-wallah who lives only to test. The Testing Nerd, for so we shall term him (another sexist slight, but this one is always male and usually wears glasses) is never satisfied with any response data. 'I know it's looks good', he says, 'but if we had enclosed the second lift letter, included a sample of pre-1993 lapseds and increased the cell test in Glamorgan, we'd have achieved a 0.23 per cent uplift overall.' I see him now. He is tapping on his Psion as he utters.

Testing has an infernal habit of producing less-than-thrilling results. In Britain, we enjoy a tremendous privilege in newspaper advertising recruitment, for many of our papers offer genuine A/B split-run facilities with two different ads appearing in alternative copies of the newspaper. This is an exciting facility and one underpinned by statistical credence for newspaper readership figures run into the millions. All too often, though, there is scant difference in response to the two ads.

It's back to Roger Millington's leverage points. The audience is the biggest variable – which is why lists and individual newspaper titles are always worth testing. So is the offer – remember that colossal difference when UNICEF enclosed that diary.

But when it comes to format, and certainly when it comes to creative nuances, the difference in response exposed by testing tends to be sadly insignificant all too often.

Volume and only volume provides the exception to this sceptical rule. The Royal National Lifeboat Institution has a programme of loose inserts and door-drops that is subject to rigid and proper testing – even the featured coxswain in the piece has proved to be a geographic variable. But millions of pieces of print are involved each quarter and the response data is sufficiently robust to be applied thereafter. Charities with lower-volume programmes rarely need to saddle themselves with such ambition.

The rules of direct mail testing can be prolix. Joseph Kachorek's book *Direct Mail Testing for Fund Raisers* runs to nearly 200 pages that contain just about every testing procedure you could ever consider. But its introduction makes an important point. '… improper use of testing can lead to confusion, inefficiencies, unproductive mailings and a decline in revenue. Not testing is a bad idea, improper testing is worse.'

Amen to that! My version of improper testing can probably afford to be simpler than that of Mr Kachorek. It would involve any test that offers less-than-statistical validity, any test incapable of rollout and any test involving too many variables.

For these are the substantive points about testing.

● You should only test something that you can apply later. There is little point in testing variable paragraphs in the letter copy unless they are still going to be valid on the next mailing.

● You should only test one thing at a time. Test the letter signatory, or the length of the letter, or the involvement device, or the outer envelope message if you have to. But not all at the same time. Only the Testing Nerd will be able to cope with the variables.

● You should only test quantities that give *response data* of statistical validity. The difference between 154 responses and 173 responses is statistically meaningless despite the fact that the responses may be derived from an apparently valid mailing quantity of 5,000.

● You should only test things within significant volumes. It is daft to test half of a list of 5,000. Believe me, I have seen it done.

● You should remember that testing against a control package or ad is usually a decision to raise less money. Beating a control is, by definition, a difficult thing to achieve. Trying to do so is an optimistic act and a professionally dutiful one, but it will not often be successful. Remember: we are fundraisers and not rocket scientists. Our daily duty is to raise money for our causes, not to expand the field of human knowledge. I know that this is dire conservatism that takes a lot of the boyish excitement out of the process, but I have often watched charities agree to use the control package on only half of their list, subjecting the other half to a battery of tests. No mail order direct marketer would so consciously sacrifice raw turnover to the gods of testing.

One final note of scepticism for a sceptical section, the inexorable law of testing. It says that, 'The rollout never performs as well as the test'. I don't know why this is always true but somehow it is.

Keep the Testing Nerd at bay. You probably have better things to worry about.

Timing

Everyone asks for money at Christmas. Every charity has a Christmas appeal. The public expects it and the public responds to it. But are there other seasonal patterns for fundraising?

Echo answers no. Up to a few years ago many charities also ran an Easter appeal in the fond hope that people were similarly motivated by Christian philanthropy. I even had a client once – a nonreligious one – who insisted not just on a Whitsun appeal but on an appeal that coincided with the Christian Whitsun, not the secular one that has succeeded it. This wide-eyed adherence to the traditional ecclesiastical year has largely been dissipated by surly lack of response from a public that now thinks of spring as a time for garden centres and do-it-yourself emporia. The Easter seals campaigns in North America have earned their place as a cultural institution and Marie Curie Cancer Care promises to do the same with its daffodil campaign in the UK. But these are the exceptions. Easter has no particular fundraising resonance in contemporary society.

There is a lot of research available in the States on fundraising seasonality but it is both geographically specific and, inevitably, self-justifying. It is claimed that 40 per cent of charitable contributions from individuals are received in the last quarter of the year, but this appears to be little more than a reflection on fundraising appeal activity. A survey produced by the Kleid Company, a New York list brokerage, offered this monthly percentage breakdown of fundraising mailings for the years 1986 to 1990.

Month	Monthly % of total mailings
November	17.0%
February	14.3%
August	10.6%
October	10.1%
March	9.0%
September	8.5%
January	6.3%
December	6.1%
April	5.3%
July	5.2%
May	4.7%
June	2.9%

So, 35.6 per cent of fundraising mailings are released between September and November. That 40 per cent statistic begins to look a little less remarkable.

Frankly, I have never learned anything that begins to offer a model for fundraising seasonality outside the Christmas period. And even the Christmas period has a great deal of elasticity to it. I have already recorded that prime time for the launch of a Christmas catalogue is at the end of August. It was during the sixties that we learned that ads placed *immediately after* Christmas pulled the best for Oxfam, post-wassail guilt being a powerful thing. NSPCC – as I shall report later – has brilliantly exploited the same phenomenon.

Common sense guides you best. A mailing that arrives in the two days before Christmas is unlikely to get the reader's full attention. An appeal launched in late July is likely to fall foul of the fact that people are on holiday or about to be, and that newspaper readerships plummet. Major media events such as a general election, the Olympic Games or the World Cup can all divert the public's attention from your appeal.

These days I find myself advising clients to communicate *when they have something to say,* or *when their cause is in the headlines.* Often the two things coincide. Greenpeace hogged newspaper and television news through the summer of 1995 with its action on the Brent Spar oil rig. When the action was complete, and successfully so, the simple mailing to supporters was a natural thing, though it came at high summer. The astounding amount of money raised by the British Labour Party by mailing and telephone campaigns just before the 1992 general election is another example of the power of important events to maximise fundraising. Any overseas disaster such as a famine or earthquake underlines the point yet again. *Fundraising works best when the need is seen to be urgent.*

Many charities are saddled with a fundraising calendar that comprises a schematic list of traditional appeal activities. Thus, a January mailing, an April mailing, a September mailing and a Christmas mailing. It may make an orderly programme but it is finally a bureaucratic convenience, nothing more.

'What shall we say in our April mailing?' says the harassed fundraiser. It is a depressing question. It means that the key interrogative question has gone unanswered. No one has asked 'Why?' And no one has created that sense of event.

Finding new supporters

Botton Village's decision not to undertake further recruitment in the near future is almost unique in fundraising. Most charities see recruitment, acquisition and prospection (try explaining these terms to donors) as key to their fundraising health.

The reasons are obvious. Perhaps four per cent of your donors will die or move away this year. Indeed, a statistic produced in the heady days of the housing boom in the UK indicated that 11 per cent of us were changing our address every year. We may do the decent thing and inform the charity of a change of address, but it is always going to be a decency confined to a zealous minority. Most of us will happily flee the avalanche of mailings.

Few charities have the confidence – or wit – to live with a static or declining number of supporters. The 'leaky bucket' theory of fundraising, whereby desperate and expensive efforts are made to 'top up' the supporter numbers, is a woeful process that often involves indefensible amounts of money and extraordinary organisational effort. It is vested in that strange fundraising fallacy to which I have previously alluded, the one that assumes that a donation is a sign of lifetime commitment. We have even invented the grotesque word 'attrition' to describe the purely human process by which tens of thousands of people get bored with what we say and the way we say it.

Be that as it may, fundraising involves a continuing need to find more new people to ask for support. Each of the available media offers different characteristics. Press ads work at times of emergencies but rarely otherwise these days. Similarly with radio and television, though current legend has it that broadcast-recruited donors are less responsive to direct mail appeals. The telephone is probably denied you in this mode.

So, sadly and inevitably, the best medium for supporter recruitment is direct mail. The great heyday of mass-recruitment mailings for charities has now passed, the victim of absurd over-mailing and consumer resistance. Percentage response and payback rates both plummeted in the early nineties. These days a recruitment programme that does better than one per cent response, or that offers a break-even payback in the first year is a rare and happy event, though such sightings are becoming more common at the time of writing.

But, who do you mail? These days the fundraiser is surrounded by a plethora of options, ever more sophisticated ways by which you can target the potential donor. There is a lot of science about.

It has meant that we often overlook the simplest means of mailing people. The national electoral roll is, after all, updated every year and actually represents the most complete database in the United Kingdom. CACI's Acorn database, which stems from it, contains more than 40 million names and addresses, neatly organised into 54 accommodation-based segments. CACI also offers the delightful Monica analysis that enables you to target priority age groups according to their Christian names, for most Scotts are young and most Ethels are old. You can identify near-neighbours of your existing supporters, or young people who have come on to the electoral roll in the last year. You can target people who have lived at the same address for a number of years on the basis that they are likely to be older, mortgage free and have greater disposable income. In all this, you will clearly need the help of the database proprietors but the electoral roll is too often overlooked by fundraisers in their search for greater and greater demographic sophistication.

That sophistication has been marked by the emergence of lifestyle compilations, based on huge questionnaire operations where gleeful consumers in search of a prize draw are happy to answer dozens of questions about themselves, their habits, interests and beliefs. They enable you to mail those who affect environmental awareness, those who read broadsheet newspapers, those at given income levels – and to match these characteristics against what you know about your existing supporters by way of profiling. All that worries me about lifestyle consumer lists is the self-selective nature of the questionnaire respondents – smart and worldly middle-class people tend not to participate. Having said that, lifestyle-based lists undoubtedly work – you will always find them at the top of any league table of recently tested lists.

Then, there are the traditional response-based lists culled from someone else's files. Thus, you can rent lists of magazine subscribers, buyers of various mail order products or services, purchasers of theatre tickets – or even cakes from Texas.

You need to be artful in choosing such lists. Subscribers to posh magazines may sound fruitful but rarely offer cost-effective recruitment – too many of them are men and too many of them are 18-hour-a-day businessmen. And, while buyers of mail order cosmetics may be pronouncedly downmarket, they are at least female and mail-responsive. Canny interpretation on lists usually pays off – customers who take out insurance on their dog or cat are saying something both about their disposable income and their love of animals. As such they make a promising list for an animal charity. And I meant it about cakes from Texas – the Collin Street Bakery list is usually more productive than Female Investors.

The world of cold lists is inevitably a world of developing technology, changing consumer patterns, an excess of lazy anecdote and a dearth of credible published response data. Frankly, you will need a good guide to see you through this jungle – a list broker with experience and probity. The choice is limited. But don't enter the jungle without them.

Even with a good list broker to machete through the undergrowth for you, you will still be playing a game of small percentages – one where the response rate will usually be measured in decimal points either side of one per cent. There is only one alternative to such demeaning response. It involves putting your own supporters' list on the market.

Swap people – you know it makes sense

It's another wonderfully insensitive word. Reciprocals – it suggests a regimen of tablets or an ice-dance routine. But it is merely the proven practice of swapping the names and addresses of your supporters with those of other charities.

This is still heresy in some quarters – many major charities still refuse to participate, preferring to pursue the costly grapeshot tactics of the open market rather than the greater precision offered by list swaps. As I say, the practice is now proven by just about every charity that ever participated in a reciprocal programme – that notional one per cent response from a cold list is always likely to be tripled, quadrupled, or otherwise multiplied in a list swap. Mark Gilden from Occam Direct Marketing, an outfit that engineers many reciprocal deals, reports a band of four per cent to 11 per cent as standard.

The reasons are obvious. The people on your list are nice people, people who give to charity by post, that minority of the population who have publicly testified to their decency. They are simply the most likely recruits for another charity. Which, for some charities, is exactly the problem. If they give to another charity, will they stop giving to us?

It is that touching fallacy again, the belief that donors are somehow 'owned' by their charity proprietors, that they are totally and singly dedicated to one cause or organisation. We have recently begun to enjoy the data that disproves the fallacy once and for all. The aforesaid Occam produces 'promiscuity' reports that can project how many other charities a supporter gives to. In some cases the totally monogamous donor represents just 15 per cent of the whole list and rarely rises above 50 per cent. 37 per cent of the supporters of one well-known charity give to five or more other charities. In the States it is believed that 50 per cent of active donors are simultaneously giving to *15* other causes.

So there should be no issue of principle here, other than that of acceding to the request of some donors that their names should not be swapped. And there is no evidence that donors react differently to your appeals after a reciprocal mailing – indeed. such evidence as exists indicates a slightly better donor performance after a reciprocal mailing.

Just three caveats. First, you must have the numbers with which to play the reciprocal game – anything less than 25,000 names is probably a waste of both parties' time. Second, make sure that like is being compared with like. You should only swap active donors with active donors on the same basis of definition – beware any list more than two years old. Third, look for the organisations that offer the most likely symmetry with your own organisation. Charter 88 runs a mutually fruitful reciprocal programme with the likes of other 'progressive' groups such as Amnesty and Greenpeace, but tends to founder when the reciprocal party is a more traditional charity.

But do it if you can. If you think that your supporters are unique to you, you are beguiling yourself. If you think that they will be offended, you will be pleasantly surprised. If you can suggest another way in which you can recruit new supporters as cost-effectively as reciprocals, just tell me.

Don't try to squeeze blood from turnips

Isn't that a glorious sub heading? I just found it in a chapter of an American fundraising book on database segmentation. It combines a mixed metaphor,

vulgarity and offensiveness – a formidable combination of verbal excess that is somehow typical of most writing on the subject of segmenting your donor file.

The Segmentation Tendency are a rum lot, close cousins of the Testing Nerd. Proceeding from the oft-repeated commonplace that 'there is no such thing as an average donor', they drink deep from the draught of database potential and hallucinate about the wonders that it can achieve. Thus, segmentation can eventually allow us to redraw response devices to make them convenient for left-handed donors. It can have us dropping in Burns quotations for Scottish donors. It can have us offering topic preference whereby a donor who has given to a service delivery appeal will not be asked to give to a research programme.

I jest, but only just – that last example is taken from another textbook. Not for the first time, technological possibility collides with operational reality. Who in their right fundraising mind would *want* a database of 100 segments? Only the Testing Nerd would thrive in such a segmented utopia and he will shortly need an assistant or two.

Database segmentation is a great way to increase the return from your fundraising programme as long as you keep the process simple and as long as you keep your pragmatic wits about you. For too many segmentation programmes assume that segmentation is a finite process, discharged the once and forever changeless. But the very point of a database is change and the ability to capture that change. Apart from the obvious changes such as ageing and relocation, people do all sorts of things that affect their relationship with you. They marry, they have children, they change jobs, get fired, become born-again Christians, discover the string quartets of Ariaga... And you are never going to know about these changes, be your database mightily relational and meticulously segmented.

But you need to capture the changes that you can know about – the change from a one-off donation to a standing order, the change from a standing order to a covenant, the change from regular giving to irregular giving (a process that is sadly as common as the reverse). These changes do not just give you a pattern of donor support – which is a statistical construct. They give you the chance to say something to these donors – which is a human opportunity. Too often database segmentation presumes on a static situation and demographic information (the word demographic merely means 'a picture of people' and nothing more mathematically rigorous) is seen as an eternal truth. This is how someone who gives you £250 becomes forever a major donor though he may have gone bankrupt in the last year. And how a low value donor is always believed to be simply and perennially poor.

Not for the first time I exaggerate to make my point. Segmentation makes obvious sense if it allows for change and if it concentrates on the few things that matter. Those few things are simply recency of donation, frequency of donation and size of donation. This holy trinity of factors is the key to successful database segmentation. The donor who has just given is the most likely person to give again. The donor who has given frequently is the most likely person to give to a committed giving scheme. The donor who has given a large donation is the most likely person to give another large donation. It is when the technology coincides with common sense that we see the best rewards from the process.

Scan the last few paragraphs carefully and you will quickly spot an apparent paradox.

I am commending the traditional importance of frequency, recency and donation value on the one hand and simultaneously making the point that people – and their circumstances – change. There is no real contradiction between the two observations – the first is a proven index for successful database fundraising, the second is simple human observation. Too much database technique salutes the one but ignores the other. As such, it suppresses the true

potential of the computer to produce effective communications, to give wider choices to the supporter, to build better relationships.

And no one should sneer at the ability of segmentation to do something horribly negative – expel non-respondents from the file. Or, as our American friends would have it, ceasing the attempt to get blood out of turnips. Most charities I know are either deeply sentimental about this process of expulsion or indefensibly wedded to the numbers on their database. Certainly, most charities retain too many donors on file long after they have effectively announced their resignation. Hope springs eternal in the fundraising breast and it is often an expensive emotion. These days I would not mail anyone who had not responded in the previous year (presuming a regular appeals cycle at least), except in very special circumstances. I know of no charity currently prepared to be this ruthless. Not for the first time the fact of mailing is confused with the fact of fundraising.

There is no such thing as an optimum segmentation for a fundraising database, though Botton Village offers a model of donor-driven segmentation whose success has already made a regular appearance in these pages. But Joe Saxton, shortly after he left Oxfam, wrote a piece in the much missed *Donors* magazine that reported Oxfam's traditional segmentation of its database. It went like this.

- Members of the Project Partners committed giving scheme.
- High value covenantors.
- Medium value covenantors.
- Bankers order donors.
- Give as you earn supporters.
- New supporters who entered the database in the last three months.
- High value donors.
- Medium value donors.
- Low value donors.
- Trading catalogue donors.
- Trading catalogue customers.

This seems to me to take the process of segmentation just about as far as it can profitably go. It enshrines all three of the holy trinity factors of recency, frequency and donation size and adds in other relevant – and usable – segments. But it takes a big charity to make such segmentation worthwhile. For hundreds of thousands of names are being segmented here – by an organisation whose income from the process was reported at around £15 million annually from direct marketing.

But, even here, the word donors is allowed a credence that it may not deserve. Probably the most useful verbal segmentation that a charity can deploy is the one that acknowledges the difference between a one-off donor (probably a majority of names on the file at any one time) and donors who have given more often. Perhaps the word 'responders' is a fairer description of what the first group has actually done. If we formally admitted as much in our segmentation, we might just be able to communicate with them with a little greater intelligence.

All in all, let common sense be the most powerful input in any segmentation programme. And beware the Segmentation Tendency, for they are purists and you can rarely afford to be.

Time to go...

There comes a time when it is implausible to carry on mailing people who refuse to give you money. I have already recorded my own brutal timetabling of the process – a year's inaction should qualify for expulsion.

Fundraisers create a great deal of fuss about this. Again, the very vocabulary used is presumptive. We talk of 'lapsed donors' as if non-response was a carefully considered action akin to resigning from a club. We talk of 'attrition' as if some chemical process was worming its way through the database. All that happens is that people get bored with us. Statistically most people get bored with us. Or,

of course, were never that committed in the first place. It doesn't make them bad people.

But persuading them to give again – 'reactivating the lapseds' – I fear, is a regular task for the fundraiser. It is simple financial responsibility to want to curb excess mailings that are not going to produce a reasonable return. It is not unusual to mail three or four times and intersperse the mailings with a telephone call. The percentage responses are tiny but can amass to a worthwhile programme. In the United States the process can be slightly hysterical – I know of one major cause group there that has a series of eight lapsed mailings and still contrives only a 35 per cent annual renewal rate.

You might as well be candid when you write to donors at this stage. I can see little point in an over-long or over-flowery letter; I can see much virtue in finding variants on the battered cliché that says 'We just can't go on like this'. A good letter can tell the donor why.

This is the start of one I wrote for a small charity called Womankind in November 1995.

Dear Former Supporter,

That's probably the least elegant way to start a letter you can think of. But it's a form of words I'm forced to use.

For I know just two things about you. First, that you once asked for information or made a donation to Womankind. And, second, that we haven't heard from you for an awfully long time. And my sad purpose in writing is to tell you that we will have to delete your name from our supporters' file unless you feel able to respond to this letter. I am sure that you will understand that a tiny charity like ours cannot afford to keep writing unless we feel that a response is likely.

But you once wanted to support our campaign to help women in developing countries and I can't think that your passion for the cause of women has waned in the meantime...

The letter produced a respectable 2.5 per cent response and a modest amount of cash. But a couple of months afterwards, the client faxed me in a high state of excitement to tell me that the letter had produced a belated donation of £10,000 from a guilt-stricken former supporter. You cannot guarantee such windfalls with lapsed mailings, but it proves yet again how careful and sensitive we need to be with donor segmentation. After all, a lapsed donor just turned out to be a major donor.

This is the chapter where I have tumbled headlong into the language of direct marketing tradecraft. Lapseds, payback, acquisition, attrition, cell tests, reciprocals... I can only apologise for such verbiage. For they each describe the brute mechanics of a business that starts with a common act of decency and kindness and should be sustained in those same terms.

Direct marketing happens to be the most viable way of communicating with lots of people cost-effectively. That is the justification for this last chapter. But direct marketing for fundraisers badly needs ethical redefinition. The 'leaky bucket' theory is distinctly troubling for it treats causes and donors as commodities and digits. An American fundraiser told me recently that 'We'll do anything to keep the numbers up'. We should not want to live in a fundraising world where such things can be said and meant. We have become altogether too absorbed by the pursuit of numbers.

It's time, anyway, to look at other means by which we can communicate.

Stop press: Remember the spoon mailing where I promised to keep you up to date with my £15 donation on February 14? I received a personalised thank you letter on March 6 and six weeks later another appeal mailing. Again, it's bright – it's based around an armband that goes round the arms of malnourished children to check on the degree of malnutrition. It happens to be an old idea and I'm not quite sure that they know that.

But I haven't given again. I am therefore joining the swelling ranks of one-off donors. I'm not proud of that but I don't think they've asked properly.

Stop stop press: Oh dear, on September 20th I received another mailing from them. You'll never believe this, but it contained another plastic spoon.

CHAPTER NINE

WHO NEEDS ENVELOPES?

The surge in direct mail usage has dominated the very vocabulary that we apply to describing the process of communicating in print. No one should be bedazzled by that vocabulary for it often masks sheer common sense. And it is almost always fruitful to see how else you can ask millions of people for money.

Press advertising

The first job I ever did in fundraising was to write ads for Oxfam, then the Oxford Committee for Famine Relief, under the tutelage of Harold Sumption. I don't mind you knowing that this was in 1962.

Harold had practically invented the charity press ad single-handed in the forties and fifties. Though you can find fundraising ads that date from the latter half of the nineteenth century, Oxfam was the first charity to make itself famous by regular and adroit use of this one medium. For its growth was astonishing in the sixties and that growth was made possible by press advertising. No one who was around at the time could have missed these ads – Jeremy Shaw of Smith Bundy says that he first heard of Oxfam through seeing its ads pinned to the school notice-board every day. And the ads certainly became a sort of cultural icon of the times. I remember seeing one of them used in a Sadler's Wells production of the Brecht/Weill *City of Mahogonny*

opera and I can also remember being asked by the producers of the Julie Christie movie *Darling* for permission to use another ad as a poster in the film.

No charity will ever get as lucky again with press advertising. Frankly, we had the field to ourselves for few other charities dared to use a medium that was so totally dominated by Oxfam. We spent several hundred thousand pounds a year on the process – the equivalent of a couple of million pounds today. We ran the ads in just about every newspaper and a fair number of magazines. We ran classifieds, title corners, small spaces, full pages and every space in between. We advertised in the little books that contain postage stamps and we must have kept many religious magazines in business. Heady days!

For the response to the ads has never been seen since. We budgeted overall for a 3:1 payback on every ad we ran. When an overseas emergency struck, we could do 12 or 15:1. There was actually an ad that raised 31 times its cost in a month. The fact that Oxfam's first computerised mailing list in 1966 comprised 400,000 names was a tribute to the power and reach of this extraordinary programme. How much mailing would you have to do to recruit 400,000 names?

The ads were crude, homespun and usually typeset by the newspapers themselves, never with a coupon in those early days. The headline would often

HAVE YOU SENT YOUR GIFT *To Help Suffering Refugees?*

[HELP QUICKLY] [FOOD & CLOTHES - URGENT]

THOUSANDS IN GREAT NEED

Despairing victims of war and intolerance still crowd the refugee camps of Europe, the Middle East and Korea. Now 2,500 a day have been pouring into Berlin. Many are in desperate need, especially children, the sick and elderly. Please help one such family.

SEND YOUR DISCARDED CLOTHES TO:

Oxford / Companion Relief, c/o Davies, Turner & Co., 50a, Bourne Street, London, S.W.1.

GIVE 10/-

TO SEND FOOD OR CLOTH-ING TO ONE DESPERATELY NEEDY FAMILY.

Money is needed for the early dispatch of food and medicines to those in great need, and for the inevitable expense of packing and shipping donated clothing. (10/- sends enough for one family : £10 will send 700 garments). Please help—*Now*. Groups and individuals can help a whole village by organising a local collection—leaflets and posters supplied on request to 17, Broad Street, Oxford. Remittances to: Hon. Treasurer, Companion Relief, Barclays Bank, Old Bank, High Street, Oxford.

United Nations Relief and Works Agency Photo

The plight of this Arab baby in Jerusalem is typical. If funds from international sources cease many such babies would be left to die.

OXFORD COMMITTEE FOR

FAMINE RELIEF

(Regd. War Charities Act, 1940)

SUPPORTERS INCLUDE:
Rev. Roland Brown; Dr. Maude Royden-Shaw; Rev. Dr. N. Micklem; Rev. H. R. Moxley (Chairman).

A typical Oxfam ad from the 1950s. Note the 10-shilling ask – 50p in decimal terms.

just say 'Terrible Hunger' and the words 'desperate,' 'needy' and 'heartbreaking' were in constant use. Always they featured a photograph of suffering and almost always that photograph was of a child. We had invented the 'starving child' ad, though we had learned to dispense with it by the end of the decade.

No one should kid themselves that Oxfam ads in those days were in any way sub-professional. This was a sophisticated programme that regularly tested media, spaces, creative treatments and everything else. Individual ads did not last very long if only because the publicity manager at the time was a slightly crazed individual who would never be satisfied with mere overwhelming success – there must always be something different and better we could do. Space was negotiated and bought with terrifying vigour. The week's response data, by the way, arrived on your agency desk on the Monday morning, immaculately typed in Oxford at close of play on Friday. Mysteriously, such prompt reporting does not seem to happen in these days of computers and faxes.

It was, of course, a very British phenomenon. All our major newspapers are truly national in circulation and 90 per cent of Brits read a daily or Sunday newspaper, a penetration probably unequalled in any other country. We were lucky, too, that direct response and mail order ads had always been a feature of the British press – readers were used to sending money away to press advertisers. But, whatever the analysis of opportunity, timing, professionalism and sheer good fortune, we learned that press advertising was a powerful weapon in the armoury of fundraising.

It still can be. Not so often, not so regularly and hardly ever at the response rates we saw 30 years ago. But press ads can still recruit new donors cost-effectively and they can still offer an incomparable way to present a message to the public. At the time of writing, Sight Savers is recruiting successfully at better than break even with whole pages in weekend supplements and ActionAid still seems to find sponsors almost exclusively in the press. In fact, 156 British charities placed ads in the national press in 1995 – 2,506 ads in all. And they spent a lot of money on the process.

Some current statistics

Smith Bundy and Partners know more about charity press advertising than any agency in the country. They should do, having been intimately involved in such advertising for over 20 years. They now offer a Fundraising Advertising Monitor, an information service that captures every non-profit ad that appears in the British national press. All my statistics are taken from it.

It lists the top charity advertisers among many other things, telling you how many ads they took during the year. It is a slightly surprising league table. Would you have thought that the Royal Society for the Protection of Birds was the country's leading charity advertiser, numerically at least? Bear in mind, though, that the number of ads is not the same thing as expenditure. To get a handle on that, you'll need MEAL (Media Expenditure Analysis Ltd) figures. Even then you need to discount the figures, for MEAL records rate card costs and no charity in its right mind buys its space at rate card.

The top nine, anyway.
- RSPB 161 ads.
- ActionAid 122 ads.
- Blue Cross 100 ads.
- Cancer Relief Macmillan Fund 100 ads.
- Feed the Children 98 ads.
- Help the Aged 97 ads.
- WWF 93 ads.
- Red Cross 71 ads.
- Oxfam 66 ads.

In other words, RSPB was running an average of something over three ads a week during 1995 and Blue Cross virtually an ad a fortnight. Given that all the charities on this list are veterans of the press advertising process, you can reasonably assume that these programmes are successful.

Where the ads go is pretty predictable. Everyone has learned to concentrate their efforts on the broadsheets, particularly those of liberal persuasion. Here is where 83 per cent of those 2,506 ads went
- The *Guardian* 371 ads.
- The *Independent* 328 ads.
- *Daily Telegraph* 324 ads.
- *The Times* 246 ads.
- *Daily Mail* 203 ads.
- *Daily Express* 163 ads.

- *Financial Times* 160 ads.
- The *Observer* 123 ads.
- *Today* 86 ads.
- *Sunday Telegraph* 74 ads.

The top two titles, therefore, carry more than one charity ad per average day. The *Observer,* which is of course a Sunday title, carries more than two per issue. The liberal broadsheets may seem like a ghetto of charity advertising but they continue to offer the best setting for a fundraising appeal, as they have done for generations past. The two widest-circulating newspapers in the country – the *Sun* and the *Daily Mirror* – hardly ever carry a charity ad.

The Fundraising Advertising Monitor also tells us about the spaces used by charity advertisers. It is not information that will surprise anyone who has ever been involved in such advertising, for 1,185 of the ads – a full 47 per cent of the total – occupied that familiar 20-cm-across-two-columns space. There were, though, 310 whole pages taken by charities – a surprising average of nearly six per week across the whole of the press.

A summary, then, of British charity press advertising in 1995. A lot of charities took space but very few at any rate of frequency (94 of the 156 took 10 spaces or less in the year). Most of the ads were clustered into the up-market broadsheets and almost half of them occupied the familiar 20-cm double-column space. It is a market dominated by large advertisers, charities who tend to know what they are doing with rare precision. You are unlikely to take two or three ads a week unless you do.

Is it compulsory?

I say this because the discussion sometimes gets congested. Press advertising is a very public medium compared with direct mail, a fact which leads many charity managers to pine for its visibility. Trustees, too, tend to be full of views on the subject, often offering the dreaded 'chairman's wife' anecdotage

whereby the good lady only ever reads the *Daily Mail* along with positively all her friends. Similarly chaps in the City only ever read the *Financial Times,* which must therefore be the only sensible receptacle for charity ads. Only such dangerous deference to lay judgement can explain the 160 fundraising ads which that paper carried in 1995. All of them would have died the death.

You need to keep the anecdotage at arm's length and know precisely what you are trying to achieve with press advertising.

Raising money with press ads

There is no point in slavering over the response figures I quoted from the Golden Age of Oxfam advertising. They are as relevant to contemporary fundraising as half-tone blocks, or carbon paper. No charity will ever again be able to rely on making more money from a press ad than it spends on it. If you are a normal charity making a normal appeal on a normal day, you will now be lucky to recoup 25 per cent of your investment.

The exceptions are obvious and familiar. If your organisation is in the forefront of a news story that simultaneously occupies the front page of the same newspaper and one that was on last night's TV news, then it may be worth advertising in the expectation of raising money cost-effectively. Emergency advertising in other words, the sort that offers an immediate conduit for public concern and desire to help. Wars, natural disasters and famines will always make immediate press advertising by development agencies and aid organisations successful. An oil spill, or a beached tanker is a boon for environmental organisations, or animal charities. It is as if the Four Horsemen of the Apocalypse were the patron saints of fundraising advertising.

But even in these situations, speed is of the essence. The natural disaster will dominate the headlines for no more than a day or two and your ad

URGENT

THE BLINDED OF BHOPAL NEED YOUR HELP

UP TO 50,000 PEOPLE MAY BE BLINDED WITHOUT IMMEDIATE MEDICAL TREATMENT

THE ADVANCE RCSB MEDICAL TEAM, INCLUDING ITS MOORFIELD'S CHEMICAL BURNS EXPERT, ARRIVED IN BHOPAL YESTERDAY WITH 10,000 TUBES OF VITAL EYE OINTMENT

The catastrophe which has hit Bhopal is the worst man-made disaster ever. More than 2,500 are dead. Hundreds of thousands are sick. Tragically, children and old people are suffering most. Already experienced workers from the Royal Commonwealth Society for the Blind are there bringing help where it is most needed.

THEY NEED YOUR HELP RIGHT NOW

PLEASE SEND WHATEVER DONATION YOU CAN TODAY

RCSB BHOPAL BLIND APPEAL

FREEPOST 5, HAYWARDS HEATH, RH16 3AZ

Telephone Enquiries (0444) 412424/455683

This advertisement was subscribed by Keeler Ltd, suppliers of ophthalmic equipment to RCSB for 20 years

Ken Burnett's Bhopal ad. It was merely a list of facts but it raised over £100,000.

must appear in the immediate wake of the news coverage. Three days later will be too late – as many charities advertising on the Sunday after a disaster find to their cost. Move quickly or don't move at all.

Creatively, such ads can afford to be simple, very simple. If there is time to assemble a news photograph, use it. If there isn't, just rely on the news tag and try to use reporters' quotes from the field. The words 'Bosnia' and 'Shetlands Oil Disaster' are satisfactory headlines; you are making an announcement, not going for a creative award.

When Bhopal in India was turned into a disaster zone by emissions from the Union Carbide plant there, the Royal Commonwealth Society for the Blind phoned the young Ken Burnett at home and asked him to put together an immediate press ad, which he did in a matter of hours. I reproduce it here in all its less-than-creative glory. The headline just says 'Urgent'. The body copy is just reportage. It raised over £100,000 at a cost that I fancy was in the hundreds. An ad like this serves as a public service notice-board, for people want to respond to an atrocity like Bhopal. Giving them an ad by which to do it is not a process that need be encumbered with anything more than the facts.

Finding new supporters with press ads

We have seen the role of direct mail in recruiting new supporters. It is likely to remain the staple means of recruitment for some time to come. Sometimes, though, you can find new donors more cheaply with press ads. The emergency ads reported above are an obvious example but there might be others.

But you should know a lot about the true worth of a donor before you proceed. An acquisition cost of £30 through direct mail or press advertising may sound frightful but it can make sense if you know that the donor will likely continue with you for a number of years, will sign a standing order or covenant, will be a likely candidate for a committed giving scheme. There is plenty of evidence that donors recruited by press advertising are actually more robust in their support than those recruited by direct mail or broadcast advertising – perhaps because they feel that they took the initiative themselves, found their own envelope, licked their own stamp.

The child-sponsorship agencies rely heavily on press recruitment. It makes sense because the sponsorship 'product' is relatively expensive, allowing the charity to make an investment in recruitment that would rarely make sense elsewhere. An ActionAid sponsor now pays £180 a year, usually covenants that sum and usually stays a sponsor way after the four-year span of a covenant. The total worth of a new recruit can therefore be predicted with confidence. The number of replies that ActionAid gets to its well-honed ads is its secret, but their regular and familiar appearance tells us all we ought to know – that press ads are producing new sponsors at an acceptable rate.

I predict that there will be a revived use of press advertising for the new generation of committed giving schemes. Here again, the 'product' is expensive and the allowable recruitment cost can afford to soar beyond the traditional norm. But I think it will need a more adventurous creative treatment to optimise the equation and almost certainly larger spaces. ActionAid can afford merely to show those wide-eyed children in 20-centimetre double columns. Other charities looking for a sizeable commitment will have to apply new creative thinking to the process. They will almost certainly have to earn their way out of the small space ghetto with flair and imagination.

Creating awareness with press ads

Think hard. What exactly do you mean by 'awareness'?

Do you want to be as famous as Oxfam? Do you want your agenda to be as well known as that of Greenpeace? Do you simply want to go up a few points on a piece of spontaneous-recall research? Or do you regard such advertising as a piece of morale boosting for your current supporters?

The word 'awareness' has probably extracted more money from charity coffers than any other in recent times. It is usually a false god, demanding regular financial sacrifice, and most charities should stop worshipping it for they cannot afford to worship it properly. I think of the many British charities who regularly unleash a couple of hundred thousand pounds on the process. They hire a smart advertising agency (almost always one that knows bugger all about fundraising), they run a short campaign (almost always comprising large spaces and usually whole pages), they produce wondrous and thrilling creative executions and they wallow in a sense of new-found importance.

Sadly, it is always a private wallow. Twenty full page ads do not an awareness campaign make. They may impress the trustees but the public will barely notice. A regular press advertiser such as a retail store will probably take 20 full-page ads every week, spending tens of million pounds annually on the process. It is a foolhardy charity that pretends that it can be a contender in this expensive contest for public attention.

Awareness takes years to accomplish. If you want to achieve it by press advertising, you must be prepared for colossal investment over the long term. How much? I know of two major health charities who have indeed secured greater awareness of what they do and why they do it by use of press advertising. That awareness is regularly checked in tracking surveys and other forms of research, and there can be no doubt in either case that it has given a sound basis for grass-roots fundraising. Each of these charities has spent approximately three-quarters of a million pounds for the best part of 10 years on its awareness advertising. If you cannot afford this kind of entry fee to the process, you are best advised not to bother.

READ THIS YOU PIECE OF SHIT.

If you're offended by this advertisement, you should be.

Nobody should be treated like this.

Yet unfortunately, there are millions of people around the world who are.

For many, a verbal lashing is the very least they have to worry about.

In Brazil, for example, Amazonian estate workers face a punishment called 'the trunk'.

A man who hasn't felled his quota of trees, is stripped, tied up and left in a hollowed out tree-trunk for three days.

As if that isn't punishment enough, the trunk is first smeared with honey to attract ants and other insects.

In India, children face similar horrors. Kids as young as six are sold to work in carpet factories.

When the loom-masters can't find enough children to buy, they kidnap them.

The kids are made to work all day. If they slow down at all, they are not allowed to sleep at night. If they make a mistake, they are beaten.

One child was doused with paraffin and set ablaze because he asked for time off. Six others were so viciously beaten for just playing, one of them died.

In Nepal, slavery is just as widespread. Ten year old girls are abducted and sold into prostitution in India.

First, they have to go through a 'grooming' period. Stripped naked, they are locked in a tiny room for days at a time without food.

They are burnt with cigarettes, beaten and raped until eventually they become totally submissive. Only then will they fetch the highest prices from Bombay's brothel keepers.

Just as prostitution can be a form of slavery, so can marriage.

In many parts of the world parents still control who their daughters wed. Who they choose very much depends on what the groom's family offers in exchange. The bride's welfare matters little.

Consequently, there are many women forced to marry against their will. Some even as young as nine. One twelve year old Nigerian girl hated her husband so much, she kept trying to run away from him.

To stop her, he hacked off both her legs. As you can see, slavery isn't a thing of the past.

Nor is it just a problem of the Third World.

In Britain alone, there have been 1700 cases of abused domestic servants reported since 1987. Most of them are young girls from poor backgrounds overseas. They see working in Britain as an answer to their problems.

But when they get here, they are often treated no better than animals. Many are made to sleep on the floor and just fed scraps. They have to work an 18 hour day. If they complain, they're beaten or caned. Some aren't even allowed out. Some are raped.

The list of atrocities goes on and on.

There are still over 100 million slaves in the world. Each one probably has a story as pain-filled as these.

Anti-Slavery International campaigns for the abolition of slavery. We know that it's only by making the facts of these people's lives known and by bringing slavery out into the open that we'll ever destroy it.

Indeed, by lobbying and by raising world awareness of these issues, we've persuaded governments and the UN to tackle the problem.

In some countries like Thailand, India and Pakistan we've even pushed them into changing the law.

None of this would have been possible without the help of our supporters. They have sent letters and asked questions of individuals, companies and governments all around the world.

To keep the pressure on them, we need your help in our forthcoming campaigns.

If you'd like to be involved, fill out the coupon below and become a member. In time, we'll make sure no one knows what it feels like to be treated as a slave.

ANTI-SLAVERY
INTERNATIONAL

Anti-Slavery International, Stableyard, Broomgrove Rd, London SW9 9TL. Tel: 0171 924 9555. Fax: 0171 738 4110.

I would like to join ASI. £15 Individual membership ☐ £5 Student, Unwaged ☐ I would/would not like more information. Name ____
Address ____ Postcode ____ I would like to donate £ ____ Payment can be made by cheque or postal order (payable to Anti-Slavery International) or by credit card. Mastercard ☐ Visa ☐ Amex ☐ Diners ☐ Number ☐☐☐☐☐☐☐☐☐☐☐☐☐☐☐☐ Expires ☐☐☐☐

The epitome of the pseudo-clever 'awareness' ad. It would have made its creators modestly famous for a week or two in the advertising trade press. But it won't have done much for the Anti-Slavery Society.

Press advertising is an option and not a responsibility for charities. There are many major national charities who never seem to advertise in the press. But then, Marks and Spencer and the Body Shop never seem to advertise anywhere. Each of them is a reasonable role model when it comes to awareness.

Reminder advertising

Smith Bundy's Fundraising Advertising Monitor reveals the soft underbelly of British charities, the simple majority (94 out of 156, remember) who took 10 spaces or less during 1995. Unless they had a good reason for these occasional utterances, they were almost certainly wasting their money.

I have often heard the use of low-frequency advertising rationalised as 'reminder' advertising, the apparent responsibility of keeping your name in the public eye. As with awareness advertising, the practice confuses good intention with fact. Advertising is a mass medium or it is nothing. Frequency is critical. If you cannot afford it, then you should face the simple fact that you are achieving absolutely nothing with an ad that appears in one title every six weeks or so. For no one is noticing you. You are probably spending tens of thousands of pounds on this ritual. You have better uses for the money. Well, haven't you?

Products, services and events

To be fair, some of those infrequent advertisers will have a good reason for their sporadic programmes. They might be publishing a mail order catalogue, advertising an affinity card or promoting a fundraising event. Most of the WWF ads in 1995 either advertised a sponsored walk or offered its booklet on legacies. In fact, the two-stage promotion of legacies now represents a growing proportion of press ads produced by British charities.

They do of course create awareness as much as the larger and more florid awareness campaigns. And they probably act as a reminder. They will rarely produce any direct money of course. But they do at least have a proper sense of function.

Campaigning advertising

I sneered at awareness advertising earlier. But there is a kind of awareness ad that bobs up every now and again, which is usually produced by those smart advertising agencies I deplored, which occupies the whole pages which I questioned, which is probably destined for an advertising award. And which I admire totally, without equivocation and with a deep sense of envy.

I refer to campaigning ads, ones that take an issue and dramatise it with all the power and all the panache that good creativity can apply. I can easily rationalise my apparent lack of consistency. For what these ads do is to take a background news story, or a story that *should* be in the headlines and revitalise it in a way with which few newspaper editors would feel comfortable. They are doing the same job as the overseas aid charities do with their disaster advertising, but they are doing it at slightly greater

The ad that changed the public face of the RSPCA. I suspect it raised a lot of money as well.

ON MAY 2ND THIS YEAR, Norway began commercially killing minke whales. This was despite its own admission that the scientific "evidence" it uses to justify the slaughter, is wrong.

Next week the International Whaling Commission is meeting in Dublin and the Whale and Dolphin Conservation Society (WDCS), is determined to expose the Norwegian whalers for the fraudsters they are.

Can we count on your help to stop the Norwegian whalers getting away with murder? Murder of whales that may swim in UK waters too?

WHY NORWAY IS WRONG TO KILL WHALES

Norway has always had what it sees as "the perfect excuse" for continuing whaling. Scientific "evidence".

But now WDCS can reveal that this evidence is a sham.

We have a copy of a leaked letter, in which the Norwegians openly admit that their estimate of 86,700 minke whales in north east Atlantic waters is hopelessly wrong. The excuse this time? Computer "error".

The true figure is more likely to be in the region of 53,000 minke whales – a difference of over 33,000 animals.

So why is Norway still whaling?

In a cynical move to get its quota of 301 minke whales in before it could be criticised by the International Whaling Commission, Norway brought its hunt forward a month, despite the fact that many whales would be in calf.

Indeed, pregnant females are likely to be the main targets as they yield more meat and are easier to catch because they are slower.

The Norwegian Government has since lowered the quota from 301 to 232 whales. However, in open defiance of their Government and of world opinion, the Norwegian whalers have rejected the new quota, declaring their intention to slaughter 301 whales.

Officials in Norway are now desperately trying to justify the present kill by quoting their own scientists as saying their botch up (the one their whalers are conveniently choosing to ignore) only entails "small errors on the data programme".

But the agonising deaths of 301 minke whales can hardly be described as "small".

WE'RE DETERMINED TO STOP THESE MURDERERS, BUT WE NEED YOUR HELP

Here are some other Norwegian "facts" which might help to convince you.

Norway has always claimed a "traditional" right to hunt minke whales. But minke whaling on a commercial scale in north west Norway only began in the early 1930s – and even then that was in the face of years of opposition from their own fishermen.

Norway states its whaling is for domestic use only. So how do they explain that their own customs officials failed to notice 3.5 metric tonnes of whale meat labelled "Norwegian Prawns" being shipped out of Fornebu airport to the "Far East" in October 1993?

Norway decided to resume commercial whaling in 1993 for "scientific and fisheries management purposes". We believe the real reason, leaked to the Norwegian Telegram Agency by an official in the Prime Minister's office, was that it was a vote winner for the Government.

It seems rather too convenient that the Norwegian Government made the decision to [re]sume whaling just one week [after] an opinion poll showed [substa]ntial support for another [politi]cal party in an area of [the c]ountry where whaling [is do]ne.

[D]espite the latest [revelati]ons about their [figure]s, Norway is still [saying] it can be trusted to [monito]r its own whaling [activit]y. They can't even [control] their own whalers, who [are] whaling right now in [defianc]e of the Norwegian [Govern]ment. How can we [trust] them to control any [othe]r aspect of their bloody [trad]e, let alone ensure that it [is be]ing run correctly and [withi]n the law?

For a long time now, [WD]CS, amongst others, has [bee]n calling for Norway's [wh]aling activities to be [clo]sely monitored by [inte]rnational inspectors. So [far] Norway has resisted all [att]empts for their sick [tra]de to be opened up to [su]ch scrutiny. Hardly [su]rprising when you [co]nsider what they've [be]en getting away with!

LIES, LIES, AND YET MORE LIES

Norway has already proved that it is no respecter of international regulations on whaling. It simply takes up its own as it goes along. But then not surprising when it even be fined for the it is committing against whales right now. The whalers can never be trusted again.

WILL YOU HELP US MAKE SURE THEY'RE NOT?

Murder of the innocents: a whale foetus is held up for display before being tossed onto a pile at its mother's entrails.

Get your Bloody hands off our whales, Norway!

Minke whales swim in British waters too. Shouldn't the people of Britain then, also have a say in their future?

LET US SPEAK UP FOR THE WHALES

There's no time to lose! The serious talking at the International Whaling Commission meeting begins on the 29th May in Dublin and only lasts for one week which is why we need your support NOW. The Norwegians have already made it abundantly clear on many occasions that they intend to start whaling on a massive scale again.

That could mean as many as 2,000 whales being killed each year by Norway alone.

How long do you think it would take for other whaling nations like Japan to follow suit?

PLEASE SEND US AN IMMEDIATE, URGENT DONATION TODAY

We'll use your gift to campaign for a better deal for all whales and dolphins. At the IWC meeting we will confront the Norwegians and demand the following concessions from them for the sake of every whale still left alive.

1. Norway must immediately stop slaughtering minke whales in the north east Atlantic.

2. Norway must fully admit in public that they got their figures wrong and should not be hunting minke whales right now.

3. Norway should be subject to an unlimited moratorium on all scientific and commercial whaling. (Ten years has been suggested – we demand a total and final ban for ever!)

LET US KNOW YOU SUPPORT US

If you agree with all of the above, then we need to hear from you by Wednesday 31st May if we're to stop the Norwegians in their tracks.

The IWC won't meet for another year. How many whales do you think Norway will get away with killing in that time? This is our only chance. Don't let us miss it!

We are legally required to protect this whaler's identity. We only wish the laws on protecting whales were just as stringent.

SEND £25 AND RECEIVE A SPECIAL WDCS REPORT

If you can send £25 today we will send you a special, in-depth report of the case we will be putting to the IWC, as a thank you. Packed with facts and figures, you'll find the behind-the-scenes story of our campaign to save the minke whale from slaughter, a riveting read.

GIVE US A HAND

There's another way you can help us too. You can sign and return the "hand" on the coupon below and we'll use it to give the Norwegian whalers a message from the British public they can't ignore.

To get their hands off our whales once and for all!

DON'T LET NORWAY GET AWAY WITH MURDER!

PLEASE support WDCS with a gift for as much as you can spare today! Complete and return the coupon below immediately to: WDCS, Alexander House, James Street West, BATH, AVON BA1 2BT.

Thank you!

SUPPORT OUR CAMPAIGN TO EXPOSE NORWAY

The Whale and Dolphin Conservation Society (WDCS) is the world's largest charity devoted solely to fighting for the protection of whales and dolphins. Set up in 1987, we expose and confront those responsible for the needless slaughter and suffering of these precious and beautiful animals.

We do this by:

● Actively and vigorously campaigning for an end to all commercial and scientific whaling.

Just last year, we helped convince the IWC to agree to the adoption of the Southern Ocean Whale Sanctuary, dealing a mortal blow to the Japanese whaling industry.

● Remaining totally opposed to the capture of whales and dolphins for display in marine parks and working tirelessly to bring an end to it.

WDCS is currently helping to fund the release of captive dolphins in Florida. Now we're set to help release the first ever orca - Keiko - star of the film Free Willy, back into his native waters.

● Engaging public support for our campaigns to stop the deliberate killing of cetaceans, including pilot whales in the Faroes and dolphins caught in tuna nets. The boycott we helped set up against Faroese fish, has so far cost that industry £12m in lost or unplaced orders.

● Funding over 35 projects worldwide to aid whales and dolphins at risk.

In 1994 alone, Canada's Harbour Porpoise Rescue Team - just one example of a successful project supported by WDCS, saved 41 porpoises and one minke whale, from agonising deaths in herring traps.

WE NEED YOUR HELP

Looking at our many activities and achievements, you may think we have a lot of money. But unlike the whaling nations, we are not rich and we are not armed. But we do have one powerful weapon - more powerful even than the electric lances, exploding harpoons and flensing knives the whalers use to decimate whales.

WE HAVE PUBLIC OPINION ON OUR SIDE.

People in this country don't want the blood of whales on their conscience. Why should we stand by and let a small minority of people flout international regulations and continue to kill whales which don't even belong to them?

Don't let Norway get away with murder!

PLEASE REPLY BY MAY 31ST 1995

I'm with you! I won't stand by and let Norway do this to our whales.

Name: _____
(Mr/Mrs/Ms/Miss/Other)
Address: _____
_____
Postcode: _____
Telephone: _____

I enclose a cheque/postal order (payable to WDCS) for:
£_____ Please write in the amount of your gift here.
Thank you!

We want to leave it up to you to decide how much to give, but you may find the following suggestions helpful.
[Please tick the box of your choice]

☐ £10 ☐ £15 ☐ £25

Give this amount and receive a full report on the case we put to the IWC.

I prefer to give by Access ☐ Visa ☐
Mastercard ☐ CAF CharityCard ☐
Card No: _____
Expiry Date: ___/___
Signature: _____

Use your credit card to make an instant donation, call 01225 334511 NOW.

Please return this completed coupon, together with your signed protest and gift, in an envelope to: WDCS, Alexander House, James Street West, BATH, AVON, BA1 2BT.

Please sign your name where shown and we will put up your hand of protest to prove to the Norwegian whalers that killing whales when they know they shouldn't, was the worst mistake they ever made - and one the British public are not about to let them repeat.

HANDS OFF OUR WHALES, NORWAY!

SIGNED: _____

WHALE & DOLPHIN
CONSERVATION SOCIETY

Registered Charity Number: 1014705
Company Registration Number: 2737421

---

leisure and with significantly greater budgets. It is often an admirable social process for it shocks and informs us about things that go on in the world, evils that we tend to relegate to the back of our minds. Their function is genuinely educational.

And they can change the public's perception of the charity concerned. The Royal Society for the Prevention of Cruelty to Animals had been part of the country's social wallpaper for 100 years before it was seen to bare its campaigning teeth with a series of extraordinary ads produced by Abbott Mead Vickers. A charity largely believed to be peopled by ladies in flowery hats showed you a photograph of 1,000 dead dogs to make its point about the need for dog registration. The RSPCA ceased to be a 'nice' organisation overnight. It became a pressure group with regularly expressed views on every aspect of animal welfare, views that would be dramatised in press advertising and backed by adroit public relations and lobbying technique. And they remained the thirteenth largest charity in the country in terms of voluntary income.

Advertising this powerful will rarely be missed by the public. Not so much because they are ads of the highest quality but because they scratch at the surface of a public anxiety that is already there. The Whale and Dolphin Conservation Society can only get away with a headline like 'Get your bloody hands off our whales, Norway!' because Norwegian whaling practice has long been reported in debates on the subject. And the ad made sense because the International Whaling Commission was due to meet the week after. More headlines, more coverage, more noise… and the ad plays a part in the whole campaigning process.

But some news is always in the background, unlikely ever to give the charity or cause group that headline-based platform from which to mount an appeal. That is the problem so admirably confronted by the whole page ads that Amnesty International has run for the past few years. We have become inured to violations of human rights, insensitised to them because they are always with us. They also tend to happen, at least in their more lurid form, a long way from home. All in all, Amnesty has a difficult job to discharge. It can rarely report good news, it can only bring you stories of ugliness and unbelievable cruelty. And it can only offer you membership of the organisation. It is not a job that could be discharged in any conventional ad space, or through application of any of the conventional rules of the game.

And it isn't. The ads, always written by the brilliant Indra Sinha, tell a story at great and powerful length. The 'Shock horror' ad is a grim litany of the appalling treatment of Liu Gang, a political prisoner in China. The body copy must run to over 1,000 words, punctuated by subheads that are headlines in themselves – '50,000 volts through a naked man' and 'Forced to eat soap from a toilet'. The typography is a masterful demonstration of that little-appreciated art. The total effect on a newspaper page is devastating – I have often watched extremely unlikely rail commuters pausing when they come to an Amnesty ad. They pause and they read – from top to bottom. There can be no greater tribute to a press advertisement. And no more powerful creation of genuine awareness.

I rarely deal in superlatives but I am quite happy to record my belief that these ads of Amnesty's are the best that anyone has ever produced in the field of non-profit press advertising anywhere in the world. I say that not just in admiration of their verbal and graphic power but because I know a little of the response they produce.

For they *are* fundraising ads. Most cause groups would be willing to accept a pitiful cash return on such powerful issue advertising but Amnesty cannot afford to be so prodigal. It expects a 60 per cent to 70 per cent immediate return on these ads. And gets it. It gets a lot else too: the respect, however passive, of a public that knows it should be told things it doesn't really want to hear.

Shock horror.

Here, exactly as they were brought out of China, are three objects which have inflicted more pain and terror than you can ever imagine.

They are electric batons, smuggled out of the Chinese prison, where they were being used to torture prisoners.

The dirt on them is real.

The man who brought them out took a terrible risk. He was desperate to show the world what is happening in China's prisons.

The baton on the left is shaped for easy insertion into the body.

When the black button is thumbed, the three metal bands around the shaft become alive with electricity.

The chunky object looks like a curling tong, but when it touches you, there's a crackle of blue flame and a shock powerful enough to burn skin and damage internal organs.

It was made in the Jing Jiang Radio No. 4 Factory, in Jiangsu, one of many such works in China mass-producing electric truncheons, cattle-prods and other items, which they then proudly advertise in glossy brochures.

In Chengdu city, for instance, the Mensuo factory specialises in ironware: shackles, chains, handcuffs, thumb-cuffs and leg-irons.

Some of these gruesome objects are immensely heavy, others are ingeniously designed to cause the maximum pain.

This torturer's toolkit is used daily in China's prisons to punish those who have called for the democratic freedoms we often take for granted.

The torture of Liu Gang.

Liu Gang is a Physics graduate student from Beijing who took part in the 1989 pro-democracy demonstrations in Tiananmen Square.

One of the 21 'Most Wanted' students in China, he was jailed in 1989 and later sentenced to six years imprisonment for 'counter-revolutionary' crimes.

Liu is what Amnesty calls a 'prisoner of conscience', that is, someone locked up in prison for expressing his non-violent political views.

Not just imprisoned. In a letter smuggled out of China last year, Liu claims that he has been repeatedly tortured.

The Chinese Government denies this, but no impartial investigation has ever taken place.

Its denial might carry more weight if the vicious tortures Liu Gang and other prisoners describe were in the slightest bit unusual, but, sadly, they are not.

A catalogue of horrors.

We now begin a catalogue of horrors that some people will find upsetting.

Please read it carefully. The information has come directly from prisoners who want the world to know what they are suffering. Often they have taken great risks to get the details out.

Liu Gang was one of 11 political prisoners held at Lingyuan No. 2 Labour-Reform Detachment in Liaoning province.

Their ordeal began when they angered the authorities by refusing to admit that they were 'criminals'. Six were taken away to be tortured.

When the electric baton being used on Tang Yuanjuan ran out of power, the guard began kicking him with tough leather boots and broke two of his ribs.

Leng Wanbao remained silent when questioned, so they forced open his mouth and stuck the electric truncheon in.

Kong Xianfeng was attacked in a special way. The guards applied their electric batons simultaneously to different parts of his body and he started bleeding behind the ears.

When Liu Gang's turn came, they applied the electric batons to his genitals.

He was put in leg-irons weighing about 20 pounds - he wore these for several weeks.

Liu was also forced to sit without moving on a bench for as long as 12 hours a day - leaving his body in agony.

50,000 volts through a naked man.

On the second anniversary of the 1989 massacre in Beijing, a prisoner called Li Jie staged a one-day hunger strike in memory of those who had died in Tiananmen Square and elsewhere calling for democracy - many of them mown down by machine guns, some crushed by tanks.

He was stripped naked and dragged onto a stage where the prison's Brigade Commander shouted and blustered at him before applying a huge 50,000 volt electric baton to his inner thighs.

Two other guards gave him high voltage shocks to his head, neck, shoulders, armpits, chest, stomach and fingers.

Li Jie went into spasms and passed out.

'Su Qin carries a sword on his back.'

To complement their skill with electric batons, many Chinese prison guards are shackle experts.

They have invented several tortures with fancy names like: 'Bending three wheels', 'A string of bells', and 'Su Qin carries a sword on his back.'

In 'Su Qin', one arm is bent back over the shoulder, while the other is twisted behind the back.

The hands are pulled together and the wrists tightly shackled.

A prisoner manacled in this manner can be hoisted by his wrists and left hanging for hours, till he loses all feeling in his arms.

'Chain-shackling' is the science of cuffing a prisoner's hands and feet together.

One especially cruel method is as follows: find the smallest handcuff that fits the prisoner's wrist, then cram both wrist and ankle into it, using pliers and hammers to snap the cuff shut.

The pain of this torture is indescribable. The prisoner reportedly screams all the time he or she remains shackled, until silenced by hoarseness.

Screaming, of course, can make matters worse, if it irritates the guards.

At Mian County Detention centre, in 1990, one young prisoner was left shackled this way for several days.

He screamed and wailed all day, and all night, so loudly and pitifully that no-one could get any sleep.

The shackles finally came off to reveal, apparently, rings around his wrists and ankles of red, rotting flesh.

'The old ox ploughing the land.'

In the same jail, Xie Baoquan and another prisoner were to be punished for fighting. They were handcuffed back to back and a rope was tied around them. A group of prisoners was made to run with the rope, pulling them along.

One of the pair was able to crawl forward as fast as he could. Xie Baoquan was pulled along on his back over the rough concrete.

This activity, picturesquely called 'The old ox ploughing the land' continued until the concrete was covered with Xie's blood and his back was one massive wound from which the skin and flesh had been scraped.

He was put back into his cell without any medical treatment, his back left to suppurate.

Xie's cell mates covered his back with a cotton blanket which became soaked with pus from the wounds, and which filled the room with the stink of rotting flesh.

Forced to eat soap from a toilet.

Some prisoners were playing chess with pieces carved out of soap.

Spotted by a guard, they quickly threw the soap chessmen into their toilet bucket. The guard forced them to fish out every piece and eat it.

In Gutsa Detention Centre, Lhasa, Laba Dunzhu, a young Tibetan who had taken part in a pro-independence protest was taken out into the prison yard and made to kneel.

A guard placed a boot on his neck and forced his face down into the filthy water of the latrine.

Meanwhile, others beat him.

Laba Dunzhu died of a ruptured spleen.

She woke to find herself dying.

In Seitru Detention Centre, also in Lhasa, 26 year old Sonam Dolkar was being questioned after having been arrested on suspicion of being a Tibetan independence sympathiser.

Tiring of her answers, her captors stripped her naked, wrapped electric wire around her and plugged it into the mains.

Sonam convulsed and passed out. When she regained consciousness, she was lying in the same room. Her skin had turned blue.

Often she was beaten with electric batons. Once, Sonam awoke to find that her body was covered in bruises and that two ribs were broken. They had hit her as she lay unconscious.

Like Liu Gang, she was kept in leg-irons for months. The torturers applied electric batons to her face and every part of her body, including inside her vagina.

Eventually, Sonam was vomiting and urinating blood daily.

We only know of her suffering because when she was moved to a police hospital, she managed to escape and flee to India.

You can do something to help.

If you're as upset by these things as we are - and we're sure you must be - there is something simple and effective you can do right here and now to help. Join Amnesty.

Even in China, our voice is heard.

The stronger we are - and the more pressure we can bring to bear on the Chinese Government - the more likely it is that the torture will stop.

The more powerfully we tell the world of the horror in China's prisons, the more difficult it becomes for governments in the free world to turn a blind eye to the prisoners' plight.

This does work.

From other countries all over the world, we receive scores of letters every year from prisoners and ex-prisoners who have been helped by our campaigning. These include people who had been living in daily fear of torture or death.

For them, Amnesty's intervention has brought renewed hope and relief from pain.

Liu Gang is still in prison.

Years of torture had left him suffering from a prolapsed anus, haemorrhoids, psoriasis and heart and stomach trouble.

Although only 32 years old, his hair had started falling out.

Until just over a year ago, he had had no medical treatment and had been allowed only five baths in two years.

But since summer 1993, international pressure appears to have improved his situation. His family have once again been permitted to visit him and they report that he seems to be in better health.

Earlier this year, foreign journalists were allowed to visit the prison where he is being held, but weren't permitted to talk to him.

A letter to each of us from Liu Gang.

Last year, Liu Gang managed to smuggle a letter out of prison. Here is an extract:

"Handcuffs and shackles won't frighten me. Electric batons won't silence me. Force-feeding and brain-washing won't affect me. Forced labour won't change me. Solitary confinement and torture won't ever terrify me. Regardless of what is done to me, I shall continue to use all peaceful and non-violent means at my disposal to fight against tyranny and abuse."

Liu faced his ordeal with such courage that his fellow prisoners called him 'The Iron Man'.

He and others have taken incredible risks to tell the world about their suffering.

Surely it's impossible that people who enjoy the very freedoms which they are denied, could learn about their suffering and do nothing to help.

We're not trying to point a finger at you - this means all of us.

Liu's letter to us all ends with these words: "I have no option but to fight with all my body and soul. Please don't let me down."

There's a coupon immediately below this sentence. Please use it now.

PLEASE TAKE A COUPON

AMNESTY INTERNATIONAL

The creative aspect of press advertising

I'd like to pretend that the process of creating press advertising works to a different rule book than the one I offered on direct mail. It doesn't.

The AIDA formula still applies, only more so. You have exactly two seconds to catch the reader's eye. You are denied the solitary relationship that you enjoy with a direct mail piece. Your readers have not bought the newspaper to read your ad. They have bought it to catch up with the politics, read about last night's football, or do the crossword. Think of yourself as a fundraiser standing in the street with a collecting tin. People are rushing past you, averting their collective gaze. How do you catch their attention? How do you secure their interest and cultivate their desire? How, above all, do you lead them to action?

I will repeat what I said in a previous chapter about my apostasy in the matter of homespun visuals and kitchen-table graphics. Their days are over, their power restricted to those occasions when the audience will subliminally allow of amateurism because the need is seen to be urgent. For the rest, you are looking to slug it out with all those other smart and clever ads for cars and banks, with all those offer-led ads that promise beauty, comparative wealth, a sparkling new kitchen and holidays on palm-girt beaches. Being a charity gives you no privilege of communication amidst this print babel.

The visual will probably reign triumphant for some time yet. You can record its rise by comparing that Bhopal ad for The Royal Commonwealth Society for the Blind in the early eighties with the ad currently being run by the same organisation (it has changed its name to Sight Savers in the meantime). The 'Blinking Hell' ad from Smith Bundy derives its power not just from a catchy headline but from the marriage of that headline to a startling graphic that shows barbed wire affecting a pair of human eyes. You are at least intrigued by this image, startled even.

Read on and you can understand the imagery. Read further on and you realise that you can save someone's sight. The coupon is a logical point of action at the end.

An appeal in the wake of a Bhopal disaster could probably still thrive on the simplicity of that old Ken Burnett ad. But most of the time successful fundraising ads now need an increasing amount of that 'glossy professionalism' that we used to think was the mark of Cain.

There is just one point on which I wish to revert to the curmudgeonly mode. Coupons. Art directors, or at least the new wave of that distinguished breed, don't like coupons. They are a functional irritation in the process of producing great art, a bit like having to include a lavatory in a cathedral. This is how they get to be tiny, strangely shaped, absurdly mannered and altogether donor-unfriendly.

You don't actually have to have a coupon in a press ad. But, if you do, just make sure that it is easily filled in with the longest address you can think of, and by the oldest and shortest-sighted donor in the world. If such dull utility offends your sense of aesthetic, don't have one. Just make sure the readers can read the address of the charity concerned.

Buying the space. The most creative thing of all?

Behind every successful fundraising ad stands a person buying the space that it will occupy. What this person can achieve is quite the equal of what the creative team can achieve.

By this I do not just mean that skilful media buying can enhance the fundraising equation, dramatically lowering the cost of the exercise so that the chances of a proper return are optimised. This is a truism, though it is still less than totally appreciated in many charities.

But every charity advertiser should know the extraordinary difference that the size and position of an ad within a newspaper can make. That astonishing concentration of charities in 20-centimetre double-column spaces is no coincidence. It actually stems, as so much else has stemmed, from our experience with Oxfam in the sixties, when the efficacy of that size of ad was proven time and again (though the very best ad space of all was the old five-and-a-half inch double column next to the crossword in the *Daily Telegraph*).

But the point about the 20-centimetre double-column ad is less its non-threatening size – which may or may not assure donors that money is going unwasted. It is where those spaces go in the newspaper make-up. The ads on the front page of a broadsheet newspaper are always this size and you will very often find them on the back page. Such spaces are much sought after.

But the rules on ad placement are obvious. Right-hand pages are better than left-hand pages. Early in the newspaper is better than late in the newspaper. Avoid special-interest pages such as financial, fashion, or sport. Look for adjacence with parts of the newspaper that guarantee high general readership – the crossword certainly and perhaps the weather forecast, or the television listings. Never ever buy 'run of paper' unless you are truly desperate. You will probably find yourself part of an advertising supplement on Malaysian banking.

Powerful graphics and a snappy headline make a highly efficient ad for Sight Savers.

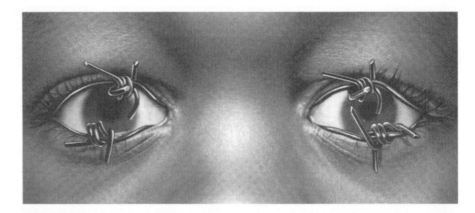

Blinking Hell

At first it's not too bad.

And it's easy to see how it's spread. Just watch a child for five minutes. They don't sit still for a moment. They're always poking their fingers into something they shouldn't, then rubbing their eyes with grubby fingers.

And that's all it takes to spread trachoma.

You only notice there's something wrong when the child's eye starts to itch and swell up

It's not terribly nice but it's bearable, and the infection will 'burn' itself out after a few weeks, leaving just a small scar on the eyelid.

The trouble is, it'll be back. And it won't just come back once. It will strike over and over again, with every reinfection burning and scarring the child's eyelids a little bit more.

In the end, after years of suffering, the eyelids become so scarred and disfigured that the eyelashes turn inwards, into the eye. Until, agonisingly slowly, you go blind.

Imagine, every time you blink, you scratch your eyes

Think about it. You've probably blinked a dozen times since you started reading this. What if you'd scratched your eyes every time? You'd be in agony and you'd be desperately trying to stop. But how do you stop blinking?

You may never even have heard of trachoma before, but 6 million people in the developing world are blind because of it. And millions more are carrying the infection. It makes life impossible for young mothers trying to raise children. Fathers and husbands can't work to support themselves, let alone their families. So the whole family suffers.

The utterly horrifying thing is, this suffering is totally unnecessary, because trachoma can be treated very quickly and cheaply in its early stages with Tetracycline ointment.

It costs as little as £1.20 to treat one person

But this is still far too much for many people in the developing world, which is why Sight Savers is asking you to help.

With £12 you can help relieve the suffering of ten young people with trachoma.

You can even help with the more advanced cases. £5 is all we need for the operation to turn back the ingrowing eyelashes, so they stop scratching the eye. A donation of £50 will help save the sight and relieve the suffering of ten more people.

Wouldn't you pay a hundred or a thousand times that if it were your eyes at stake? Please help by sending a donation with the coupon to:

Sight Savers International, FREEPOST, Haywards Heath, West Sussex, RH16 3ZA

Or you can call our credit card hotline (Access/Visa/Amex/CAF charity card) on 0700 01 42020

Delivery Guaranteed
WE PROMISE YOUR GIFT WILL SAVE SIGHT

YES, I want to help:

My gift is ☐ £10 ☐ £20 ☐ £50 ☐ £100 ☐ £250 ☐ Other £ _____

Please make your cheque payable to Sight Savers International, or if you wish to pay by Access, Visa, Amex or CAF charity card enter your card number in the boxes below.

Card expiry date ___ / ___   GU48

Signature _____

Mr/Mrs/Miss/Ms _____   Initials _____
(BLOCK CAPITALS PLEASE)

Address _____

_____ Postcode _____

Please return this coupon with your donation to: Reg. Charity No. 207544
Sight Savers International,
FREEPOST, Haywards Heath, West Sussex, RH16 3ZA

SIGHT SAVERS INTERNATIONAL
Reg. Charity No. 207544

Larger sizes? There is a dangerous hinterland between the proven smaller sizes and the exhilarating whole pages. Such spaces come in standard formats such as 28 centimetres across three or four columns, or 38 centimetres across six. The bigger they get, the more page impact you achieve, the greater the chance of a true solus position. But there is an increasing premium to be paid at every stage and you will rarely be rewarded for such adventure in response. The differential in costs between the standard 20-centimetre double-column space and these larger spaces can be threefold, fivefold, or more. It is not often recouped.

But it is always worth seeing how you can make *unconventional* use of press advertising. Weekend supplements were thought a graveyard of fundraising until charities found that you could buy black-and-white whole pages dirt cheap on occasion – Sight Savers has luxuriated in such spaces. And in the autumn of 1995, the Labour Party, through Evans Hunt Scott Eurocom, ran a colour ad in the *Observer* which used a plastic membership card as a tip-on – a brilliantly audacious recycling of a facility created for commercial advertisers. It recruited over 1,000 new members.

The Royal National Lifeboat Institution began an equally spirited advertising campaign in the summer of 1996, reporting its message and function regularly in visual integration with the part of the newspaper most relevant to the boating community – the weather forecast. Plenty of non-boat users will also see this regular deployment of the RNLI message in a fixed spot. It is a low cost campaign but it is another example of the value of taking a lateral look at the possibilities of newspaper advertising.

In all this, you will need a guide through the jungle as surely as you do with cold mailing lists. The guide is a called a media buyer and you find them in advertising agencies. You will find high-powered ones in those smart above-the-line agencies but you will find the most appropriate ones in direct marketing agencies, particularly the handful with true fundraising credibility. These are people used to dealing with the press on a daily basis, wheeling and dealing by the hour, spending their Fridays negotiating space for the weekend. The phenomenon of 'distress space', bought at the last minute, is one that often passes larger agencies by in their pursuit of leisurely media schedules, television rating points and colour spreads. Fundraisers can hop along like cheerful sparrows in their wake, nourishing themselves on what appear to be the crumbs of the media business.

The media buying function is truly a creative one. It could be the *most* creative one.

A 'tip-on' membership card. Who would have thought that the Labour Party could get this adventurous?

Loose inserts

In 1982 I convened and chaired a conference for the then British Direct Mail Advertising Association, now the DMA. In my search for interesting new direct marketing applications, I was advised to seek out a man who had started using loose inserts in Sunday newspapers for a development charity. The inserts had a clever leaflet/envelope format and were being used on some scale, indicating a thorough testing process. I located the pioneer concerned and he made his considerable debut on a British direct marketing platform. This was how I met Ken Burnett, then a braw Scottish lad, much given to tank tops and other affectations of garb.

Yet again the pioneering was slavishly copied. Soon, fundraising inserts began to fall out of newspapers and magazines throughout the land. Ken and I joined forces to produce a wide-scale insert campaign for ActionAid that tested regional edition against regional edition, format against format, creative treatment against creative treatment. These were the days when the more sophisticated print formats had to be bought from the States and shipped here in bulk, such was the conservatism of a British print industry faced with the demand for more than one fold in a piece of paper. By now the commercial sector had joined in. Credit cards, banks, building societies, retailers and mail order companies were all making heavy use of the loose insert and advertising sales departments were rubbing their hands at this unexpected surge in incremental business.

The inevitable happened. Response rates dived. I remember one insert campaign for Greenpeace that had been costed at a 0.65 per cent response rate. Suddenly we were looking at a quarter of that figure. So was everyone else. Readers were seen emptying their magazines of inserts before proceeding. They still comprise an informal carpeting arrangement on the floor of many branches of W. H. Smith.

The potential advantages of loose inserts are obvious. They offer space to tell a long story, they offer a self-reply format, they offer a distinctive bite into massive newspaper and magazine circulations on a regional basis. They remain the staple of a recruitment campaign like that of the Royal National Lifeboat Institution that runs into millions annually. Practically all newspapers and magazines now offer the facility.

But beware the Testing Nerd. It is tempting to make a long list of available and apparently pertinent media and spray inserts around them. Many magazines will look extremely relevant but will boast circulations in the low tens of thousands. A reasonable response from a loose insert in a magazine whose circulation is 25,000 will probably be around the 50 mark. Was it worth the delivery costs of the inserts? I only ask.

A similar inhibition attaches to national and Sunday newspapers. The regional testing facilities are mouth-watering and they lead many charities to try 50,000 inserts here and 25,000 inserts there. The response data generated must always be slender, the chances of informed rollout minimal. A lot of fundraising loose insert campaigns seize up at this point because not enough has been learned to engender greater confidence in greater numbers. It is statistically inevitable. Sadly, loose inserts have become a volume option – you now need to plan distributions in the millions to get full value from the medium.

Creatively, I would return to my earlier theme of giving the reader too many words. Just because a loose insert gives you the space does not mean that you have to fill it with a thousand of the things. The time is ripe in my judgement for a loose insert that eschews words in favour of graphics, that is prepared to make its case with photographs and purely visual devices, that even – heresy of heresies – uses full colour (WWF UK already does). The black-and-white charity insert is predictable, successfully predictable in some cases. But someone needs to attack the convention just as First Direct did with the medium – ironically by replacing the florid colour of a standard bank leaflet with the stern use of monotone.

Distinctiveness is everything with a loose insert. You are very rarely these days going to enjoy the privilege of solus distribution that we often enjoyed in the mid-eighties. Any charity insert is now going to be one of two, or three, or six pieces of paper, each of them risking the irritation threshold. You need to be clever to overcome the risk.

In buying terms, you must demand to be at least the only fundraising insert in that edition. Head-to-head competition with another charity or cause will diminish a percentage response rate that was always going to be a low one to the point of embarrassment. You can always wait for the next charity-free edition.

I used to say that a loose insert campaign should offer a unit cost that was a tenth of direct mail and a percentage response likewise. Both media have become increasingly congested since then and the variance on all such rules very marked indeed. But, if you want a rule of thumb, it probably still applies.

Household distribution

The blandest means of communication is probably just to stuff something through someone's letter-box – unaddressed, unnamed, apparently untargeted. The facility of 'door-drops' was long a province of the grubbier end of the communications' trade, much used by distributors of soap coupons and the like. In fact, it occurs to me that practically all political and electoral communication takes place through door-drops. So it's still grubby.

These days it gets to be called 'household distri-bution' in deference to the vast strides made in the sophistication of the medium, largely at the behest of the Royal Mail which has proved adroit in its development of direct marketing communication.

Household distribution now enjoys an honoured place on the media menu. In parts of Europe, it is probably the means by which most fundraising messages are imparted.

For it is relatively cheap. It offers massive targeting and testing facilities and it is a particular boon to anyone mounting a regional appeal. It has become the standard means of distribution for those 'survey' packs I recorded earlier.

The NSPCC has used door-drops for a long time. But until 1990 it used simple leaflet formats. They did not work – perhaps because a random leaflet is just about the most dismissable item you can send anyone. But put something in an envelope and the rules seem to change. Indeed, WWAV Rapp Collins, NSPCC's agency, adapted a successful cold mail recruitment pack and used it as an unaddressed door-drop. The result? A 57 per cent increase in response from previous household distribution and a 20 per cent better performance than the average use of cold lists at the time. The NSPCC's door-drop package at Christmas 1995 is a first cousin of its current cold mail recruitment. No less than six items were enclosed – including a decal – within a plain envelope addressed 'To the Occupier'. It is effectively an unaddressed mailing package.

Other charities do this on a scale of distribution – if not of production – that suggests the medium has grown fast in the wake of the growing failure of increasingly expensive cold direct mail recruitment. And I have seen recent experiments that put a regional spin on a national appeal and produce response rates that are at the top end of any reasonable presumption about current direct mail performance – at a fraction of the distribution cost. It could well be that household distribution has already overhauled direct mail as a means of recruitment for British charities. If that is the case, then the ugly duckling will indeed have turned into a swan.

This would be pleasing indeed. For the cycle of fundraising fashion would have turned full circle and

Fed, walked
and loved
for 12 years...

...THEN
ABANDONED

INSIDE: Your chance to help abandoned dogs like Mutley

Delivered by hand to Dear owner
Registered Charity No. 227523

VIOLENT END TO TOT'S
SAD LIFE OF CRUELTY
'The secret shame'

Child sex abuse reports
double but it is still
the 'tip of the iceberg'

THE number of cases coming to light of children
sexually abused almost doubled last year. The
cent—and that was only
...today.

DAD 'SHOOK
BABY DEAD'

A small boy was killed by his father when his brain
was shaken "like a blancmange in a bowl", a court
...day.

Starving baby too weak to cry

LITTLE Bobby was found lying on his rotting cot, too weak
to cry. He had never been washed—and never had a clean nappy
to the the six months of his life.

Boy 'kicked to death
over a dirty nappy'

A THREE YEAR OLD boy
died after being kicked in
the stomach and...

LITTLE GIRL WORE SAME
DRESS FOR FIVE YEARS

Police find children alone at home

To: The Occupier

The RNLI
invites you on
board...

Royal Mail

If undelivered please return to
Royal National Lifeboat Institution
West Quay Road, Poole, Dorset BH15 1HZ

Lifeboats

Yes, I want to help a child in
Brighton today

Name
Address

Please send £6
Or, if £6 is too much, a smaller sum: £
Or, if you can afford more, there is
sadly no shortage of children who £
need our help.
I will try and send in my donation by 30/1/94
£ ...... payable to NCH

Household distri-
bution – it could be
overhauling direct
mail as a
fundraising
technique.

we would again be confronted by the agreeable prospect that simplicity can coincide with cost-effectiveness. And there is another reason why I am happy with the rise of household distribution, for it could mean that we will increasingly revert to a medium that falls within the power of intelligent volunteers to manipulate. The old-style house-to-house collections depended – and still depend –

on the trudge of countless Doctor Woods to a million doors. It would be good to offer them a little more guidance and a little more science. It is now 30 years since Oxfam distributed eight million 'family boxes' throughout the realm. The enclosing was handled by a mailing house, the distribution done by tens of thousands of volunteers. It might be an idea worth revisiting.

CHAPTER TEN

I JUST CALLED TO SAY
I LOVE YOU

I have already recorded my own historic foresight in the matter of telephone fundraising. I said it would not work in conservative and sensitive Britain.

I was wrong. Dead wrong. It has emerged as a key medium for donor development in the UK and throughout Europe. I therefore devote a slim chapter to its astonishing power.

Indeed, talk to a telephone fundraiser these days and you will wonder why any other medium ever gets used. Take these recent stories.

- Christian Aid rang 1,200 new donors who had given to their emergency appeal for Rwanda – 100 of them took out covenants. Return on investment: 19:1
- The League Against Cruel Sports rang ordinary donors and asked them to commit to a monthly giving scheme – 64 per cent of those contacted sent a donation; 27 per cent signed a bankers order.
- The Terrence Higgins Trust rang covenantors and asked them to make a legacy pledge – 38 per cent did.

I owe these stories to Personal Telephone Fundraising, Pell & Bales and Rich Fox respectively. They demonstrate a medium of awesome power but one that many fundraisers keep at arm's length, or at least at the margins of the process for reasons of subjective discomfort and organisational disquiet.

For the telephone occupies a metaphorical 'below-stairs' status in the sociology of fundraising. It is a function discharged by companies who lack the corporate glitz of advertising agencies, where transient actors are given lines to learn, where the premises are strangely quiet before six o'clock at night. The nine-to-five fundraiser is often slightly unnerved by this twilit underworld, with its strange language of pre-call letters, number tracing, effective contacts and so on.

Anecdote deepens the negativism. Everyone hates getting a fundraising call. It always comes when you're preparing the dinner. It is always crass, intrusive, pushy. Remember the old lady who got a fundraising call hours after she'd just buried her husband? No, neither do I, but it's a very resilient fundraising myth.

Of all the fundraising media, the telephone is the one that constantly forces us to reconsider our basic conservatism, our habit of staying where we comfortably are rather than where we want profitably to be. Telephone fundraising probably now works more cost-effectively across a whole range of uses than any other medium. It really is about time we acknowledged the fact.

Move the co-ordinates!

British fundraisers tend to use the telephone grudgingly and in areas where they can no longer deny its efficacy. It has become a convention for covenant renewals and lapsed donor programmes but there are few signs that it cannot be used cost-effectively in everything we want to do, with everything we want to communicate.

Consider,

● Using the telephone to say 'welcome' to a new donor. The mailed welcome pack has become standard issue with many fundraising programmes. A human voice can probably do the job better and produce a quicker financial return on the process. It may cost five times as much; it is not inconceivable that it could produce 10 times the immediate revenue.

● Information gathering. As I have suggested before, people like to be asked questions. The telephone call is always going to be a better way of getting answers than the arid questionnaire and sometimes better than the self-conscious research group. If you are serious about wanting to know more about your donors, about why they gave, about how they feel about issues over which you preside, about the depth of their commitment... then the telephone will always give you a high quality set of answers. And do so more promptly.

● Campaigning. Earlier I was fairly rude about the worth of persuading your supporters to send postcards to jaded politicians and legislators. But the telephone sometimes adds a new dynamic to the process. Shelter's campaign against the Government's Green Paper on Homelessness in 1994 targeted 'campaign-oriented' supporters by telephone and generated more letters to the Department of the Environment than had ever been seen on a single issue – the Green Paper was swiftly withdrawn.

And Rich Fox lovingly tells the story of the campaign he ran for the RSPCA on an issue that few of us would have regarded as a social priority: sow tethering. Sows, female pigs that is, were being tethered. The RSPCA sprang into action.

They telephoned 6,000 supporters and asked them to contact their MPs to express their concern about the practice. 90 per cent of them agreed to do so and MPs received more post on the subject than they received on another high-profile event of the time – the Gulf War. This is how sow tethering got banned. I know you were wondering about that.

● For legacies. Yes, that final barrier of taste has also been breached. Just as we have learned that people do not mind being talked *to* about legacies, so we have learned that people do not mind talking *about* legacies themselves. The legacy leadership concept of Rich Fox proceeded from everything else that had been learned about soliciting a bequest. But it had the nerve to do the job on the telephone. The programme offered a pre-call opt-out letter – and was used by just five per cent of the donors involved. The rest were called, offered a public inscription of any legacy pledge, treated to a later service call and generally talked through what is believed to be the most difficult request a fundraiser can make. The concept was also tried successfully for a religious charity and a health charity – sometimes to lapsed or low value donors. It worked everywhere.

These are perhaps the furthest reaches of practical fundraising application for the telephone. For most charities, the regular use of the medium will be in more prosaic areas. But always the results seem entrancing.

The Cancer Relief Macmillan Fund rang supporters to ask for help in house-to-house collections, to take part in its 'World's Biggest Coffee Morning' promotion, or to renew or upgrade their covenants. 31 per cent of those asked agreed to run a house-to-house collection and 75 per cent agreed to become involved in some kind of voluntary activity. Over half the lapsed covenantors agreed to renew

Amnesty contacted 10,000 people whose membership had lapsed in the previous two to four years. 25 per cent of them agreed to renew and over half of them agreed to do so by direct debit at an average rate of £52 a year.

ActionAid has used the telephone since 1988 as part of their sponsor-get-sponsor programme. Existing sponsors are simply called and asked to act as 'advocates'. If they agree, they are supplied with a case history of a child and asked to recruit another sponsor from friends and family. Most of them don't – but they do tend to enclose a donation when they return the case history, a significant subvention of the cost of the telephone activity which underpins the entire programme. It is claimed that 18,000 new sponsors were recruited in this way in five years. From what I know about the lifetime value of ActionAid sponsors, the total revenue accrued must have been in the tens of millions of pounds.

These are all success stories – indeed they are all plucked from the promotional materials and presentations of telephone fundraising companies. Doubtless there are failures in this field, but they are as likely to be failures of nerve as of performance. I know many charities who run screaming for the exits at the first whiff of controversy caused by telephone fundraising. For some people do complain. They do write letters to local newspapers about it. They do alarm those trustees who are given to scorn any communications process that came after Marconi. But they are few, very few, these complainants.

And every telephone fundraiser tells me that there is one regular complaint that comes when you call charity supporters. It is the fact that the supporter receives too many mailings!

Enjoy the irony. I do.

Talking to people

That's all telephone fundraising is. Beneath all the necessary segmentation, the proper pre-calling courtesies and all the mechanics of fulfilment, there lies the potential enchantment of a personal conversation. This is why the telephone works.

If our telephone never rings, our self-esteem plummets. If my answerphone does not indicate half a dozen calls a day when I return from London, I pace the study and think myself a has-been. If my 16-year-old daughter fails to receive her wealth of calls in the evening, she mopes to her room, a social outcast. Phone calls cheer people up.

Simon Pell of Pell & Bales makes an interesting point. Often, he says, it is older people who respond best to a telephone call for they receive fewer than most and are glad to feel the more relevant and useful because of the call. There is certainly plenty of evidence that apparently low value donors can be sparked into greater activity better by a call than through the mail. It would be perfectly logical, for a mailshot is always an inert thing while a telephone call, however crass, is always a personal thing. Then, there is the virtue of singularity. A fundraising mailing will always appear in a batch of other mailed communication; telephone calls come one at a time.

But we should admit that many – if not most – telephone calls made in the fundraising area are indeed crass. To quote Simon Pell again, 'Tired thoughts and messages sounding more tired in the mouth of a bored caller.' The clash between the inevitable script and the need for verbal enthusiasm in imparting it is the classic dilemma of the telephone fundraiser. Even the resting actors and aspirant writers who so often make the calls are tested to the full if they are simply tasked to make the same scripted call eight times an hour night after night. As the regular recipient of their verbal entreaties, I would urge a greater freedom from the scripted process. We should not imagine, incidentally, that telephone companies are immune from concern about the creativity of verbal fundraising – an internal discussion document from Pell & Bales talks of creative space, depth structure and renaissance rhetoric. Such terms are rarely used in advertising agencies.

Again, I sense fusion between what I have said about direct mail and press advertising and what should be said about telephone fundraising. It occurs to me again how important is that sense of event, that need to give a communication urgency and relevance if it is to prosper. It may already exist but it can often be convened.

Of all the odd examples I have come across in this field, nothing surprised me more than the use of the telephone by the dear old Campaign for Nuclear Disarmament, a cause for whom I first marched in 1958 and which has survived an inevitable cycle of success and failure for nearly 40 years. The connection between the Gulf War and unilateral nuclear disarmament was not exactly a close one, but the sight of a multi-national army massing to take on Saddam Hussein was a troubling one for many who had lived their lives in fear of a world war. It certainly enabled CND to call its supporters during this time with the successful message that simply said 'Don't let CND die'. It thrived because people's anxiety levels made it a proper time to ask.

Political fundraising is a proven arena for telephone appeals. The British Labour Party persuaded many thousands of members to give by credit card before the 1992 general election as a result of telephone fundraising and the greatly swollen number of party members can expect more of the same next time. But even here, where the reason for the ask is so obvious, it often pays to be specific and to express the need with colour and with drama. These are excerpts from a Pell & Bales script for that 1992 election.

Last week our advertising team came up with one of the most effective political posters we have ever seen. It's so good and so positive that we think it will give us the final push we need... Have you seen it? Believe me, it looks stunning in colour.

...Because it's the only hope of getting the poster up, we're calling everyone back to ask for one last donation to help break the deadlock. Is there any way you could match your last donation?

... Believe me, we wouldn't ask if we didn't think that it will make such a difference. This poster will set the tone of the campaign in the last week and it could well swing enough wavering voters to help win the marginal seats we need.

Anything at all would be wonderful. We only need £15 to ensure the poster is up for 12 hours.

...That's brilliant. In that case, can you send your donation back with the form in the letter from Larry Whitty – so we can commit your donation to the poster campaign in the next two days.

I don't know how many Labour Party members solemnly believed that they were actively commissioning a poster display when they responded. What I do know is that this is consummate fundraising – dramatic, urgent, specific. Above all, it answers that question 'Why?' that I insisted on all those pages ago.

It also underlines an even earlier point I made. About not getting what you don't ask for. About the donor's willingness to give more if the time is right and the asking done properly.

For the people who received the telephone call above had already given to the Party's election fund just a few weeks previously. This call was made on the weekend before the election. It produced a 90 per cent response. Only the fact that the Tories won that election spoils the story.

What to expect

Telephone fundraising carries the highest unit cost of any mass communication. Call cost is measured in pounds not pence. Add in the cost of number tracing, a pre-call letter and two stages of fulfilment and it is several pounds. But it is the only medium where you can ever expect that most people will respond to your appeal. Not always, I grant you, but at a far more honourable rate than with any other medium. Simon Pell goes on record as saying that an active donor list should perform at 40 per cent to 65 per cent. Indeed, he offers a rather comforting band of likely response rates, agreeably specific in its forecasting.

A donor upgrade programme should work at between 20 per cent and 60 per cent; a membership renewal programme at between 30 per cent and 60 per cent; a house-to-house recruitment programme at between 20 per cent and 80 per cent; a committed giving programme at between 15 per cent and 30 per cent. These are obviously large differentials but they do help refine the process of determining likely payback. For you can of course test the telephone in small quantities of calls, a facility impossible with direct mail. You can even do it yourself – the NSPCC telephone programme is entirely conducted in-house.

And you can certainly ask for large sums of money. In the fast-growing field of alumnae fundraising a request for a pledge of £50 a month is far from unusual on a telephone campaign.

But it took Karl Holweger, director of public affairs at RNID, to dispel any lingering inhibitions a fundraiser might still have about the use of the telephone. Karl is both a telephone nut and a customer-care nut. His presentation at London's Direct Marketing Fair in March, 1996, used a glittering array of statistics proven by his own programmes.

He compared a 9.5 per cent response rate through the mail with a 30 per cent response rate from the phone. And an average donation of £13.50 and £26.00 respectively.

He reported a 0.1 per cent response to a covenant appeal by mail and a 10 per cent response to one conducted by telephone. A differential of precisely 100! And an average covenant size of £25 by mail and £45 by phone.

He reported that donors who had been telephoned continued to perform much better in subsequent mailing appeals than those who had not been called, 31.6 per cent playing 18 per cent on the first such mailing, 15 per cent playing 7.0 per cent on the fifth.

For the case he was making was not for the total and exclusive use of the phone in a fundraising programme. Rather, it was for the sensitive and progressive use of phone and mail in conjunction. Which is the sort of motto to which we all subscribe, but which we too rarely apply. In many charities the managers of phone and mail programmes are often different people, running different empires with different terms of reference no matter how frequent the ritual salaam to integration.

It is all very simple really. If you phone people they like you better and they give you more money. You can prove it as simply as the John Groom's Association for Disabled People proved it. It rang a group of supporters to ask them to watch out for its next appeal. Those people responded to the subsequent appeal at 32 per cent with an average donation of £16. The ones who were not phoned responded at eight per cent with an average donation of £14.

QED, I submit.

What happens next?

It seems to me that we stand at the same point with telephone fundraising as we stood with direct mail fundraising 10 years previously. The technique is proven, the technology developing fast. A fashion cycle looms.

It is a dangerous time for we risk doing exactly the same with the telephone as we did with direct mail. We could overuse it, desensitise it, betray another personal medium by transforming it into an impersonal one. As so often, we can look to the States to see the potential horrors of telephone fundraising. There, a computer can call you with a pre-recorded call. Agree to give and you are asked to tell the computer so that your donation can be processed. One company bases its telephone strategy on no less than nine successive 'asks', starting with a request for $1,000 and sliding down to $25 – say no to that and the question is 'But isn't there *anything* you are willing to give?' Tactics like these might just make sense on the bottom line of a financial equation, but at what cultural expense?

We had better apply everything we have learned about relationship fundraising to the next generation of telephone communication. In doing so, we need to acknowledge people's growing irritation with the telephone generally. The hideous invention of Voice Mail may be a bureaucratic good practice, but it is an infuriating reaction to most callers. The sound of a recorded voice telling you that you are in a telephonic queue punctuated by electronic Mozart is a familiar one for a caller trying to reach a public utility, but it suggests organisational incompetence rather than technological wizardry. I mention these things because charities have latterly begun to subject me to them. When I phone someone, I want a voice at the other end, not a recorded message, or a Voice Mail menu. I am not impressed by charities who hide behind electronic screens.

But, if we wed the technological possibilities to the power of the human voice, then it must be a fruitful marriage. There is now a computer programme that can whizz donor records on to a screen by virtue of automatic number identification. It will probably become a regular facility for those taking inbound calls. I just hope that it is administered by a nice, friendly person. Perhaps she will be called Mavis, for this is what telephone operators used to be called. That or Brenda.

We should be careful too, about over-saturation of the market and acknowledge the speed with which we killed the goose of direct mail, a goose that was previously laying golden eggs. No one knows how many fundraising calls are now made a year. Estimates range as high as 15 million in a country of 27 million households – the vast majority soliciting help with house-to-house collections. All this activity will be properly targeted, which can only mean that a majority of households will receive no calls and a small minority lots of calls. There will be an irritation threshold here as well. I already begin to feel it.

We still have time to optimise the power of the telephone. As with direct mail, it will mean making fewer calls not more, making them better, making them more personal, listening to people as much as talking at them. Longer calls, in other words. For, of all the ways in which we can communicate, only face-to-face solicitation and its first cousin the telephone give us the opportunity of dialogue.

'It's good to talk' is the slogan behind British Telecom's current advertising campaign. It will have been diligently researched and offers us a truism of great application for fundraisers. When the Labour Party started telephoning supporters in 1988 it was with considerable diffidence and embarrassment. How on earth could these hard-sell techniques work with such hidebound and doctrinaire socialists (the word was still used then)?

The Party took a deep breath and asked. The answer was 'of course'. 42 per cent of those called responded with a donation. It was a moment of modest historical importance in British fundraising.

One last point. The telephone may finally prove to be an *empowering* medium. As with household distribution, it is a technique which can easily be acquired by the committed and trained volunteer. In the Auckland offices of Greenpeace New Zealand, I watched the telephone team come in of an evening and overheard them calling supporters with details of a committed giving scheme. It was a process made more potent by the fact that the callers were members of that same scheme themselves. For they were Greenpeace supporters and activists. The telemarketing company had been tried and found wanting.

You can of course empower yourself. How many charity directors have ever copied that example of Guy Stringer's and rung donors to say 'thank you' on a regular basis?

All of them could do it. All of them should.

Why not start this Friday?

WHAT PRICE TV AND RADIO?

It was only at the back end of 1989 that the Independent Broadcasting Authority announced that it would be relaxing the rules that had previously debarred charities from advertising on commercial radio and television. It seems a generation ago.

Creatively it *was* a generation ago. The first wave of charity TV commercials was commissioned from above-the-line agencies who dealt in imagery rather than response, in brand awareness rather than direct selling. These commercials were the equivalent of the narcissistic whole-page ads about which I was previously so peevish. They had the same effect. They allowed the charities concerned the same wallow in self-esteem. It was later calculated that the average return on a charity TV commercial in 1989/90 was exactly 12p in the pound. Dozens of British charities had been involved and another piece of conventional wisdom immediately set in. Television advertising did not work for fundraising.

Until it did, of course. In 1991 the NSPCC assigned their direct marketing agency, WWAV as was, WWAV Rapp Collins as it has become since, to produce a commercial. It recouped its costs in full. In April/May 1992 a further test was undertaken. It recruited 9,000 new donors and produced a 1.79 return on investment. A mould was broken.

WWAV's fundraising commercials have become famous, rightly so. They feature regularly at British advertising awards ceremonies for they are much gonged. When they are shown, an audience that has been imbibing freely for hours falls silent and respectful. For to be other than respectful would be distasteful – these ads impel respect. And, in doing that, they evoke a fundraising response.

For there is no crudity about these ads, no production short-cuts, no shrieking voice-overs. Lighting, art direction, camerawork and cutting are all of the highest professional standard. The music may be Elton John or Nat King Cole; the mood is always sober, the narrative economical and powerful.

For the best of these ads do tell a story, do give you a set of pictures, which can be added to the repertoire of irresistible images of need that charities have given society. Who can forget the image of Ellie as her face transforms from that of a belligerent ill-treated child in black and white to a smiling thankful child in full colour while the final ask is made on the voice-over? Who can forget the neglected dog retreating to his shabby kennel as the rain comes down, or the RSPCA inspector arriving to cut the rope that tethers him? These are moments of true artistry.

But they are not the whole story. Watch any show-reel of charity commercials from around the world and you will see dazzling technique on all sides. Every trick of the film-maker's trade can be

WHAT PRICE TV AND RADIO?   173

used to depict need, to shock, to illuminate an issue, to create horror even. I have seen a cinema audience wince at a commercial produced to highlight the cutting down of the Amazonian rain forests. And I have seen an audience roar with laughter and delight when they realised that the funny little cartoon character who cloaks himself in a condom is part of an AIDS awareness message from the Terrence Higgins Trust. It is rare to see a charity commercial that does not have impact.

But deriving a fundraising response from such technique is altogether something else. As so often, creativity is merely the jam on rather dull bread. Blessed are the bread-makers. For jam looks pretty silly on its own.

What really matters

I hope WWAV would be prepared to admit that its triumph with the NSPCC commercials was as much to do with diligent planning as with the final creative execution. Maria Phillips, the creative director there, tells me that she and her colleagues still research up to six storyboards preproduction. And the target audience for that first commercial was selected after careful profiling of current NSPCC donors – elderly for the most part and profitably congregating in lunchtime and afternoon spots. It is still rare to see a charity commercial at any other time than off-peak.

For media planning and buying is the art that occasionally makes it possible to procure a cost-effective response with a fundraising commercial. Anecdote tells of one brave failure with a fundraising commercial in the UK's peak-time soap *Coronation Street,* an experiment never repeated. Fundraising television spots must be cheap.

It is a lesson learned simultaneously by commercial direct response advertisers. On some afternoon transmissions on Channel Four you will often see a charity commercial buttressed by a direct-selling insurance commercial and a commercial for elderly health care programmes. The same audience is being targeted – comfortable, decent, retired folk who are not at work. We have probably created the equivalent of the 20-centimetre double-column ad ghetto in the press. And for the same reason – because it works.

And there begins to be emerging evidence that television breaks new ground in recruitment, attracting a different kind of donor than the middle-class norm – the shift worker, for instance. NSPCC found with its first wave of commercials that only 20 per cent of television respondents coincided with its existing donor typology.

Not that television works all the time, even now.

The biggest risk of all

Scott Fitzgerald said that 'The rich are different from us.' 'Yes', said Hemingway, 'they have more money.' The same banality applies to media – all media are the same but some cost you more money. Television, being the most powerful and penetrative of media, costs you more than anything.

It is the biggest risk you can take in media selection. Many charities have taken it in pursuit of fashion and because they do not want to be seen to be behind the game. And many of them have lost a lot of money. Being of churlish disposition, I can only develop this into an outright negative statement. I truly believe that most fundraising campaigns on television still lose money. And that many of them lose quite a lot.

Unfortunately I cannot bring you the statistics to justify this jeremiad. I know of one or two spectacular failures intimately and I have heard through the grapevine of far more. But none of the organisations concerned has felt comfortable in sharing the experience with me. The wide canvas of DRTV is currently covered only by the daubs of the regularly reported successes. Failures do not feature. We live in a half-world of anecdote and mealy-mouthed rationalisation. 'It did surprisingly well', or 'A lot of people saw it'.

Again, the charities who know what they are doing are doing it and doing it well. Plan International now spends 80 per cent of its acquisition budget on television, using three different commercials. World Vision spent £581,000 on the medium in 1994, The British Red Cross spent £975,000 and Oxfam £1,062,000. These sums would not have been deployed idly by such charities. But, is it any coincidence that the first two are sponsorship charities and the last two relief charities? The fact of an expensive 'product' on the one hand or of an emergency appeal on the other has probably affected the response statistics as completely as it does in other media. (I should point out again that these are MEAL figures reflecting rate-card time costs; the charities concerned would have paid much less.)

But 34 different charities used television in 1994 and we see the same phenomenon as we saw in the league table of press expenditure, with an astonishing number of charities spending tens of thousands of pounds to buy what could only have been a handful of spots in an outer region of the country. Were they advertising a one-off event? Or did they run scared when a tiny test failed to provide a cost-effective dividend?

I feel obliged to be this negative about DRTV for fundraisers not because I am opposed to the use of television and not because I am opposed to risk. All I am trying to counsel is a proper caution in the face of a medium that has been much hyped. I also speak with some knowledge of the direct-selling sector where DRTV has still to make its point on either terrestrial or satellite channels. The jury is still out.

But it could be that the mould will be broken again. The convention of the 90-second commercial may begin to look quaint as the number of television channels explodes via cable and satellite. All of them will be hungry for material and charity-led 'infommercials', already popular in the States, could

fill programming gaps. Some charities have already become significant programme providers. Scope produce a television programme called *Disability Today,* which is shown throughout Europe as part of the BBC Prime Channel. WWF UK has persuaded the BBC World Service to run 55-minute films and three half-hour films on the environment in the next year. All of them will be credited to WWF and feature the famous panda logo.

But this is awareness and education, not fundraising. And even here I have to be sceptical – who will be watching these channels, which threaten ever-diminishing programme quality? For we are already targeting DRTV for charities at retired folk dozing in front of an old black-and-white film on Channel Four in the afternoon. Who will watch our infommercial on a minority programme on a minority satellite or cable service? I have nothing against couch potatoes but they tend not to have too much money. The only arena for successful fundraising commercials is likely to continue to be those channels with predictively large and loyal audiences. They already include several satellite and cable channels that are used by the likes of the British Red Cross and Plan International.

Not for the first time, fundraisers will have to distinguish between awareness and fundraising. As with press advertising, charities are unlikely to be able to afford the entry fee to the process of true awareness creation. Sadly, many will continue to try. Television is a very seductive medium.

The future of DRTV

WWAV Rapp Collins has produced a successful model for a fundraising commercial. Born of its experience in direct selling generally (it remains far and away the largest direct marketing agency in Britain), it expanded the length of the commercial to 90 seconds. The call to action was emphasised throughout with vivid and regular depictions of credit

Your £15 could help
fund our Child Protection Helpline

Your £15 could help
us counsel a child

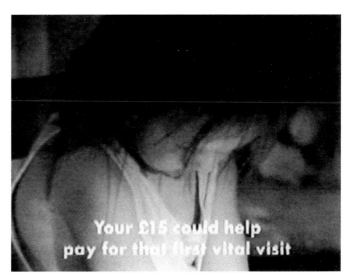

Your £15 could help
pay for that first vital visit

0800 444 222

NSPCC

VISA

NSPCC TV Appeal
Freepost London EC1B 1QQ
0800 444 222

Stills from WWAV Rapp Collins' famous NSPCC commercials, which changed the rules about fundraising DRTV.

cards, donation amounts and the telephone number. The commercial was flagged with an opening frame that announced the nature of the appeal and used the length of the commercial to report the need, explain the solution and make the call to action – repeatedly. It is a highly efficient model of communication.

But it is the slight variants on this theme that probably indicate its development in the future. WWAV's commercial for the Royal Society for the Protection for Birds pays full homage to the primacy of the offer: it offers you *Birds* magazine, visiting rights to all RSPB properties and a free bird table – all for £19! An Oxfam commercial, which seems to have been running for years, asks not for a cash donation but for a £2-a-month subscription. And an NSPCC commercial at Christmas 1994 did just a little to shift the predictive seasonality of DRTV.

For in 1994 fully 30 per cent of charity DRTV budgets were spent in the month of December. The 'Karen' ad artfully enabled NSPCC to place it successfully *after* Christmas. It tells a story again. The children are back at school and the teacher is asking them how they enjoyed Christmas. Most of the kids had a great time, but not Karen whose face dissolves into a series of ghastly flashbacks of quarrelling parents, an overturned Christmas tree, doors slamming and the misery of an unloved and lonely child. It is in black and white and is again immaculately shot. I just watched it on video and blubbed. So did lots of other people. It produced a return of 1.54:1 on investment.

The formula was merely tweaked here, just as it is in the Oxfam commercial, which so obviously eschews the traditional images of poverty in favour of positive images of development. It is these careful expansions of the DRTV formula that will mark its future. Perhaps the 90-second length will change, almost certainly to be lengthened. Perhaps the television fundraising 'product' will become the committed giving scheme rather than the one-off telephoned donation by credit card. I certainly hope

that someone will soon take a deep breath and experiment with other than the £15 ask level for it is becoming a tired cliché indeed.

But DRTV will remain a minority pursuit for fundraisers. You need two or three commercials a day for optimum impact, you need a four-week campaign to get full benefit from the process, you need to take great pains with the under-reported art of efficient fulfilment. You need to have the confidence to back a successful test with an immediate rollout – there is little point in blowing £50,000 on such a test if you cannot follow it, presuming success, with another £100,000 or so. All in all, you will – or should – spend a great deal of money.

But it is the whole process of television recruitment that deserves greater consideration. A donor who has responded to an urgent TV appeal will not be impressed by a laggardly thank you letter that arrives weeks later. The Oxfam commercial I have quoted is fulfilled with a pack that arrives two days after the donation. It also repeats the last frame you see on the commercial – of a girl running towards camera. The material is customised to the appeal that generated the donation, bestowing a greater authority on the whole event.

And there is one last negative. Donors recruited by television tend not to be mail-responsive thereafter. Perhaps the telephone (which television-recruited donors have already deployed with their original donation) will emerge as the best means of donor development.

Steam radio

My enjoyment of Classic FM is regularly impaired by fundraising ads. But then I guess that one's enjoyment of a classical music station is always going to be impaired by *any* ads.

But ours have become a ritual. 'This is an appeal by the XYZ Fund' they say with all the sonority that announces a party political broadcast. And what follows is so often a long and equally sonorous appeal, which has usually leapt from the loins of the DRTV formula. Radio advertising has a problem. It can't show you pictures. Words, which can serve as good commentary as voice-over on a TV commercial, rarely survive on their own.

Commercial radio is actually the fastest growing advertising medium in Britain. New stations abound at a rate that I don't dare quote in the knowledge that any figures I give will be superseded by the end of the year. They offer the fundraiser a multiplicity of audiences – young, old, regional, national. And they offer a far cheaper entry fee than television, for here it is possible for once to spend a sum in the low tens of thousands to some effect. In 1995 Sight Savers convened a radio campaign with Smith Bundy that spent no more than £7,455 on Classic FM and produced 376 new donors and an average donation of £17.35. It now spends upwards of £30,000 a year on radio recruitment, adding Melody Radio to the statutory classical music station and producing some of its lowest recruitment costs within a mature programme that includes well-honed use of cold direct mail, reciprocals and press advertising.

We have a lot to learn about the creative potential of a fundraising radio commercial. That very absence of visual materials is a challenge as much as an inhibition. It invites us to use sound in all its aspects rather than the mere deployment of the human voice. It offers us proximity, intimacy, drama. A radio commercial from MIND and produced by Burnett Associates, which I wrote with Marc Nohr there, depicted anguished callers to dramatise the need for their new helpline. A Feed the Children commercial, again from Burnett Associates, has a field worker memorably reporting from Rwanda, in live conversation with Marc Nohr.

These are simple games to play for they merely reflect the conventions of much radio news coverage. But they are altogether more powerful than the simple verbal message. Listen to the *Week's Good Cause,* the BBC's old warhorse of a charity spot that is still to be heard on Sunday mornings. No matter how sparkling the personality delivering the appeal, it is always dire and predictable – a mass of verbal clichés strung together to occupy the time. It raises pitiful amounts of money these days.

For just as we are now a society of visual sophisticates, so are we a society of aural sophisticates. A football commentary on radio is now punctuated by commentary from other grounds. An arts programme on radio will use soundbites from plays, films and concerts. Disc jockeys now chatter over the music that they once merely played. And everything you hear is punctuated by station announcements, trailers and general sonic irritation. It is another babel in which the fundraiser has to ask for money. Many radio advertisers have evolved their own 'sonic logo' – a jingle or theme tune that identifies the advertiser. Charities have yet to do this. They will probably do so as the need for aural distinctiveness becomes apparent.

Some might argue that the babel makes it sensible for radio charity appeals to stay simple and stay verbal. Sometimes perhaps. A radio commercial making an emergency appeal can rely on the authoritative recitation of the facts just as much as the equivalent press ad – indeed too much production trickery would demean the message. But for most routine appeals for support, it must be worth plundering the exciting and rarely used box of tricks used by other radio advertisers. Sound effects certainly, music possibly, humour even. For there are certain things you can do with radio advertising that you cannot do with any other medium. You can actually use silence to great dramatic effect. Listen to any good radio play to see how.

I regard radio advertising as an area of huge untapped potential for the fundraiser. I am as positive about it as I am negative about television. And it is cost that shades these two judgments. Radio gives you targeting, testing facilities, huge audiences, frequency (you can still get dozens of spots for £10,000), low production costs, pretty immediate access and the ability to change a creative message on a daily basis. Above all, it gives you the chance to experiment creatively at a reasonable rate. I think the best is yet to come.

We shall need to experiment more, taking charity commercials beyond those first few stations whose worth has been proven. We shall need to think of some smart way of finding a response mechanism for that considerable number of listeners who are at their car steeringwheel while listening. We shall certainly need to evolve a more sensitive means of fulfilment, moving beyond a telephone number that merely receives a donation and offering respondents dialogue as well as acknowledgement.

But all this is possible at a lower cost of experimentation than is practically possible in press advertising, in direct mail, or in television. One day soon a charity will redefine the process of radio advertising as dramatically as Oxfam did with press advertising all those years ago. I look forward to seeing it. Or rather, hearing it.

CHAPTER TWELVE

WORKING WITH SUPPLIERS

This is a short section. But it would be daft to write at this length about fundraising creativity without taking a brisk look at the help you may need to exert the lessons I have tried to offer.

I must declare an interest. I have forever been an agency man. Though I have worked with hundreds of charities and cause groups in 20 or so countries round the world, my mode has always been that of supplier. In my sere and yellow years I remain just that – an agency hack. If you notice the occasional twinge of anguish in the next few pages, you can attribute it to 30-odd years before the agency mast.

For agencies, consultants and suppliers generally are often seen as parasites on the body of fundraising. Mythology has them growing rich and corpulent while the charity-wallah remains the soul of dutiful integrity, monkish or nunnish, penurious always. The supplier is the one in the Armani suit. The charity-wallah is the one in the anorak.

The facts deserve recall. Most senior British fundraisers these days earn quite as much money as their supplier counterparts. They also enjoy comparative job security. Agencies and consultancies wax and wane and tend to die early. Charities never die. Very few advertising agencies that were around in the sixties still exist. All the charities do.

I will not elaborate the point. But there is still plenty of evidence that the imbalance of respect between charity client and charity supplier poisons many relationships that should be more fruitful. A client forever fearful that he or she is being ripped off is likely to remain wary of every aspect of the relationship. How can a test mailing cost so much? Who is really paying for all those lunches? How can their managing director afford that new BMW?

I'll let you into a little secret. Suppliers – and especially agencies – are poor, quavering, fearful sets of individuals. Their financial performance is often abysmal by most standards of commerce and the individuals concerned are unlikely to be building private fortunes – hence the occasional BMW when things look good. They live on hope – the place on a pitch list, the success of a presentation, the odd acceptance of a lunch date after a spot of networking. They work ferociously hard because they have to, because they are often the last ones down the line of production and distribution. They are in total, continuing and awestruck fear of all their clients every day of their lives.

It is this sad rabble that clients often think inhabit a world of wealth, power and esteem. The converse is true, at least in part. Clients have all the power – especially the financial power. Show me an agency with financial reserves as great as that of the average charity client – and muse over the ethics of not paying the agency promptly.

But clients rarely use this power properly. In selecting a supplier, they often behave like coquettes, circling the sad rabble with dropped handkerchieves and come hither body language. In using a supplier, they often appear bemused by the nature of the agency service. In dismissing a supplier, they often behave whimsically. When I have lost such clients in the past, it has often been at the peak of service performance – but there seems to come a time when the apparent need for a new set of faces transcends any objective assessment of performance.

The rules of the game should be transparent.

1. Decide what help you want.
2. Decide who can help you.
3. Vet the candidates.
4. Choose one and give it the job.
5. Let the organisation do the job.
6. Allow it to work profitably.
7. If it succeeds, say thank you.
8. If it fails, fire it.

So, what help do you want?

It could be none. I know of charities where perfectly professional fundraising programmes are conducted from within the payroll. A printer or a mailing house may be occasionally needed but nothing more overwrought.

Most charities, though, need someone at some stage. It might be purely creative help, the ability to write and design a mailing pack, an ad, or a poster. If the need is occasional, the most cost-effective solution will probably be a one person creative service or a consultancy. Always make sure, though, that the appointee knows about fundraising. Most creatives don't. It is a specialist art.

As your needs grow – either in terms of regularity or in terms of plurality – you will begin to need a more formal commercial relationship. Advertising agencies beckon. You have a wide choice of rabbles.

If your programme has a heavy direct marketing component, you are wasting your time talking to anyone else but a direct marketing agency. Even here you could be wasting your time, for few direct marketing agencies know anything about fundraising. In Britain this gives you the choice of a couple of dozen reputable suppliers. It is quite enough to meet your needs.

Now, select. In *Dear Friend,* an American textbook on direct mail fundraising by Lautman and Goldstein, a valuable chapter on choosing a supplier lists these six key questions to be answered.

1. Does our cause philosophically mesh with your firm?

There is no point in being silly about this. Agencies inevitably take on the characteristics of their proprietors and management, just as dogs start to look like their owners. Some will move in 'progressive' political circles and others will have a client list that better reflects captains of industry and the like. A cancer charity is unlikely to be relaxed with an agency that works for a tobacco firm. My own agency would never have taken on the Conservative Party – and would never have been asked. Comfort is a mutual process.

2. How do you charge?

Which is probably the key question because clients seem either uninterested in the subject, or dazzled by the nuances of agency remuneration. Like is rarely compared with like in this field.

It should be easy to say how much it costs to produce a mailing pack. It should be, but it isn't. How can you quantify five sets of revisions and authors corrections at every stage of setting? How much should you pay if the work stinks? This is so often the friction field of an agency/client relationship. Mutual respect and understanding can ease the pain but it still should mean a more formal agreement on who pays as work changes.

If the work is continuous, if the work demands a true and regular partnership, if you need the strategy of the process as much as the execution, then the agency should be receiving a basic annual fee. This in itself will give them a cushion against which to bounce the inevitable accidents of approval and disapproval. But it also gives them a feeling of commitment, the sense that they are senior partners in your fundraising programme and not just occasional contributors to it. I would not these days agree to offer a full-agency service to any client who havered at the thought of a basic retainer.

For the client runs a considerable risk in denying such a relationship. Most agencies still make most of their money on commissions and mark-ups. In other words, the more they can persuade the client to spend, the more money they make. This can be dangerous, very dangerous, in fundraising. A good agency should often persuade the client *not* to spend money and they should not feel financially challenged when they offer such ideological largesse.

But there will always be commissions and mark-ups and they should be clarified in advance. Should the agency hang on to all its advertising commissions or should it pass on a percentage? What will be the precise mark-up on production work controlled by the agency? All these things should be clarified in advance and all of them should be contractual between the two parties. What's in the basic fee and what's not? How many agency hours are predicted to mount a campaign? Who pays travel costs?

Both parties need a menu of explicit financial agreement, the tighter the better. And both parties need regular budgetary control as the relationship matures lest things get too sloppy. Burnett Associates must send out dozens of estimates a week, often for dumb things like 2,000 envelopes. It is doubtless tiresome but it is good discipline and proper courtesy.

The potential client should always be prurient in advance about the supplier's charging practices.

The potential agency should always be totally candid in the face of the prurience.

One last observation on charging by suppliers. If the supplier offers to work for nothing, look for the exit sign. Suppliers are not part of the voluntary sector in this sense. The promise of free creative work in particular should have you studying the production bills with great care. *Pro bono* are two very deceptive words.

3. Who are your clients?

No problems here, for the supplier is going to bend your ear with their names anyway. But, why not take it a stage further? Ask for permission to approach those clients direct and ask supplementary questions. What's good, what's bad, what's brilliant, what's insufferable? Always tell the supplier if you intend to do this. It is good manners.

4. How long have you been in business?

This is probably more important in the United States than it is here, for they worship more fully at the shrine of corporate longevity.

But if a supplier has been around for a few years, it does indicate a certain professional stability and a certain greater experience. Remember though, that good people are breaking away from older suppliers all the time to start their own businesses. Don't dismiss them because they are corporately junior. Maurice Saatchi's outfit is technically a newcomer but you'd have a reasonable expectation of professionalism.

5. Who will work on my campaign?

Much more important, this. Famously, agency presentations are headed up by high-profile proprietors who melt away after the pitch to be replaced by unknown nerds. There is no need for this in the size of supplier company that is relevant in fundraising. Always feel free to ask these questions explicitly. Who will write for you? Who will be the art director? Who will manage your business? It is the client's right not just to ask such questions but to demand some time with members of the putative account team. They are going to have to work closely with the client and there is nothing self-conscious about interviewing them accordingly.

6. May I see samples of your work?

Again, no problem – the supplier is probably willing to bang on about previous work until the pubs open. Know, however, that what you will hear will always be success stories. Make a nuisance of yourself. Tell them – but tell them in advance – that you want to hear about some failures as well.

Failures are often as indicative as successes – we all have them and we would all benefit more if we shared them.

Meetings, bloody meetings

I always used to say that meetings were what you were doing when you weren't working. They remain the regular ceremonial of the client/supplier relationship and a terrifying abuse of everyone's precious time. The average fundraiser now spends most of his/her time in meetings. Everyone knows there are too many meetings, no one does anything about it. This is why commuter trains are now full of people working – they have been in meetings all day.

The achievement of a meeting is often a poor return on the cost of assembling the audience. For many of the people at a meeting usually form an audience – they contribute little except their presence, they make simultaneous notes in similar notebooks, they nod and smile.

Office diplomacy and personal sensitivities are usually responsible for swelling the meeting audience. Benjy needs to be there if Sharon is invited and Malcolm from planning needs to be there in case Wendy from donor development says anything daft.

All I can suggest is wariness in the face of this familiar phenomenon, for meetings have a habit of multiplying like rabbits. And meetings cost money. If the charge-out rates of six agency people are £60 an individual hour, then the actual cost of having all of them in a whole-day meeting is over £2,500. Match these numbers with a client team and you are evoking an event that somehow is costing the charity thousands of pounds. Was it worth it?

At least work out the terms of reference of a meeting and be prepared to admit that they are not working cost-effectively, or that they could work better. Otherwise they merely become a ritual and a tiresome one. A well-planned monthly meeting, punctuated by regular personal communication in between and with an explicit set of objectives, should be all you need. Always find room in these meetings for some liberated discussion on what might be rather than what is. A meeting should be able to explore new ideas as well as monitor existing ones.

If creative work is to be discussed, the creative team members should always be there. They should always receive a brief direct and always have the responsibility of explaining themselves and their work when the ideas are presented. Account managers will always do this diffidently and imperfectly, no matter how good a sales technique they may have acquired.

Above all, insist that both parties prepare properly for meetings. There is nothing worse than a ritual gathering of senior people where no one has read carefully produced papers (or had no time to) and where everyone flounders for three hours to sustain the ceremony.

How to approve creative work

Quickly.

Most clients agonise over creative work. They feel a responsibility to worry about every nuance of the mailing pack or the ad, to declaim a point of view lest their clienthood is seen to be less than virile. The psychology of a meeting is such that people start agreeing with meaningless points of view. A whole negative and useless momentum starts. It is rarely productive or helpful. It goes like this.

Senior client: I like it a lot, but I'm not quite comfortable with this headline. And I think the pictures could be larger.

Less-than-senior client: I think I agree with that. Actually I think we could have chosen better pictures.

Really smart junior client: And there's no mention of our new policy on community development. Was this deliberate on the part of the agency?

Agency hack: Er, er...

Senior client: I certainly think that community development should be in. And we should make more of GiftAid as well. Come to think of it, it's very big – isn't it?

Less-than-senior client: Just what I was going to say. I think it's too big, much too big. And do we really need the second colour?

And so it goes. The client would be more helpful if he/she just said, 'I don't like it. Do it again'. Posturing and role playing rarely make a positive contribution to good creative work. I think of the long lost client who would narrow his eyes every time he was presented with a visual and say 'Now, what is this envelope really *saying* to me?' It was the sort of thing he thought he ought to say. In fact it marked him out as a complete prat.

Anyone approving creative work has only three questions to answer.

1. Is it accurate?
2. Is it on brief?
3. Does it coincide with the budget for the job?

All the rest is subjectivity. And there is little point in trading subjectivity with people you have hired to do a specialist job. If the doctor diagnoses an ailment and prescribes a course of antibiotics, you do not question the judgement and engage the quack in endless discussions about whether the ailment might really be mumps rather than a broken ankle. If the

lawyer suggests a certain course of legal action you do not idly demand a treatise on case law precedent. No one should pretend that the professionalism of the agency hack is in the same class as these worthier trades, but fundraising suppliers do deserve a version of the same trust. As I say, if they do not prove that they deserve the trust, fire them.

For they are not always right. And they are not always successful. But the client always has the power to rectify this situation. Believe me, all I'm trying to do here is to save you time.

But suppliers posture too

I have already begun to personify the supplier as the sort of advertising agency with which I am most familiar. There are other breeds. You will probably need them – list brokers, database specialists, corporate design firms, maybe media buyers.

Don't let your suppliers posture beyond their means. A full-service agency will boast creative, production and media departments, but even this panoply of experience may not always meet your needs sufficiently. Does the media department have experience in broadcast media for example? Can the production department deal with complex print formats? Be prepared to ask these needling questions and hire additional suppliers if the answers are less than convincing.

Suppliers do not know everything and should not be allowed to pretend that they do. It is likely that your database expertise will be superior to the supplier's. It is likely that the specialist art of telephone fundraising demands a specialist supplier. Similarly with reciprocal mailings. Agencies can co-ordinate these functions, can buy these services for you. But they are not the prime sources of supply.

And apply the same worldliness the other way around. Don't let smaller suppliers pretend that they are generalists. A mailing house proffering creative services usually has a freelance team on occasional tap. A list broker who claims expertise in above-the-line media buying usually has a mate at a friendly agency. Very few suppliers are prepared to admit technical inadequacy. Show them a budget figure and they have an awful habit of slavering at the noughts.

The two cultures

I offer you a paradox: charities change more continuously and profoundly than suppliers.

The supplier toils on year after year, doing broadly the same things in the same way. The client list grows or refines but, in these troubling times, staff turnover is a lot less than it used to be.

It is the charities who have become more volatile. Staff turnover has become marked in the last few years as salary levels have increased dramatically throughout the sector. Reorganisation and restructuring seem to be a permanent factor in many charities – one year's decentralisation followed by another year's centralisation. Regional fundraising reports to the director of communications, then it reports to the new regional fundraising director, then the regional fundraising director becomes the deputy director of communications with special new responsibilities for public relations (regional) and education (national). Does this sound familiar?

Then there is the computer system, which is always perennially outmoded in any charity I have ever known. A new system is coming on stream next year. A new system is always coming on stream *every* year. Yours too?

Even the priorities of the organisation can change dramatically, usually as a result of a working party which produces a report with a big title like 'Toward the Millennium: A Mid-Term Strategy Plan for the XYZ Fund'. This is entirely proper, for a charity should examine what it is doing on a regular basis. All I can ask is that charities try to explain all such changes to their suppliers. For it is they who seem forever in flux and not the suppliers.

Sue Wilkinson of the National Trust gave me a wonderful quote on all this.

We trained hard; but it seems that every time we were beginning to form into teams, we would be reorganised. I was to learn later in life that we tend to meet any new situation by reorganising and a wonderful method it can be for creating the illusion of progress while producing confusion, inefficiency and demoralisation.

Did I hear you say 'ouch'?
I didn't say it. Gaius Petronius said it. In 66 AD.

WHERE DO
WE GO
FROM HERE?

'The past has revealed to me the structure of the future.'
Letters from a Traveller, Pierre Teilhard de Chardin

THE TWO GREAT
PRIORITIES

The old Irish joke is probably politically incorrect these days but I'm going to repeat it anyway. It is highly relevant to fundraising.

Lost traveller: How do you get to Sligo?

Local Irishman: Well, I wouldn't start from here.

This peasant-like wisdom applies to much current fundraising practice. We have confused ourselves with our own tradecraft, blinded ourselves with pseudo-science, dazzled ourselves with minutiae whilst missing more useful and central truths. All in all, we shouldn't start from here.

We recruit donors expensively, attempt to retain them expensively (and usually fail), subject them to hysterical blandishments when they don't respond and pretend that all this aggregates to cost-effective fundraising.

It aggregates to no more than the unthinking pursuit of convention. Like all convention, it has merit. And like all convention, it should be regularly challenged. We can either decide that our job is to raise funds, or we can decide that our job is to administer fundraising programmes. If we are serious in believing in the first rather than the second of these two statements, then regular bouts of lateral thinking and head clearing are necessary.

It is in such a mood that I will take my life in my hands and suggest that there are exactly two great priorities in the next decade of fundraising throughout the world. They are each products in the sense that I described many pages ago. Their financial potential and their cost-effectiveness dwarf any other kind of giving. They are universal, simple, customer-friendly and utterly proven.

They are committed giving and legacies.

We need to concentrate more on each.

Isn't it odd that both things are seen as specialist subtexts of the fundraising process? Isn't it odd that fundraising departments will often have marginalised officers dealing with them? For to many donors, they are merely the natural ways in which to give to charity. Our denial of such simplicities is extremely strange. It is as if the Ford Motor Company were to give priority to spare parts and spend less time on making cars.

The common sense of giving regularly

It's time to deconstruct the fundraising vocabulary again. We talk of 'committed giving' or 'monthly giving'. The donor probably talks of a 'subscription' and increasingly of a 'bankers order', or 'standing order'. In other words, what to us is an advanced technique is merely a commonplace habit to the customer. We need to de-mystify the whole thing and humanise it, to demonstrate the sheer common sense of regular giving. We need to wean ourselves away from the theology of the one-off donation.

In the States there is a particular problem, born of the low penetration of electronic funds transfers – American fundraisers are always perplexed by the proclivity of Europeans to sign direct debits from their bank accounts. But again the American fundraising vocabulary often stands in the way of marketing vision – a 'monthly pledge programme' or a 'sustainer programme' is an intimidating description of a human habit best left simple. By the time there is a formal job called a 'sustainer clerk' (and there is), then words are betraying meaning.

Why monthly giving makes sense to the charity

It shouldn't need listing. But here goes.
● Because it gives you regular and more predictive money.
● Because you get lots of it.
● Because donors actually like it.
● Because it's easy and cost-effective to administer.
● Because it helps build supporter loyalty.
● Because it offers a good source of volunteers.
● Because it offers automatic renewal.
● Because it gives you a reason to stay in touch with the donor.
● Because you can still send additional appeals.
● Because it gives you a better base from which to upgrade the commitment.
● Because it gives you a natural track to legacy giving.

And why it makes sense for the donor

- Because it's convenient and easy.
- Because they mostly get paid monthly.
- Because they mostly pay their bills monthly – mortgages, rent, credit cards.
- Because it's easier to find £10 a month than £120 a year.
- Because it answers that 'need to belong'.
- Because it is seen to reduce administration and fundraising costs.

Faced with this dazzling array of benefits to both the charity and to the donor, it is quite astonishing that monthly giving enjoys a position fully half-way up the famous donor pyramid, a formal bridge between a first donation and the eventual hoped-for legacy. By placing it there, by insisting that it is a product somehow to be *earned* by the donor, we lose sight of the fact that it is the product *preferred* by many of the people we are talking to.

Again, step outside the fundraising ghetto to see the point. Why do some people prefer to take out a charge card with a store rather than settle each individual transaction with cash or cheque? Why do some people buy season tickets for a concert series or a football season? Why do some people subscribe to a magazine when it is freely available on news-stands? It is a combination of factors obviously – convenience, a certain desire for status, a certain commitment. All these are human instincts entirely relevant to fundraising. Especially when the donor is announcing that he/she has more disposable cash than most.

Charities need season-ticket holders. All evidence suggests that the season ticket merely needs articulating.

Who are the monthly givers?

I now believe that three to five per cent of any supporters' file will join a committed giving scheme if asked properly. A couple of years ago Amnesty UK recruited 550 committed givers to its 'Partners in Freedom' scheme at £20 a month from its top 10,000 donors. The Stromme Memorial Foundation in Norway recruited 10 per cent from a 15,000 list. And Greenpeace UK's *Frontline* scheme now has over 4,000 members giving at £10 to £20 a month – they are responsible for a full 10 per cent of that organisation's total income. The analogous 'Friends of Rainbow Warrior' from Greenpeace Australia had 25,000 members in 1994, giving an average $15 (Australian) a month.

Don't think, please, that people who join monthly giving schemes are automatically your richest supporters. They are to a great extent your most *committed* supporters, an important distinction. And, beyond that first segment of the truly committed – a segment that every charity has – there is a growing legion of people who will give in this way because of its sheer convenience and because it offers them better emotional reward. With regular giving you become an investor in the process of doing good, an explicit stakeholder in the process. I use these fashionable words with caution for I do not want to build a new theology on the foundations of something so very simple. I only use them to try and get committed giving out of its apparent closet.

For £5 a month, or even £10 or £20 a month, is no big deal for the middle class who form our constituency. It is the sum of money that your teenage children regularly ply from you when they go out. It is a round of drinks, a cup of coffee a day, a week's newspapers… and it is no coincidence that these homely examples of spending are regularly used

£5 A MONTH, OR EVEN £10 OR £20 A MONTH, IS NO BIG DEAL FOR OUR CONSTITUENCY.

by charities whose entire existence is dependent on monthly commitment. There are probably nearly half a million people in the UK who give these amounts in support of child-sponsorship charities. That one figure alone tells us about the scope for committed giving. It tells us, too, that we need to evolve a product strategy around such schemes. Just asking is not enough.

Belonging better

Sponsorship charities have it relatively easy. There is the child, the whale, the dog – these are specific objects of the donor's support, be they literal or entirely metaphorical. But even here, when a sponsorship scheme tries to move beyond the purely personal, it often founders. One child-sponsorship charity of my acquaintance has regularly failed to secure support for a village-to-village programme. And I doubt that NCDL's dog sponsorship scheme would work as well if the object was a dog's home rather than the individual. The donor wants Trevor, not his domicile.

Other charities lack the provenance of the one-to-one appeal. To secure regular giving they need to answer all those basic questions that I posed in an earlier chapter. Particularly the brute one that just says 'Why?'

Finding a justification for a committed giving scheme is perfectly easy. Evil, injustice, poverty, disease… these are the things we exist to combat and they will not quickly go away. The donor knows that subliminally. The donor should be told that explicitly. If you are serious about the environment, or heart disease, or poverty in the developing world, then you know full well that the one-off donation is a gesture to the process of combat – a creditable gesture to be sure but still a gesture. By proposing a committed giving

Components of the
ground-breaking
Greenpeace
Frontline campaign.

relationship you are merely suggesting that the donor should have the greater courage of his or her apparent conviction. Charter 88, who so often lets me out on a long leash, has profited by such apparent verbal aggression. Its 10,000 standing order donors are in place not just because they are good and committed people but because I have been regularly licensed to tell them that a standing order is simply the most likely way to achieve constitutional reform.

So the sheer *importance* of a committed giving scheme may be the only point you need make in selling it. Presume intelligence on behalf of your supporters and prey on it. Tell them that you need committed income to balance the books. Tell them that you need it to plan better and more cost-effectively. Tell them that it does indeed reduce your administration costs. Tell them that it will create an emergency fund.

This is what Greenpeace UK did with *Frontline*. To quote from a recruitment letter dating from February 1995.

> *Greenpeace* Frontline *is a major initiative that provides us with a much-needed 'priority fund' – giving us instantly available resources that we can turn to whenever a need presents itself: for example, when an ongoing campaign escalates into an urgent priority.*
>
> *The Greenpeace* Frontline *priority fund isn't a reserve fund. We'll spend the money as we get it because our campaigns are central to our work*
>
> *Priority campaigns funded by Greenpeace* Frontline *do of course involve taking a large financial risk. But we know from experience that taking risks when the stakes are high can produce dramatic results – results such as the Antarctica Treaty, an international accord that has saved Antarctica from oil and mineral exploitation for at least 50 years. By making this campaign a priority, we gave it all we had – and we won.*

There's a certain inelegance about this letter (resources? ongoing? escalates?) but its point is well made. Greenpeace needs to move fast when it needs to move and it will move faster if it's got the dosh. A few months later the Brent Spar happened. Presumably the support of *Frontline* members made a little of it possible. I hope so anyway.

But it is the final line of that letter that summarises the spirit of the appeal. It simply says 'It really is the most important thing we've ever asked you to do'.

Any charity can offer this promise of personal importance. For that is what a committed scheme implies. It is not just a means of raising money. It is a means of conferring greater status on the donor, giving them a greater role in things. It enables people to belong better. It is when we see it as a human relationship rather than a mere scheme or spreadsheet that we can perceive the full value, the full joy of committed giving. It becomes a season ticket to 'good'.

Creating the committed giving product

It needs a name. It will not thrive if it is just called the £10 a month club.

Greenpeace has *Frontline* and Friends of Rainbow Warrior. Oxfam has Project Partners. WWF UK has Animal Watch. All these names suggest a greater intimacy with the organisation's programme, a greater responsibility on behalf of the donor. The name of your scheme needs to offer a suggestion of both. But don't get into too much of a state about this. Product names have a habit of easing their way into the public consciousness – Esso and Shell are pretty silly names for oil companies.

Then you need to define its specific purpose. As I have suggested, this can often be as easy as spelling out the long-term nature of your charity's programme, or your need for free funds, or your need for an emergency fund. Sometimes you may want to make it project specific. The choice is yours. But there should always be a reason, one that you can explain with professional probity and with excitement.

Lastly, you need to define some sort of reward structure for the committed giver. He/she should not be taken for granted. Which is not to say that they need be regularly bombarded with goodies. A certificate or a decal usually makes sense and you should not begrudge these good people a Christmas card or an annual report. For the rest, you can merely offer them access to material that is going to be around the office – internal reports, special studies, a new piece of research. Inside information, in other words, whatever it takes to give donors the feeling that they have an 'inside track' with you, that they are confidantes.

Greenpeace *Frontline* did this with characteristic flourish. The videos were cheaply produced compilations of existing footage for the organisation has its own state-of-the-art studio and editing facilities, but they were thrilling to watch – genuinely exciting and informative depictions of Greenpeace campaigns around the world. Not many organisations would be able to replicate this degree of ambition but they could certainly offer the other things received by a *Frontline* member – the press releases, the staff newsletter, the campaigning updates. They all give the supporter that better sense of belonging.

FIND A REASON TO GET TOGETHER WITH COMMITTED GIVERS. THEY DESERVE THE COURTESY. YOU DESERVE THE EDUCATION.

And so does personal contact. Greenpeace was astonished at the numbers who turned up when they invited *Frontline* members to the first campaign briefing. They were also astonished at the human variety – nurses sat with policemen, middle-aged ladies with students... it was a dramatic depiction of how diverse our supporters are and how dangerous it is merely to scan them through the lens of the database. Always find a reason to get together with committed givers. They deserve the courtesy. You deserve the education.

Not all of them will need all this reward. In fact Greenpeace found out in the early stages of *Frontline* that members were becoming overwhelmed with such material and cut back the information supply accordingly. Give the new recruit the chance to opt out of the information stream. Some will take it – and you will save money.

And think about a special hot-line telephone service with a named individual at the other end. Few will ever phone it but it adds to the sense of being a friend at court.

How much to ask for?

When *Frontline* asked for £20 a month in 1992 it sounded like science fiction. In a world where the £15 donation had become a self-fulfilling norm, how on earth could you ask for £20 a month? Especially from supporters who were already paying an average subscription of £18 a year and often making donations on top of that? Especially when you were asking for the commitment on standing order ?

Let's say it again. *You don't get what you don't ask for.*

I now see committed giving schemes that ask for £2 a month, £5 a month, £8 a month. I fancy that these giving levels emerge from diligent research groups where respondents are allowed to say that £15 or £20 a month is too much for most people (an obvious but not very helpful truth). But I think that they also emerge from that strange caution that affects so many charities, the fear of being seen to be hysterically demanding.

But £15 a month is what it costs to be an ActionAid sponsor – and there are usually over 100,000 of them at any one time. An average sort of insurance premium is £20 a month. I repeat: such sums are no big deal for the minority of the middle-class supporters who form the market for committed giving schemes. The difference between £5 and £20 a month for such people is rarely troubling and it is therefore signal underachievement to ask for the lower sum. For you will surely get that lower sum.

The difference in long-term payback is enormous. Annie Moreton of Greenpeace reported to the International Fund Raising Workshop in October 1994 that *Frontline* would be worth £5.5 million to the organisation over the next 10 years. If the ask had been for £5 a month, the take-up might have been slightly higher but the overall return on the process would have been a fraction of that £5.5 million. It is all very simple really. You could even argue that all such schemes have been underpriced. Who is to say that £30 a month is inconceivable?

It does depend of course on how the supporters pay.

Standing orders – and only standing orders

Read up about monthly giving programmes in the United States and your heart sinks. There, it is still common to base such a scheme on mailing reminders every month, usually with a less-than-heartwarming financial statement. Some smaller non-profit organisations ask donors to send 12 postdated cheques. A 'tip' in one textbook suggests sending monthly pledgers 12 self-addressed envelopes and pledge forms and 12 calendar stickers to remind donors of when their cheques are due.

In Europe we are privileged. In America electronic funds transfer has only been approved for inter-state banking since 1979 and many Americans remain wary of it. But in most parts of Europe standing orders, autogiro and direct debits have been part of everyone's lives for nearly a generation. In 1967 I launched a monthly bankers order scheme for Oxfam called Ploughshares – it was unremarkable even then.

Direct debit is fast becoming the traditional way of being paid, of paying regular bills such as those from public utilities and of paying just about any membership subscription. Any charity that offers an annual membership subscription and that has been doing its job properly is now likely to have 70 per cent of such members paying by direct debit. In some countries it is already unusual to pay in any other way.

A direct debit to a monthly giving scheme is therefore deeply conventional. It will join a small collection of other monthly payments automatically deducted from the bank account in exactly the same way. Greenpeace in Germany receives over 60 per cent of its very considerable income via the automatic electronic route. It is the future, nothing less.

And, for the fundraiser, it has another and obvious virtue. Direct debits rarely get cancelled – indeed one of the main reasons for cancellation is the perfectly excusable fact of death. Short of that, anyone cancelling a direct debit to a charity is somehow announcing that they are either suddenly poor or suddenly mean. Few do it.

I know of one charity that gets 94 per cent annual retention of direct debit members and where it can calculate member life in terms of 11 years and rising. It is the sort of statistic that puts so much other fundraising practice into perspective. Why do we continue to look for the single donation when the mechanics and the provenance of the regular donation on direct debit are staring us in the face?

Don't give monthly givers any other option. Don't give them a cash alternative. Don't try credit cards. Don't let them send you cheques. Just ask them to sign a direct debit. You know it makes sense. So do they.

But who are they? And how do you find them?

Committed givers will self-select themselves out of the more obvious parts of your database. Regular, frequent, recent and higher-value donors are the most likely sources for cost-effective recruitment. Be careful not to ask those handful of people who are already giving more than you are asking for with a monthly scheme. And remember the primacy of direct debit – anyone already giving a smaller sum in this way is a good prospect for increasing the monthly amount. Keep inching out the recruitment beyond the obvious segments – it is even possible to sell such schemes successfully to a 'lapsed' file!

For you can afford a much higher recruitment cost with committed giving. You are not confined to your own database. These schemes have yet to make a regular appearance in newspaper ads, but they will. And recruitment for Oxfam's Project Partners seems to thrive on television. In Austria, a major environmental organisation actually sells such a support scheme on the street – in little booths in town centres where people are enjoined to sign direct debits on the spot.

This might prove to be a little risky though. Door-to-door canvassing has been much used for Greenpeace committed giving schemes in the United States and in Australia. It works – but it often carries the seeds of its own decay. The drop-out rate on canvassed Friends of the Rainbow Warrior in Sydney was a frightening five per cent a month. Members recruited by direct mail lasted six times as long and the lifetime value of such members was calculated at $1,388 (Australian) in 1994 – a figure similar to the one we might expect in Europe.

Adventures in recruitment technique aside, it is likely that you can recruit satisfactorily just by using direct mail and the telephone. If your supporters' file is properly segmented and if you select intelligently, that opening prediction of three to five per cent take-up still applies. And so, I guess, does Simon Pell's predictive band of 15 to 30 per cent for a telephone recruitment campaign.

What are you waiting for?

For, if I am right, every charity that has a supporters' file of 20,000 has a chance of persuading 1,000 of those people to give at a rate of £15 a month. Simple arithmetic (the only kind I can cope with) says that that will produce a fund of £180,000 a year. The most conservative prediction of direct debit performance says that it will eventually produce a fund of more than £1,000,000. Deduct recruitment and servicing costs and you are still looking at one of the more benign fundraising equations you will ever see.

I repeat: what are you waiting for ?

'Whoopee, we're all gonna die '

I once started a legacy presentation in Vienna with that subhead on a slide. 'Do you recognise that line?' I asked with proper diffidence. 'Yes, of course', said the young Austrian fundraisers, 'Fixin'-to-Die Rag by Country Joe and the Fish, Woodstock, 1968.' They smiled knowingly. I smiled like a fond uncle. It is comforting that pop music can still bond the generations.

But it wasn't an accidental choice of song. I used it because I get irritated with the maudlin ceremonial with which fundraisers choose to surround the greatest donation anyone ever makes – the legacy. Just about a third of all income to British charities still comes in the form of legacies. Yet we plod around the opportunity as if we were undertakers ourselves, clad in black with crêpe bands hanging from tall hats. We need not just to admit the scale of the legacy opportunity but to admit its joy, its promise, its inherent customer satisfaction. For it is the only donation that never reflects in the donor's current account. It is the only donation that most of us will ever make in thousands, tens of thousands, hundreds of thousands of pounds. It is the only donation that just about everyone *can* make.

> IT IS THE ONLY DONATION THAT JUST ABOUT EVERYONE CAN MAKE.

For the only 100 per cent statistic that you can apply to the human race is the one that applies to death. Whatever advances are made in medicine or on cryogenics, however longer we are allowed to plod along beyond three score years and 10, whatever our zeal for lentils rather than beef, whatever our increasing use of the exercise bike, whatever our cessation of naughty habits... we are all going to keel over at some stage and shuffle off the mortal coil.

So, whoopee, we're all going to die. I myself seem to have about 1,500 Saturday nights left. How about you?

Whose will is it anyway?

In 1995 the number of wills made in England and Wales on estates over £5,000 was 181,332 – a further 50,104 people died intestate, failing to make a will. (All the many statistics I shall use in this section come from the extraordinary repository of knowledge that is Smee & Ford, a company that reads every will deposited at Somerset House every day and that, therefore, provides British fundraisers with research data unequalled anywhere in the field of fundraising worldwide.)

The total probate value of those 181,332 wills was a breathtaking £15.7 billion. But here's the rub for fundraisers; only 25,236 of those wills made a charitable bequest, giving a total number of 71,643 charitable legacies in the year.

Let us pause right there for we are already faced with the central and most absorbing statistic about legacy marketing. It says simply that *the vast majority of people making a will leave no money to charity.*

In 1995, the number of charitable wills was just 13.5 per cent of the total. It is a percentage that has barely moved in the last five years, despite all the careful and assiduous legacy marketing programmes mounted by charities. Put simply, people left a total of £12.3 billion in wills that made no charitable bequests whatsoever. Fundraisers should slaver at this opportunity.

For, when legacies can be developed and when those bequests are made, the volume income becomes quite astonishing. These were the top 10 legacy earners in Britain in 1995, showing the proportion of legacy income to total voluntary income.

1. Cancer Research Campaign £39,300,000, 70 per cent.
2. Royal National Lifeboat Institution £38,400,000, 66 per cent.
3. Imperial Cancer Research Fund £32,700,000, 72 per cent.
4. National Trust £24,600,000, 32 per cent.
5. Royal Society for the Prevention of Cruelty to Animals £23,300,000, 73 per cent.
6. Guide Dogs for the Blind £20,100,000, 81 per cent.
7. Salvation Army £20,000,000, 51 per cent.
8. Royal National Institute for the Blind £18,600,000, 71 per cent.
9. British Heart Foundation £16,700,000, 59 per cent.
10. Barnardo's £16,100,000, 47 per cent.

I fancy that this league table would not have changed much in the last 10 or 20 years. Other charities tend to see it as a rather tribal list, convincing themselves that these charities are somehow the natural historical repositories of bequests from the generation just gone. Perhaps they are, and perhaps the apparent dependence of some of these charities on legacy income is a dangerous thing. But that dependence has been long lasting – it was in the sixties that I was told that Barnardo's was too dependent on legacy income. A dependence on tens of millions of pounds a year is a reasonably happy dependence in a troubled world.

Not that I want to get parochial just yet. I just want to chant the statistics again so that we can get a grip on the scale of the legacy opportunity.

- Over 86 per cent of people making a will leave no money to charity.
- Thus, no more than five per cent of people who die leave money to charity.
- Even so, this minority provided 33 per cent of all charity voluntary income.

In other words, the legacy market is still largely untapped by charities. We could actually double the financial size of the voluntary sector if we made a dramatic change in the way people dispose of their wealth when they go.

Dismissing the negatives

Not so long ago, a legacy was the gift that dared not speak its name. A charity may have had a leaflet about legacies, usually worded in sepulchral tones and aimed at solicitors. There may have been a suitably inhibited display of austere ads in the legal trade journals and the occasional reticent small ad – often a classified indeed – in the broadsheets. 'Remember us in your will' these ads would say. One heard a nervous cough as they said it. My personal high spot was to be asked to book an ad in the *Funeral Director* on the presumed basis that undertakers would put in a good word for the charity whilst overseeing the burial.

It was both an inhibited and a deferential area of fundraising – inhibited because a barrier of good taste was supposed to apply, deferential because professionals were believed to be the route through this good taste barrier. It is a wonder that so much money has been left in legacies since, for the donor can rarely have been asked direct.

But I still hear the familiar myths about legacy marketing. They are no more than easy rationalisations regularly paraded by people and organisations who simply feel uncomfortable working in this area. One look at the copious information we have about this market destroys them all.

'People don't like to be reminded about their mortality.' Simply untrue. People – especially old people – are entirely level-headed about the facts of life and death.

'It's a very long term business.' Not like it used to be. Forty-nine per cent of all charitable wills that came through in 1995 had been made in the last three years, 23 per cent in the last 12 months. The will-makers are updating their wills all the time.

'It's too unpredictable.' It can afford to be, given the scale of the rewards. But is it any more unpredictable than other means of fundraising? Smee & Ford can tell you where legacies came from county by county. It can tell you which are the prime months for legacy-making. It can tell you the average size of any kind of legacy. No other area of fundraising offers this quality of research data.

'Our supporters are too young.' Nearly five per cent of charitable wills in 1995 came from people who died between the ages of 18 and 59. A minority obviously, but a fairly valuable one. And young people do get older.

'People only leave money to "safe" causes.' Older people obviously tend to leave money to causes and charities that have been familiar throughout their lives – hence the rather stately nature of the current legacy top 10. But things change. Oxfam received £6.1 million in legacies in 1995. WWF UK receives nearly 27 per cent of its income in the form of legacies. Environmental or development charities now receive 6.5 per cent of all British legacies, a proportion that will surely increase as years pass. Greenpeace USA has already been notified of one legacy gift of $8 million.

'Only your existing supporters leave you money.' Baloney! Seventy per cent of legacies come from people unknown to the organisation concerned.

'You can't ask elderly trustees, members of staff, or volunteers.' More baloney! These are the

THE TWO GREAT PRIORITIES

first people you should ask. Especially the trustees. Especially the elderly ones. Especially the elderly ones who are female. It's called targeting.

'Solicitors are critical in helping guide a charity bequest.' It may once have been true that little old ladies timorously entered the solicitor's office in such a state of unworldliness that they needed professional advice on where to direct their charity bequests. Only the continued power of this pleasant little picture can explain the extent to which solicitors' offices are awash with calendars, diaries, bookmarks and other gewgaws bearing the names of wide-eyed charities. Only continued subscription to the myth can explain the absurd expenditure on advertising in the legal trade press and handbooks.

There are 11,000 solicitors' practices in the UK. In 1995 only 38 per cent of them acted as executors on *any* will. And 1,800 of that 4,000 did it just the once. Apply the known statistics of charitable against non-charitable wills and you will see how seldom they ever played any part in guiding a legacy to a charity. Apply common sense and you will see how very seldom they ever guided a legacy to a *particular* charity.

A charity needs to make use of the legal profession. Supplying a list of legal practices that will make a will for supporters at a discounted rate is a proper service for it takes some of the mystique out of the process. But the idea that solicitors are instrumental in charity selection on any scale is simply daft. Banks already have three per cent of the executor business and it is reasonable to expect that the new self-assessment rules of income tax will enhance the role of accountants in such matters. But the role of professional advisers will always be utterly marginal and mechanical.

They don't nominate the chosen charities. It is your legacy marketing that gets you on the list of bequests. The professional adviser just looks up the address.

More statistics

Smee & Ford is knee-deep in them. Let me quote some more in the hope that they will persuade you to attack this market with vigour.
- Two-thirds of will-makers are women.
- The average number of bequests in a charitable will is currently 2.8. Few legators leave money to only one charity.
- The average pecuniary bequest is currently for £3,230; the average residuary bequest is for £20,040.
- The most popular area for charity bequests is currently the nursing/care charities. They received 23.5 per cent of all charitable bequests in 1995 – 16,810 in total. The second most popular cause was animal welfare – 15.2 per cent of the total with 10,890 legacies.

• The most popular month for will-making is March when 9.5 per cent of wills appear to be made. Don't ask me why.

• The average age of death for those who make a charitable will is 82 years and 6 months if you are female, 77 years and 6 months if you are male. The equivalent figures for those making non-charitable wills is 80 years and 5 months and 75 years and 8 months respectively. It is a fascinating differential.

And it is quite the best statistic of the lot. It proves beyond peradventure that people who leave money to charity live two years longer!

A new mind-set – legacies are fun!

I made my own will not so long ago. The man from the National Westminster Bank sat on my settee and tried to be lugubrious about my responsibility to dispose of my wealth with care, tax-effectiveness and stern precision.

It was a shorter session than he wanted. I made my dispositions to the family and then started leaving money to good causes. Within five minutes I had given away more money than anyone except a building society had ever shaken out of me. But the point of this story is not what a wonderful old philanthropist I have turned out to be. It is how good I felt after I'd enacted all this largesse.

I beamed, I stroked the cat, I dusted kitchen surfaces to the point where the wife wondered out loud whether I had had early access to the hooch bottle. The explanation was far simpler – I was happy because I'd given a lot of money away, because in doing so I had become aware of the *privilege* of doing so, because I suddenly felt myself twice the man I had been before. And the absolutely amazing thing about this sudden power surge is that it had cost me not one apparent penny – my miserable little piles of money in my bank accounts remained completely untouched by the avalanche of philanthropy.

I enjoyed the process so much that I am fully capable of doing it all over again – and at regular intervals. Which is what presumably a lot of legators are doing all the time.

Only a legacy offers this 'feel-good' factor. For, if I give a significant sum of money to a charity during my lifetime, I am still going to be haunted by the thought that it might waste it or let it disappear into diffuse areas of operation of which I might disapprove. With a legacy I am haunted by no such inhibitions. They can spend it all on whole-page awareness campaigns for all I care. I am dead, after all.

So, a legacy makes you feel good, makes you feel powerful and often makes you carefree to boot. How else can you explain some of the wills that Smee & Ford has captured over the years?

Wills like that of Hensley Nankivell in 1987 who left £400,000 between 15 different relatives but only on the basis that they passed 8 O levels, or qualified as airline pilots within two years of his death. Most of them were over 70 at the time.

Or like that of the 46 year old whose will was read in March 1996. After a dutiful charity bequest, we read this, 'I desire that my body be cremated and the ashes be placed in an empty red Absolut vodka bottle and be thrown out to sea from some point chosen by my executors.'

But the man I'd really like to have met included this in his will, 'To my first wife, Sue, whom I always promised I would mention in my will – hello Sue!'

I use these examples to embroider my point. Leaving money in your will makes you feel good and powerful. Leaving money to charities makes you feel good, powerful and altogether wonderful. Legacies are fun.

Target, communicate – and keep communicating

David Ford is very restless with much legacy marketing. He is allowed to be, having proselytised the idea so very vigorously over the last decade or more.

He says, 'People think they can just dip into it. They think you can just write a letter and sit back. But donors can't just be ignored for 20 years.'

Amen to that! Legacy marketing is just like any other kind of fundraising. It deserves flourish, imagination, sensitivity and perseverance. But, because it is the last rung on that donor pyramid, because it is the last reward for relationship fundraising, many fundraisers seem to favour a minimalist approach. Securing the legacy pledge is often seen as the end of the process, not the beginning. Dignified silence somehow enshrines the process at that point. It is as if we had persuaded the legator to pray in church – when we see him/her in the pew we tiptoe quietly away, leaving the new convert to find his own way out of the church. We are still guilty of that nervous cough.

But the whole process, like all processes of communication, starts with targeting and a modest amount of research. You can build a model of your potential legator, either from your existing legacy records or from the copious data available from the world outside. Is it a she rather than a he? Does she or he tend to live in the south of the country rather than the north and in the towns where folk go to retire? Are you the 'senior' charity in a will, or are you more often one of the 'also rans'.

Get answers to these questions but don't waste too much time in trying to sophisticate the model of the potential legator – only the largest organisations will have the historic data to do it with true statistical precision. Besides, the potential of legacy marketing is surely in 'reaching out' to that vast majority of people who do not currently intend to leave a charitable will at all, let alone to your organisation.

The most accessible part of that majority is clearly on your donor list already. So, ask them to make a legacy pledge. But, don't stop there. Go looking for other means of communicating with potential legators. You can take ads in that growing number of magazines that are read by the senior members of society. You can rent lists that offer the correct characteristics – cold mailing for legacies is much under-used. You can build advertorial supplements around the proposition in local newspapers. You can deploy a dozen means of communication. But you need the correct mind-set of optimism and promise in all of them. You need to be besotted by the potential of these obvious facts.

- You are talking to people who are probably wealthier than they ever thought possible.
- You are talking to people who have probably not dreamt of leaving money to you.
- You are offering these people the chance to do something wonderful, remarkable, utterly personal and relatively painless.
- You can offer them every assistance and every comfort in doing this marvellous thing. Exciting, isn't it?

Elevating the issue

We need to talk about legacies everywhere. We need to stop apologising for raising the issue. We need to stop coughing nervously. The occasional paragraph in your newsletter is dutiful underachievement – why not produce a special legacy issue once a year? Why not devote a local committee meeting to the whole subject – just as you would with a special event?

It is a campaign like any other. So, target it. Say you want 100, or 250, or 500 new legacy pledges a year. Then go for it.

- Give it a campaign title.
- Persuade staff, committee members and trustees to pledge. Publicise their leadership.
- Set up an advisory hot-line service.
- Offer to visit people.
- Telephone major donors and tell them that you want them to be part of the campaign.
- Consider a reward structure for pledgers.
- Test cold mailings and ads.
- Set up a regular communications' programme with pledgers.

And infuse all these activities with a sense of purpose, a sense of excitement. Above all, *share* the excitement with everyone to whom you are talking. If that target of 100, 250, or

500 pledges is met, tell pledgers the good news. If it is unmet, tell them the not-so-good news – they will likely know some people who could make up the difference.

And remember that you are sowing seed on ground that has probably never yet been tilled to grow the legacy crop. It is this that fascinates me more than anything about legacies. For to an extraordinary extent, leaving money to charities is what *other* people do (a statistically valid fact, of course). When you make the point that leaving money to charity is something *you* can do, you dislodge apathy in favour of purpose.

Charities still have an awesome educational job to do in persuading their middle-class public to accept the charity bequest as a behavioural norm. Too many people are unaware of their wealth. Too many are nervous of the whole process of will-making and bequesting. Too many are plumb ignorant of the fact that you *can* leave money to organisations (the younger cause groups, often denied formal charity status, are particular victims of such ignorance).

We will not breach this educational gap with quiet dignity. We will breach it with noise and excitement and with a new sense of giving the donor what he or she wants. All in all, we need to stop whispering and start shouting.

The creative tools of the trade

You can ransack the previous pages of this book to see how you can communicate in legacy marketing. I see no need for a special language, little need for a different tone of voice. And I see plenty of application for many of the points I have made so far.

Take the standard legacy leaflet, for example. Why does it never seem to have human faces in it? Ask existing pledgers if they would object to being featured, at least verbally but hopefully photographically. Why have they committed themselves? What do they look like? These simple touches of human reportage must offer the potential legator a more easeful route through a process that is usually totally private and discreet. Remember the need to belong.

Or take my point about sharing information and talking with a new candour to your supporters. In the summer of 1995, the Royal National Lifeboat Institution became troubled about trends in the legacy market and an apparent dip in its very considerable legacy income. The temptation was to set up research groups of supporters and continue to rely on macro-market data or anecdotal anxiety. It was a temptation well resisted. It was decided instead to take the issue directly to the only people who could do anything about it – the supporters. This is the letter that came from Ian Ventham, RNLI's head of fundraising and marketing, and which accompanied the next issue of the RNLI magazine.

To RNLI Supporters only

Dear Supporter

Future funding of the RNLI

I'd like to share some thoughts with you. I am sure you are aware that the RNLI is funded totally by voluntary contributions and that legacies are our largest source of income. We are concerned about future legacy income and it seems sensible to talk about our concerns with our regular RNLI supporters as early, and with as much candour, as possible.

You probably know that we have always been able to rely, more than most charities, on the fact that RNLI supporters remember our organisation in their wills. In some years legacy income has amounted to 60 per cent of our total income, with more than 2,500 supporters making a bequest to the RNLI. This generosity has enabled the RNLI to run more than 200 lifeboat stations, to equip our fleet of lifeboats so that our volunteer crews can continue our mission to save life at sea, and to build up much-needed reserves. Indeed, it is fair to say that the magnificent service that the RNLI provides has largely been created because of this tradition of legacy-giving, alongside fundraising and subscriptions from committed supporters.

There are signs that this tradition may be in decline. Our legacy income for 1994 fell by nearly five per cent and the early months of 1995 seem to suggest a greater drop. There are all sorts of reasons why legacy income could be falling and we are trying to understand these reasons as I write. We don't yet know whether this is a 'blip', or whether it is a long-term trend. This is why I am writing to you.

If it is a 'blip', then our reserves are probably sufficient to carry us through. But, if it is a long-term trend then we may have a major problem on our hands in two to three years. We may have to dip into our current reserves – probably on some scale. We might also have to devote more resources to other kinds of fundraising, inevitably increasing the cost of raising money from the low levels of which we are currently so proud. What we must do is minimise the risk of being unable to continue the constant improvement and upgrading of our lifeboats and stations that we are planning in the second half of the decade and into the next century.

Hence our concern and hence this message to you. We are asking whether you intend to leave the RNLI a legacy. If enough of our committed supporters can give us an answer to that question – whether positive or negative – we will be in a better position to plan for the future. Let me make it quite clear that this is research and not a sales tactic, which is why I am asking the question in general and not in detail. Whether you leave the RNLI money by a pecuniary, residuary, or even a reversionary bequest, how much you leave us in your will, whether you are leaving money to other charities... all these are matters private to you, your family and your professional adviser. But we do have an obvious and urgent interest in asking the broad questions below. I hope you will understand our need for the information.

The more answers we receive, the better informed we will be about our financial future. We shall be better placed to run the RNLI at its historic level of cost-effectiveness. That is why I urge you to complete this small questionnaire. It goes without saying that your answers will be treated in complete anonymity at this office – as you will see, we are not asking for your name and address on this form. We will, of course, keep you informed about the situation as it unfolds, with regular information in our journal, The Lifeboat.

I do thank you in advance for your co-operation.

Yours sincerely

Ian Ventham

Head of Fundraising

PS. If you have already indicated your intention to leave the RNLI a bequest, please accept my apology and ignore this letter.

Over 14,000 supporters completed this little questionnaire – a 6.5 per cent response from the magazine's total circulation. Client confidentiality means that I cannot give you the breakdown of the individual answers. Suffice to say that we were very pleased indeed with the results – and not just in terms of information. For we had elevated the issue of the legacy, shared the emerging sense of crisis and talked directly and with honesty. Supporters responded with equal maturity. They answered our questions and gave us an invaluable summary of their collective will-making intentions. And let's not be coy about it – we nudged some of them into making a pledge at this point. All in all, a colossal return on a tiny investment in human communication.

CONFIDENTIAL

I have already made a will	Yes	No
I have included a bequest to the RNLI	Yes	No
I intend to include a bequest to the RNLI	Yes	No
I am considering charitable bequests to other charities	Yes	No
Date of birth		

If you would like a copy of our new Guide to Making and Changing Wills, *write to Ian Ventham, Head of Fundraising, Dept LJ/L5, RNLI, West Quay Road, Poole, Dorset BH15 1HZ*

Please return this questionnaire in the envelope provided
THANK YOU

LJ/L5

The form used by 14,000 RNLI supporters to signify their legacy intentions

More product development...

There is now a standard promotional norm in legacy marketing. It is essentially two-stage. The charity offers information on how to make a will. That information contains a pledge form. A minority of respondents send back the pledge form to the respective charity. The charity creates a distinct line of communication with these pledgers. Eventually the pledges mature into actual legacies.

It works. Charities who have marketed their legacies in this way for 10 years or more can begin to put figures on the extent to which it does work. They can quote a figure for cost per pledge and they can begin to quote a figure for the financial relationship between the initial investment, the subsequent servicing and the eventual reward. Every charity I know that has run such a programme can show an upward curve in legacy income that follows the curve of active marketing.

But there must remain the need to 'grow' the market. As we have seen, the percentage of charitable wills remains stubbornly stuck at about one in eight. We may have educated

Legacy promotion need not be sombre. This cartoon adorns the front cover of a legacy booklet from the Royal National Institute for the Blind.

How to send for your guide

You are invited to send for your free copy of the National Trust's guide to making or updating a Will.

Protect the people and the places you love – with your Will

Your free guide to making or updating your Will

THE NATIONAL TRUST

This is a summary of what your guide will tell you:

- Why a Will is vital
- When you should review an existing Will
- How to make or update your Will
- When your estate will attract inheritance tax
- Why remember the National Trust?
- How to include the National Trust
- Glossary of legal language.

How to receive your guide:

a) Complete the reply form enclosed
b) Seal in the Freepost envelope
c) Post – no stamp is needed.

THE NATIONAL TRUST

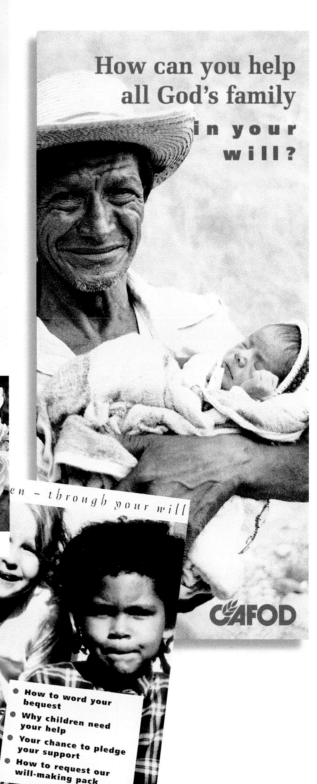

How can you help all God's family in your will?

en – through your will

- How to word your bequest
- Why children need your help
- Your chance to pledge your support
- How to request our will-making pack

CAFOD

The different faces of legacy promotion. It could be time to get more adventurous.

the minority of people who are charity supporters but we have barely touched those without such affiliations. Even the minority have failed to perform in true volume.

We should be increasingly anxious about the future efficacy of the legacy marketing programmes of the last decade. We have made the pledge our standard item of currency. But currencies have a habit of being devalued. What percentage of those pledges will actually mature? I do not wish to be overly pessimistic, but it does seem to me that we need to work harder and more imaginatively in the next few years to revitalise a market into which we have made such small statistical inroads.

We need to think again in terms of product engineering. How can we add that optimism, that 'feel-good' factor to the legacy product? How can it be made to coincide better with that array of human needs and emotions that I listed in the first chapters of this book?

Why don't we persuade middle-aged supporters to persuade their elderly parents to make a bequest? Again, we could share the problem and the promise. And who better to proselytise the charity bequest than the other likely beneficiaries of the process?

Why don't we sell the earmarked or project-specific legacy? I know that every charity sees legacies as a great source of free funds but that is a housekeeping virtue and could be a promotional vice. We approach major donors with specific needs. Why not legators?

Why don't we create a five per cent legacy product, one that simply says that five per cent of your wealth will go to charities of your choice? Such a figure would harm few estates that currently leave no charitable bequests. But it would act as a moral benchmark, easy to understand, a far happier concept than the minefield of pecuniary, residual and reversionary bequests. The legator who can say 'I have left one pound in every 20 to charity' will have said a simple and a decent thing.

And so on. The current two-stage pledge programmes have shown us the way, no more. We must continue to perfect the legacy product, to retune it to meet the needs of the donor. I could not have used such language 10 or 15 years ago – it would have seemed irreligious and modestly outrageous. But we have learned to talk about legacies out loud. We should now talk about them with greater imagination.

I think we shall have to, whether we like it or not.

The future of legacy promotion

We need to pop our heads over the parapets of our existing tradecraft with legacy promotion. We need to acknowledge what is going on in our society for it will affect legacy giving far more than any other kind of charity income.

I give you two opposing pieces of futurist rhetoric.

The first says that the middle-class people who will die in the next 20 or 30 years will be the richest people who have ever existed on earth. They may not think of themselves as rich but rich they are – stinking rich, historically rich, mind-bogglingly rich. They will be the first (and arguably last) generation to profit by a serene career path, regular employment from school to retirement, private pension plans and the inflation in property prices that marked the years from the late sixties to the late eighties. No generation has ever been this lucky.

A normal family man or woman who bought a house in 1967 for £5,000 will have paid a mortgage well within their income level for 20 to 25 years and will now, all things being equal, be sitting on a mortgage-free property asset worth perhaps £80,000, or more. If they had moved up in property terms, they could be worth three or four times that. They have probably been saving assiduously during that time, now have the children off their hands and can still look forward to tax-free payments from a pension plan and an annual income thereafter from the same source. Moreover, they stand to be the beneficiaries from any money left by their own parents. For these people I am describing can be as young as 50 years of age, maybe even less.

I repeat: these people are historically rich. But they are not merchant bankers, brain surgeons, or film producers. They are bus drivers, civil servants and teachers. They are deeply ordinary people fortunate enough to live when they did. And they are a finite blessing to the fundraiser. Their children will be unlikely ever to amass the same degree of wealth, for the property bonanza, which accounts for so much of it, will almost certainly never happen again.

So the fundraiser is working within a market that is becoming increasingly aware of its own astonishing good fortune, a market that is beginning to flex its financial muscles with exotic holidays and second cars, a market that will not give a single additional pound to charity unless we make a better case.

For the second piece of futurism is pessimistic. It dwells on the fact that this wealthy market is now traumatised – not by its sudden awareness of wealth but by its sudden awareness of the fact that it will have to plan financially for its own old age.

For it is sudden, this revelation. The people I am describing have lived their lives in the Welfare State. They have paid their taxes for decades and their expectation was that they could depend on the statutory services when they became infirm and needful. That expectation has now been denied them. At the time of writing, you do not qualify for automatic State provision in old age if your assets total more than £16,000. You will have to pay for any nursing home costs yourself. Thousands of old people's houses, perhaps tens of thousands, are now sold annually to meet this need. Thus, that historic wealth of many people is being dissipated in the direction of private health care.

Not for all of them of course, perhaps not for most of them. But the anxiety about those post-retirement years will have affected just about everyone in this generation. There is almost a moral parable here: just as you were learning how lucky you are, you learned how responsible you still had to be. And just as charities were learning to appreciate the potential of this historically wealthy generation, they learned that the potential was impaired by the new anxiety. Now you see it, now you don't.

These huge sociological shifts will shape the future of legacy giving in most Western countries. At present the omens are bleak. The best statistical forecasting models indicate a massive downturn in legacy giving in the next 15 years. It is no time to be smug and certainly no time to project those existing growth curves in legacy income ever upwards and onwards. We are going to have to think very imaginatively indeed. We need to learn as much about estate planning as our American colleagues know. We need to be more full-blooded about asking for life insurance policy payouts, percentages on pension plans and even properties. We need to persuade people to dispose of their wealth – and leave us a legacy – *before* they die.

We should continue to be obsessed by the wealth around us. We should continue to be obsessed by the fact that so few people leave money to charity. We must create a generation of new products born of such obsessions. They will be needed very quickly indeed.

I end this chapter on a sombre note. But I insist that the two areas of committed giving and legacies are the two most important in the whole area of fundraising. That has probably always been true. But it is certainly true now and in the immediate future. Any charity ignoring their potential, or of seeing them as marginal or occasional activities, is guilty of a strange irresponsibility.

FUNDRAISING IN A CHANGING WORLD

It was my sad duty yesterday to register a death. I gave the details to the registrar who dutifully logged them into a computer, a new procedure since I last had to perform this task. I presumed in my innocence that she would then print out the death certificate from the given data. She didn't. She wrote it all out again in longhand. The data, she told me, was for the national census database. The death certificate was personal and therefore handwritten.

This strikes me as a vivid example of the compromise we make between human instinct and technological possibility. We are surrounded by vast technological change but we try as individuals to find a human role for it. Why do I still write cheques when I could go full pelt into electronic banking? Why do I post letters when I could communicate by fax or E-Mail? Why do I still visit the cinema when I could wait a few months for the video? Why do I still watch sport in the flesh when I can see it better via a dozen television cameras? Why do we still have conferences when any information imparted at them could be imparted in newer, sleeker ways?

The answer, in some dim sense, is that we all need a human context for what we do. We like being with other people, we like talking to them, communicating with them. We like to see their faces, hear their voices. I cannot see that this will ever change. So I cannot really believe in a cyber-future where communication becomes merely electronic. The Internet is a wondrous thing but I retain a healthy scepticism about its role as a fundraising tool. For it is essentially an information medium, the equivalent of a massive library or museum. I know of one major charity that claims to have thousands of pages on its Web site. This may be a dutiful endeavour of information collation and presentation (though I worry about the value of thousands of pages of anything), but I cannot think that it has any fundraising potential, or at least any cost-effective fundraising potential. More means worse in fundraising as elsewhere. We will not provoke the instinct to care and to give by stupefying the donor with a mass of information, no matter how encyclopaedically that information is contrived or how excitingly it is communicated.

The resilience of traditional forms of communication is striking and under-reported. The printed book market continues to grow. The renaissance of the cinema is extraordinary. There are now more theatres in Britain than there were a generation ago. And anyone who has recently set up a public meeting will have learned that people are still astonishingly willing to turn out on a rainy night to participate in something in which they perceive importance and relevance.

I therefore predict that the major forms of fundraising communication will continue to be the ones we currently have at our disposal – the direct mail pack, the telephone, the press ad, the broadcast media which will now multiply so dramatically. But we shall be using them with a much greater knowledge of the society with whom we are communicating. For the composition of that society is changing very rapidly. We do well to take demographics seriously.

The five current donor generations

The best commentator on the changing demographics of fundraising is Judith Nichols in the United States. And no one in Europe should be so insular as to pretend that her research and extrapolations, carefully honed and updated over the last decade, are irrelevant here merely because they are based on American experience. For what Judith reports affects all Western societies.

In *Pinpointing Affluence* she repeats her findings on the five generations of donors that confront us all. It omits only the very elderly. All the figures given are the current ones from the USA.

Pre-Second World War babies (up to 1939) – 33 million people
- World War One babies (born 1910–1919).
- Roaring 20s babies (born 1920–1929).
- Depression babies (born 1930–1939).

Second World War babies (1940–1945) – 13 million people

Baby Boomers (born 1946-1964) – 77 million people
- Mature Boomers (born 1946–1950).
- Mid Boomers (born 1951–1957).
- Young Boomers (born 1958–1964).

Baby Busters (1965–1977) – 32 million people
- Mature Busters (born 1965–1970).
- Young Busters (born 1971–1976).

Baby Boomlet (born 1977–2005) – 72 million + people
- Mature Boomlet (born 1977–1995).
- Echo Boomlet (born 1996–2005).

These strangely titled demographic groups are easily explained by the fashion cycle of procreation. During and after the First World War American women seized up on child bearing – a process that continued through the depression and right through the Second World War. With its end, the pent-up desire for children was unleashed, giving a baby boom that lasted for two decades. The more cautious decade from the mid-sixties to the mid-seventies led to a declining birth level – the 'baby bust' years. Since when, and for whatever reason, we have a small rise, a baby boomlet, which is predicted to last into the first years of the next century.

The value of these statistics is to provoke a more careful shading of the bromides that we constantly repeat on population trends. Thus it is true that people are living longer, but it could be more usefully true that most living people are young. Many more Americans who are alive today were born after the Second World War than before or during it. A good half of the population of the United States were not around when President Kennedy was assassinated. The same will be true of all Western countries.

Judith's demographic analysis gives us the building blocks of an attitude to fundraising within these respective generations but it should not mean that we accept caricatures of these tens of millions of people. She herself regularly makes the point that the old are increasingly active – physically, commercially, sexually even. We should dismiss the idea that the donor in his or her seventies is a frail and infirm thing, fit only for kindly legacy solicitation. Look around at any demonstration against road building or for animal rights – the old are well in evidence.

WE SHOULD DISMISS THE IDEA THAT THE DONOR IN HIS OR HER SEVENTIES IS A FRAIL AND INFIRM THING.

Youth, too, is a moving target. My own eldest children, though I must always think of them as younger people, seem remorselessly to have turned into thirty-somethings. They are as nostalgic about seventies music as I am about that of the fifties and sixties. And even here the chronology takes a few curves. When my daughter was married, she specified some Chuck Berry tracks for the disco – music to my ears obviously. Apparently the soundtrack of *Pulp Fiction* had made him famous all over again!

I would argue that this commonality of the human race transcends chronological segmentation. For chronology is not a finite process – it merely gives us different memories, different entry points to the process of caring. I am old enough to remember the vast movements of refugee populations after the last war. Someone who is now 40 will remember the Biafran conflict from his/her childhood. Those who turned 20 in the last few years will remember the Ethiopian famine from the early eighties. All these age groups will share a memory of need, whenever it was depicted. We all end up as potential donors.

True, technological change has been frighteningly rapid. The fax, the personal computer, the mobile telephone… these are now everyday things that would have seemed like science fiction a mere 15 years ago. But their easeful acceptance into our daily lifestyles persuades me again to stress the continuum of human existence rather than the trauma of change. This book has been written on a piece of equipment that would have terrified me witless 10 years ago. I am a relative master of the fax machine. My video camera has already been dismissed from adult use and gathers dust in my daughter's bedroom. And didn't I read somewhere that the fastest-growing sector of Internet users were in fact old rather than young?

People take technology in their stride. It changes them little. They remain potential donors, fired by those same universal instincts with which I started my argument. Fundraisers should take comfort from that and beware the dangers of missing the emotional wood for the technological trees.

How will fundraising change?

By now I will have laboured a point of view of creativity in fundraising. I have tended to scorn mere tradecraft. I have questioned the rush to massification, the apparent tendency to build empires out of statistics, the deferential me-too-ism that makes so much fundraising so banal and unsuccessful. I have tried to embroider the newer themes of relationship fundraising and one-to-one marketing.

They are enormously relevant to the successful practice of our trade in the next decade. For the brutal fact of current economics is that we shall likely be asking fewer people for more money. We have done little to expand the base of permanent supporters as opposed to one-off donors and the cost of pursuing the latter is becoming prohibitive, reflecting in fundraising ratios that are increasingly indefensible. Many donors would find administration costs of 25 per cent alarming and troubling, though the percentage gleams through the thickets of many British charities accounts as an emerging average. By the time that fundraising investment increases that figure to 35 per cent or 40 per cent – and it has in some cases already – then we are faced with a moral issue and not a statistical one. Who would happily give £10 to charity if they knew that £4 would not be spent on the primary objects of the charity? American fundraisers regularly preside over such figures. 'We'll do anything to keep the numbers up' remains a terrifying quotation. I find this blind pursuit of numbers a simple nightmare. It is surely a betrayal of what we are truly here to do.

I predict that we will be mailing less and better. I predict that we will be taking product development a lot more seriously, forging better and more sensitive ways in which our supporters can commit themselves to us. And, yes, I predict that we shall be asking people for lots more money in exchange for a better, more human relationship. For the biggest thing that fundraisers have to learn is they are merely part of a human relationship. Our programmes need to ease back into that relearned wisdom. We do a simple thing when we ask for money. We have made it all too complicated and, in the process, we have dehumanised it.

We have also rendered ourselves the objects of social suspicion.

The danger of scepticism

One senses the growth of a high-powered cadre of men and women who are good at what they call 'communication' in the field of charity – professional conscience prickers if you like – whose skills are pretty much transferable between causes.

The thought comes from that excellent journalist Matthew Parris, in a piece in *The Times* in December 1995. It is an unusually articulate comment on a feeling shared by many people. The pop singer Bono put it more bluntly in an interview 'People are getting hip to what's being done to them'.

Charities would do well to heed the warnings. We live in a sceptical age. We have absolutely no reason to believe that the sanctified role that charities have always enjoyed in Western societies will continue unchallenged. Charities have become loud, opinionated and occasionally crass in their understandable search for support. It is inevitable that we will find ourselves subjected to the same examination of scepticism that has already belittled politicians, companies, sportsmen and women, and public bodies of all kinds. This is not a time of belief or respect. It is a time of suspicion and hostility, a time when a reputation earned over decades can be shattered by one act of foolishness, one stupid scandal.

For the moment, our supporters continue to want to believe in us. They still want to buy that dream that I tried to articulate earlier and still trust us to discharge it. But it will not take much to dislodge that belief and trust. Much current fundraising practice, no matter how sound it may be in statistical terms, is just about impossible to explain to the wide-eyed supporter. Our languages are beginning to diverge. We talk of brand awareness, of acquisition costs and of niche strategies. We have to talk of these things because we are marketers and because we are driven by what we see as competition. But we should remember how totally this ugly language collides with the instinct and feelings of the donor. The donor sees charity giving as a means of doing good; it is a fine and innocent instinct and it should not be disturbed carelessly by our own inevitable surge for greater numbers. We are stuck with the culture of corporate growth but we should always remember that any growth we may achieve is the growth not of sales but of a million individual dreams. I make no apology for the sentiment.

The point of all this

Turn to 1 Corinthians 13.13 in the Authorised King James Bible and you find a familiar form of words, 'And now abideth faith, hope and charity, these three; but the greatest of these is charity'. The use of the word 'charity' is the best that the translators could do with the Greek word 'agape'. Thus did the word enter the English language.

But the original Greek word was essentially Christian. It reflected God's unabounded and unconditional love and, by extension, the love that Man should have for his fellow creatures. That historic definition of our role is still worth remembering. For love is more inspiring than a spreadsheet. And fundraising is a beautiful responsibility for the human race and not a mere trade full of tricks.

It was David Strickland-Eales of Chapter One Direct who directed me to the King James Bible and I'm grateful that he did. David is a committed Christian and I am not. So it was good that we could share mutual comfort in the use of the word 'love' and a common, if diffident, acceptance that it made us do what we do as fundraisers.

David could offer a proper Christian perspective on all this. I can only offer a secular version. It just says that you need to believe passionately in what you are doing if you are to fundraise successfully, to carry on caring about good and evil, about need and ugliness, about the dream by which we can make things better. For this book may have helped you to write or construct offers, or think more positively about legacies and committed giving. But it cannot teach you to care.

And nothing I have said is as important as that.

BIBLIOGRAPHY

There is now a very considerable array of books available on fundraising. I have chosen to list only those that I have used in writing *Asking Properly* for all of them have sat on my desk during the process.

Bird, Drayton *How to Write Sales Letters that Sell,* Kogan Page, London, 1994.

Burnett, Ken *Relationship Fundraising,* The White Lion Press, London, 1992.

Flanagan, Joan *The Grass Roots Fundraising Book,* Contemporary Books, Chicago, 1992.

Fraser-Robinson, John *The Secrets of Effective Direct Mail,* McGraw Hill, London, 1989.

Kachorek, Joseph P *Direct Mail Testing for Fund Raisers,* Precept Press, Chicago, 1991.

Lautman, Kay Partney and Goldstein, Henry *Dear Friend: Mastering the Art of Direct Mail Fund Raising,* Fund Raising Institute, Rockville, 1991.

Lord, James Gregory *The Raising of Money,* Third Sector Press, Cleveland, 1990.

Nichols, Judith *Pinpointing Affluence,* Precept Press, Chicago, 1994.

Warwick, Mal *999 Tips, Trends and Guidelines for Successful Direct Mail and Telephone Fundraising,* Strathmoor Press, Berkeley, 1993.

There are also a handful of occasional and smaller booklets produced by the *Third Sector* magazine in London in association with Brann. I would particularly commend *From Mailshots to the Millennium in 1995* and *It's competition, but not as we know it* in 1996. And, having mentioned one fundraising magazine, it is seemly to mention another. *Professional Fundraising* from Brainstorm Publishing continues to report intelligently and informatively on a monthly basis.

INDEX

Achievement, sense of 33-34
Acorn database, *see* CACI
ActionAid 165
Age Concern 96
AIDA formula 78, 154
Alzheimer's Disease Society 97, 98
Amnesty International 90, 112, 154-156
African National Congress 39
American Civil Liberties Union (ACLU) 106
Audience 73, 74, 137
Audio cassettes, *see* cassettes
Average donor 57-58

Botton Village 77, 98-99, 133-134,
Brochures 101-104

CACI's Acorn database 139
Canadian Broadcasting Corporation 107
Cancer Relief Macmillan Fund 109
CARE UK 35-36,
Cassettes, audio and video 126-129
Charter 88 39, 67, 76, 88-89
Clubs 51-54
Committed giving 64, 184-194
Communications, preparation, *see also* letters
  the seven point checklist 62-71
  tick boxes (*see also* committed giving) 64-65
  making the point 68
  response device 69-71
  five sins of direct marketing copy 85
  four creative virtues 88-91
Coupons 157
Creative (as a leverage point) 73, 74, 137

Democratic National Committee (USA) 18, 125
Demographics 56, 212-214

Donor pyramid 54-56
Door-drops 124, 125 , 160-161
Envelopes 95-97

Feed the Children, *see* offer examples
Finding new supporters 139-140
Fliers, *see* brochures
Format 73, 74, 137
Fundraising mottoes 9
Fundraising Advertising Monitor 147-148, 151

Greenpeace 51, 65, 71, 72, 76, 89, 101-102,
129, 188-191
Guilt 18, 32-33

Help the Aged 109-110
Household distribution, *see* door drops

Illustrations 98-101
Involvement devices 46-47, 109-113, 131-132

KISS formula 69, 81, 90

Labour Party (British) 158, 166, 168
Lapsed donors 49, 143-144
Leaflets, *see* brochures
Legacies 28, 56, 164, 194-210
Leverage points 71-75, *see also* audience, offer,
format, creative and timing
Letters
  formula 61, 80
  matching grant 76
  Adam's letter 78
  the direct mail version 79
  Mrs Chavez letter 79-80
  first person imperative, examples 87-88
  candour, example 88-89
  rhetoric, example 89
  brevity, example 90

rewriting, example 90
reproducing news stories, example 107
involvement device, example 110
Womankind letter 143-144
legacies, example 204-206
Lift letter 97
Lists 140
Loose inserts 159-160
'Low ask' 129-130

Major donors 49, 56,
Matching grants, *see* letters
Multiple Sclerosis Society of Canada 114

NCH Action for Children 130
National Canine Defence League (NCDL) 117-119
National Society for the Protection of Children (NSPCC) 65, 160, 172
 see also offer, examples
National Trust, *see* offer, examples
Need to belong 34-36
Newsletters, *see* brochures
News stories, power of 66, 106-109, 148

Offer 73, 75-77, 78, chapter 7, 137
Oxfam 92, 145-147

Photographs, *see* illustrations
Postcards and petitions 130-131
Press advertising 145-159

Radio 174-176
Reasons for giving 15-28
Reciprocals 140-141
Red Cross (British) 110-112, 173
Red Cross (Ontario, Canada) 90
Research, how direct mail packs are read 95
Response device, *see* communications,

preparation
Reward 34-37
Royal Commonwealth Society for the Blind 149, 157
Royal National Institute for the Blind (RNIB) 125
Royal National Institute for Deaf People (RNID), 167, *see* offer, examples
Royal National Lifeboat Institution (RNLI) *see* letters, legacies examples
Royal Society for the Prevention of Cruelty to Animals (RSPCA) 64, 65, 99-100, 154, 164
Royal Star and Garter Home 107-109, 129

Segmentation 141-143
Sense of event 67-68, 71, 80, 108
Sight Savers 81, 157, 175
Shelter 164
Social Democratic Party (British) 40-41
South African Blind Workers Fund 112
South African National Council for the Blind 98, 112
Spoon mailing 46-47
Shakespeare Globe Trust, *see* offer, examples
Statistics
 total number of charities 11
 expenditure 11
 income 11, 12
 charitable giving 14
 legacies 28, 195-198
 volunteers 23
 charity shops 29
 estimated percentages of donors who give only once, or twice 37
 response rates to house mailings 45
 model of current practice 45
 press advertising 147-148
 telephone 163
Surveys/questionnaires, *see* offer, examples

Telephone fundraising 31, 35, chapter 10
Television 167-174
Testimonials 105
Testing 136-137
Tick boxes, *see* communications, preparation
Timing 74, 75, 139-139
UNICEF UK, 129, 132 *see* offer, examples
Videos, *see* cassettes

Volunteers 30
  see also statistics

WWF 52-53, 64, 76, 104, 124
Whale and Dolphin Society 154
Womankind, *see* letters, examples
World Society for the Protection of Animals
130-131

A promise from
The White Lion Press

You will have gathered from this book that the author is committed to many of the most important principles in fundraising: mutual benefit, honesty, openness, accountability and the value of a long-term relationship. The White Lion Press is equally committed to these principles. We would like to start our relationship with you on the best possible basis to ensure that it will develop into a long and mutually beneficial association. So here is our promise to you, and our offer.

Books by The White Lion Press will repay your investment many times over – and you'll enjoy reading them too. But if your purchase is damaged in any way or if you feel any of our products do not live up to your expectations simply return them to us and we will issue you with a full refund, including any reasonable associated costs such as postage. We'll ask you to tell us why, simply so we can put right anything that might be wrong, but we won't quibble. Unfortunately we can only offer this if you bought the book directly from us or from one of our recognised distributors. But even if you didn't, please let us know your problem and we'll do all we can to ensure your supplier matches our commitment to you. After all, you are our ultimate customer.

This guarantee applies to any books or videos you may purchase from us. We further promise to handle your orders and any other communications with speed, efficiency and impressive politeness.

If you wish to order any other titles from us, by post or fax, please detach or photocopy the order form that follows. We endeavour to despatch orders within 24 hours, so fax is fastest.

If you have any query regarding books published by The White Lion Press Limited please telephone Fay Buller or Mike Kerry on +44 (0)171 490 4939 or fax us on +44 (0)171 490 3126.

YOU CAN ORDER THESE WHITE LION TITLES TODAY

Relationship Fundraising: a Donor-based Approach to the Business of Raising Money by Ken Burnett.
ISBN 0 9518971-0-1

The voluntary organisations that depend on fundraising represent a vigorous, fast growing and surprisingly substantial business sector. In recent years the often counter-productive amateurism of the past has given way to professionalism in strategy, materials and approach from fundraisers.

But dangers and pitfalls lurk among the benefits of modern marketing methods. *Relationship Fundraising* identifies and defines these risks and describes a donor-based approach that is not only more appropriate but is more likely to be successful for both the fundraiser and the donor.

Relationship Fundraising is illustrated throughout by examples, donor profiles and action points.

First published in 1992 this is the classic textbook of donor development. Now an international best seller *Relationship Fundraising* has been sold in more than 35 countries worldwide. Here's just a taste of the enthusiastic praise this seminal book has received:

'Culturally revolutionary...'
John Rodd, ICFM's Computers in Fundraising

'...a different mood has swept through the fundraising world.'
Tom Smith, Teach Yourself Fundraising

'Burnett... has provided a new framework for thinking about fundraising strategy.'
Rob Paton, the Open University, in The Journal of Nonprofit and Voluntary Sector Marketing,

'This book is the fundraiser's bible.'
Conrad Lauritsen, Stroëde AB, Sweden

Friends for Life: Relationship Fundraising in Practice by Ken Burnett.
ISBN 0-9518971-2-8

Amid the widespread acclaim that greeted the 1992 publication of Ken Burnett's Relationship Fundraising was one persistent qualified comment. Essentially the question was relationship fundraising sounds very attractive, but will it help us raise more money?

In this accessible and entertaining sequel Ken Burnett describes how relationship fundaising is working in a wide variety of organisations in the USA, Canada and the United Kingdom. Their stories provide the answer: a loud and clear 'yes!'

But the ideas and experiences described in this book will do much more than just help fundraisers raise more money. It will show them how to develop and maintain strong, healthy, mutually beneficial relationships with their donors; relationships that will enable them to make friends for life.

The sequel to *Relationship Fundraising* first appeared in 1996, to acclaim:

'I'm an enthusiastic fan of Ken Burnett's approach to building friends for life. His new book builds on the practical, common-sense approach to donor development he is famous for advocating.

'Great examples, an easy read – I highly recommend *Friends for Life: Relationship Fundraising in Practice.'*
Dr Judith E Nichols, CFRE
Author and consultant, Lake Oswego, USA.

'*Friends for Life* is a witty, readable tour of donor-think from both sides of the Atlantic and brings together a unique collection of experiences and anecdotes from many world-class fundraisers. *Relationship Fundraising* is already a classic throughout the world and this sequel is sure to have a similar impact.'
Jennie Thompson
Consultant and co-founder of Craver, Mathews, Smith and Company,
Washington DC, USA

'The Botton Village case history is riveting. Its lessons have a relevance beyond fundraising. This is what direct marketing should always be, but so seldom is.'
Graeme McCorkell, author and consultant, Cheshire, UK

'*Friends for Life* has found a friend in me. It is a timely, useful and very amusing book. The basic principles of long-term donor development are truly universally applicable.'
Per Stenbeck, Chief Executive
The International Fund Raising Group, London, UK

Friends for Life video series
A series of half-hour videos from the Friends for Life sessions featuring Ken Burnett in Vancouver, Canada in July 1996. Filmed by Canada's Knowledge Network and produced jointly by Harvey McKinnon and Associates and The White Lion Press, the series will be available early in 1997. Please tick the box if you would like to receive further information.

PLEASE SEND ME THE FOLLOWING TITLES

No of copies	Title	Price*	Total
_____	*Relationship Fundraising,*	£21.00 hbk	£_____
_____	*Friends for Life: Relationship Fundraising in Practice*	£28.50 hbk	£_____
_____	*Asking Properly: the Art of Creative Fundraising*	£28.50 hbk	£_____
Post and packing cost (see below)			£_____
Total remittance			£_____

Please send me information on the Friends for Life video series, featuring Ken Burnett ☐

* If you order any two titles from this list you will be entitled to a 10 per cent discount on the retail price of each book. Orders of three copies or more will entitle you to a 20 per cent discount. (NB these offers only apply to orders placed directly with the publishers.)

   For postage and packing UK mainland please add £3.00 per copy. All other countries please add £3.50 per copy. Books will be despatched by first class post (UK mainland) or surface mail (overseas). Please contact us for overseas airmail costs or for special discounts for bulk orders.

I enclose a cheque for £_____ payable to The White Lion Press Limited.

Please bill my organisation at the address below ☐

Please debit my Visa/Amex/Mastercard Number ☐☐☐☐ ☐☐☐☐ ☐☐☐☐ ☐☐☐☐
Expiry date _____

Signature _____

Your name _____

Organisation _____ Your position _____

Address _____

_____ Postcode _____ Telephone _____

Fax _____ E.Mail _____

Please return to The White Lion Press Limited, White Lion Court, 7 Garrett Street, London EC1Y 0TY. Tel: +44 (0) 171 490 4939 Fax: +44 (0) 171 490 3126.